Wiley Study Guide for 2018 Level II CFA Exam

Volume 5: Alternative Investments & Portfolio Management

Thousands of candidates from more than 100 countries have relied on these Study Guides to pass the CFA® Exam. Covering every Learning Outcome Statement (LOS) on the exam, these review materials are an invaluable tool for anyone who wants a deep-dive review of all the concepts, formulas, and topics required to pass.

Wiley study materials are produced by expert CFA charterholders, CFA Institute members, and investment professionals from around the globe. For more information, contact us at info@efficientlearning.com.

Wiley Study Guide for 2018 Level II CFA Exam

Volume 5: Alternative Investments & Portfolio Management

WILEY

Contents

About the Authors   **vii**

Study Session 15: Alternative Investments

Reading 43: Private Real Estate Investments   3
    Lesson 1: Real Estate: Basic Forms and Characteristics, and Private
       Market Real Estate Equity Investments   3
    Lesson 2: Types of Commercial Real Estate and an Introduction to Valuation   8
    Lesson 3: The Income Approach to Valuation   12
    Lesson 4: The Cost Approach   24
    Lesson 5: Due Diligence in Private Real Estate Investment, Indices, and Private
       Market Real Estate Debt   30

Reading 44: Publicly Traded Real Estate Securities   35
    Lesson 1: Types of Publicly Traded Real Estate Securities   35
    Lesson 2: Valuation   43

Reading 45: Private Equity Valuation   51
    Lesson 1: Introduction to Valuation Techniques in Private Equity Transactions   51
    Lesson 2: Contrasting Valuation in Venture Capital and Buyout Settings   53
    Lesson 3: Valuation Issues in Buyout and Venture Capital Transactions and Exit Routes   54
    Lesson 4: Private Equity Fund Structures, Due Diligence, and Valuation   61
    Lesson 5: Risks and Costs of Investing in Private Equity and Evaluating Fund Performance   67
    Lesson 6: Valuation of Venture Capital Deals   73

Reading 46: Commodities and Commodity Derivatives: An Introduction   81
    Lesson 1: Commodity Sectors   81
    Lesson 2: Commodity Futures Markets and Participants   88
    Lesson 3: Spot and Futures Pricing   91
    Lesson 4: Three Theories of Futures Returns   92
    Lesson 5: Components of Futures Returns   96
    Lesson 6: Commodity Swaps   99
    Lesson 7: Commodity Indexes   103

Study Session 16: Portfolio Management: Process, Asset Allocation, and Risk Management

Reading 47: The Portfolio Management Process and the Investment Policy Statement   109
    Lesson 1: The Portfolio Management Process   109

Reading 48: An Introduction to Multifactor Models 117
    Lesson 1: Introduction and Arbitrage Pricing Theory 117
    Lesson 2: Types of Multifactor Models and Selected Applications 122

Reading 49: Measuring and Managing Market Risk 139
    Lesson 1: Value at Risk 139
    Lesson 2: Other Risk Measures 144
    Lesson 3: Risk Measurement Applications 149
    Lesson 4: Using Constraints to Manage Market Risk 152

Study Session 17: Portfolio Management: Economic Analysis, Active Management, and Trading

Reading 50: Economics and Investment Markets 157
    Lesson 1: Framework for the Economic Analysis of Financial Markets
        and the Discount Rate on Real Risk-Free Bonds 157
    Lesson 2: The Yield Curve and the Business Cycle 162
    Lesson 3: Credit Premiums and the Business Cycle 169
    Lesson 4: Equities and the Equity Risk Premium 174
    Lesson 5: Commercial Real Estate 179

Reading 51: Analysis of Active Portfolio Management 183
    Lesson 1: Active Management and Value Added, and Comparing Risk and Return 183
    Lesson 2: The Fundamental Law 195
    Lesson 3: Applications of the Fundamental Law and Practical Limitations 205

Reading 52: Algorithmic Trading and High-Frequency Trading 211
    Lesson 1: Trading Algorithms and High-Frequency Trading 211
    Lesson 2: Growth of Algorithmic and High-Frequency Trading 213
    Lesson 3: Risk Management and Regulatory Oversight 214
    Lesson 4: Market Impacts of Algorithmic and High-Frequency Trading 215

ABOUT THE AUTHORS

Wiley's Study Guides are written by a team of highly qualified CFA charterholders and leading CFA instructors from around the globe. Our team of CFA experts work collaboratively to produce the best study materials for CFA candidates available today.

Wiley's expert team of contributing authors and instructors is led by Content Director Basit Shajani, CFA. Basit founded online education start-up Élan Guides in 2009 to help address CFA candidates' need for better study materials. As lead writer, lecturer, and curriculum developer, Basit's unique ability to break down complex topics helped the company grow organically to be a leading global provider of CFA Exam prep materials. In January 2014, Élan Guides was acquired by John Wiley & Sons, Inc., where Basit continues his work as Director of CFA Content. Basit graduated magna cum laude from the Wharton School of Business at the University of Pennsylvania with majors in finance and legal studies. He went on to obtain his CFA charter in 2006, passing all three levels on the first attempt. Prior to Élan Guides, Basit ran his own private wealth management business. He is a past president of the Pakistani CFA Society.

There are many more expert CFA charterholders who contribute to the creation of Wiley materials. We are thankful for their invaluable expertise and diligent work. To learn more about Wiley's team of subject matter experts, please visit: www.efficientlearning.com/cfa/why-wiley/.

READING 43: PRIVATE REAL ESTATE INVESTMENTS

LESSON 1: REAL ESTATE: BASIC FORMS AND CHARACTERISTICS AND PRIVATE MARKET REAL ESTATE EQUITY INVESTMENTS

LOS 43a: Classify and describe basic forms of real estate investments. Vol 6, pp 7–9

Real Estate Investment: Basic Forms

Real estate investments can be classified into different forms on the basis of:

- Whether the investment is being made in the private or public market.
  - ○ Investments in private markets can be made either directly or indirectly:
    - A direct investment can be made by investing in an asset (e.g., purchasing a house), or attaining a claim on an asset (e.g., through giving a mortgage loan to the purchaser).
    - An indirect investment can be made through different investment vehicles (e.g., partnerships and commingled real estate funds or CREFs).
  - ○ Investments in public markets are usually made *indirectly* through ownership of securities that serve as claims on the underlying assets. Examples include investments in a real estate investment trust (REIT), a real estate operating company (REOC), or a mortgage-backed security.
- Whether the investment is structured as equity or debt.
  - ○ An equity investor has an ownership interest in real estate or in securities of an entity that owns real estate. Equity investors have control over decisions such as whether to obtain a mortgage loans against the asset, who should be responsible for property management, and when to sell the real estate.
  - ○ A debt investor is a lender who owns a mortgage loan or mortgage securities. Typically, the real estate serves as collateral for the loan, with the lender having a priority claim on the asset.
  - ○ The value of the equity investor's interest in the real estate is equal to the value of the real estate minus the amount owed to the lender.

The different forms of real estate investments are summarized in Table 1-1. This classification of real estate investments into four quadrants makes it easier for investors to identify the different risk and return characteristics associated with each classification, and to make investment decisions aligned with their objectives.

Table 1-1: Examples of the Basic Forms of Real Estate Investment

	Equity	Debt
Private	Direct investments in real estate. This can be through sole ownership, joint venture, real estate limited partnerships, or other forms of commingled funds.	Mortgages
Publicly traded	Shares of real estate operating companies and shares of REITs.	Mortgage-backed securities (Residential and commercial)

Each form of real estate investment has its own risks, expected returns, regulations, legal structures, and market structures.

- Private real estate investments are indivisible and therefore, tend to involve larger amounts.
- Public real estate investments allow the ownership or claim on the property to be divided, which makes them more liquid than private real estate investments, and also allows investors to diversify by purchasing ownership interests across several properties.
- Private equity investment in real estate requires the owner to manage the property herself or to hire a property manager. REOCs and REITs have professional teams manage their real estate investments, so investors in publicly traded real estate investments do not require real estate management expertise.
- Equity investors usually require a higher rate of return than debt investors as they take on greater risk. Their claim on the interim cash flows and proceeds from sale of real estate property is subordinate to that of debt holders. However, debt investors usually do not participate in any upside in the value of the underlying real estate.
- The return to equity investors in real estate has two components: an income stream (e.g., rental income) and a capital appreciation component.

LOS 43b: Describe the characteristics, the classification, and basic segments of real estate. Vol 6, pp 9–13

Real Estate Characteristics

> If these returns are less than perfectly positively correlated with the returns to stocks and/or bonds, then adding equity real estate investments to a traditional portfolio offers diversification benefits.

Real estate has several characteristics that make it different from traditional asset classes like stocks and bonds. These unique characteristics complicate the measurement and assessment of performance of real estate portfolios.

Heterogeneity and fixed location: While all bonds belonging to the same issue and all stocks of a particular type in the same company are identical, no two real estate properties are exactly the same. Real estate properties differ with respect to size, location, lease terms, quality of tenants, and so on.

High unit value: Real estate properties typically have a much higher unit value compared to bonds or stocks since they are indivisible. This makes it difficult to construct a diversified real estate portfolio unless large sums are available for investment.

Management intensive: Investors in stocks and bonds do not take part in the day-to-day management of the company. On the other hand, private real estate investments require active management to maintain the properties, negotiate leases, and collect rents. Property management may be undertaken by the owner herself or delegated to a property management company but in either case, these additional costs must be taken into account when investing in real estate.

High transaction costs: Buying and selling real estate entails high transaction costs in the form of fees paid to appraisers, lawyers, and construction professionals.

Depreciation: Buildings decline in value over time as a result of use and wear and tear. Further, real estate can lose value due to changes in location and design preferences of end users.

Need for debt capital: Since investment outlays for real estate properties tend to be relatively large, access to funds and the cost of funds are important considerations. When debt capital is relatively scarce and/or interest rates are relatively high, real estate values tend to be lower.

Illiquidity: Direct investments in real estate tend to be relatively illiquid. It may take a relatively long period of time for an investor to be able to sell a property at a price close to its fair market value.

Difficulties in price determination: Due to the heterogeneity of properties and infrequent transactions, appraisals are required to assess changes in value over time. Further, limited market participation and the importance of local knowledge make the real estate market relatively inefficient. Investors who have superior information and value-assessing skills can exploit these market inefficiencies. On the other hand, markets for stocks and bonds of public firms tend to be much more active and efficient.

The market for REITs has expanded rapidly over recent years as they overcome some of the problems associated with direct investments in real estate.

- Shares of REITs are more actively traded so they are more likely to reflect market values.
- REITs provide or hire professional property managers.
- REITS allow investors to add a diversified portfolio of real estate investments to their overall portfolios.

Real Estate Classifications

Real estate investments may be classified as residential or non-residential properties. Another potential classification is single-family residential, commercial, farmland, and timber.

Residential properties: These generally provide housing for individuals or families, and include single-family houses (which may be owner-occupied or rental properties), and multi-family properties such as apartments (which are usually classified as rental properties even if the owner or manager occupies one of the units). Residential real estate properties (especially multi-family properties) that are purchased with the intent to let, lease, or rent are usually classified as commercial real estate properties.

Non-residential properties include (1) commercial properties other than multi-family properties (as these are residential properties), (2) farmland, and (3) timberland.

Commercial real estate properties: Theses properties are usually classified by their end use. In addition to multi-family properties, commercial real estate properties include offices, industrial and warehouse properties, retail properties, hospitality properties (e.g., motels and hotels) and others (e.g., parking facilities, restaurants, and recreational uses such as country clubs).

Some commercial properties, such as hotels, shopping centers, and recreational facilities require more active management than others. Such properties are considered riskier by investors because of the operational risks involved. As a result, investors require a higher rate of return on these management-intensive properties.

Farmland and timberland: These properties are unique in the sense that they can be used to produce a saleable commodity. Investors can generate income by selling the commodity or leasing out the land. Primary determinants of revenue are harvest quantities and commodity prices, which are affected by factors that are outside the control of the producer. Farmland and timberland also have potential for capital appreciation.

LOS 43c: Explain the role in a portfolio, economic value determinants, investment characteristics, and principal risks of private real estate. Vol 6, pp 13–17

LOS 43l: Explain the role in a portfolio, the major economic value determinants, investment characteristics, principal risks, and due diligence of private real estate debt investment. Vol 6, pp 17–18

Benefits of Real Estate Equity Investments
- Real estate investments can generate current income by letting, leasing, or renting the property. However, the amount received by the investor is affected by operating expenses, taxes, and financing costs.
- Real estate prices may increase over time, so capital appreciation can contribute to an investor's total return.
- Real estate values usually rise in an inflationary environment, so real estate investments serve as an inflation hedge.
- Investments in real estate provide diversification benefits to investors as their performance as an asset class has historically not been highly correlated with the performance of more popular asset classes such as stocks, bonds, and money market funds.
- Investors in real estate may receive a favorable tax treatment. For example, in the United States:
  - Investors in private real estate are allowed to depreciate their properties over a time period that is shorter than the period over which the property actually depreciates. As a result, annual depreciation is higher and taxable income is lower so investors pay lower taxes.
  - REITs do not pay corporate income taxes, so investors are able to avoid double taxation.

> Publicly traded REITs have been found to have a higher correlation with stocks and bonds compared to private real estate investments. This suggests that public and private real estate investments do not necessarily provide the same diversification benefits.

Risks Factors
- Business conditions: Changes in economic factors such as GDP growth, employment, household income, interest rates, and inflation rates affect both (1) real estate values and (2) rental income.
- Long lead time for new developments: Real estate projects take a long time to be completed and market conditions can change significantly during their development. If the market weakens over the development period, rental rates can be lower and vacancy rates higher than originally anticipated, resulting in lower returns than initially envisaged by investors.

- Cost and availability of debt and equity capital: Due to the large initial outlay required, real estate investments typically require debt financing. As a result, demand for real estate is affected by the (1) availability and (2) cost of debt capital. Scarcity of debt capital and high financing costs lead to lower real estate values. As far as equity capital is concerned, higher expected returns on stocks and other investments reduce the availability of equity capital for real estate investments.
- Unexpected inflation: Real estate provides protection against inflation in the following ways:
  - Lease contracts may provide for rent increases in line with the inflation rate.
  - Construction costs (replacement cost) rise with inflation so real estate values increase with inflation.

However, if the real estate market is relatively weak, high vacancy rates and low rents could mean that real estate values may not keep up with inflation.

- Demographics: The demand for real estate is also affected by factors such as the size and age distribution of the population in the local market, the distribution of socioeconomic groups, and the rate of new household formation.
- Lack of liquidity: Real estate investments tend to have poor liquidity due to (1) the large outlays required and (2) the time taken and costs incurred to sell. Lower liquidity means that a longer time period would be required to realize cash, and there is also the risk of adverse market movements.
- Environmental: Poor environmental conditions (e.g., contaminants related to a prior owner or an adjacent property owner) can have an adverse impact on the value of a property.
- Availability of information: There is a risk of overpaying for a property if the owner makes the investment decision based on insufficient or inaccurate information. Over the last few years however, the amount of data in the real estate space has improved considerably (e.g., with the availability of real estate indices for many countries).
- Management: Management of real estate can be categorized into two levels:
  - *Asset management*: This refers to the management of an investment's financial performance and making changes when necessary.
  - *Property management*: This refers to the physical maintenance and day-to-day operations of the property.

Management risk reflects the ability of both asset managers and property managers to make the right decisions regarding the operation of the property.

- Leverage: This refers to the use of borrowed funds to finance a real estate purchase. The ratio of borrowed funds to total purchase price is called the *loan-to-value (LTV) ratio*. A higher ratio implies greater use of leverage, which leads to higher risk for equity investors since lenders have a priority claim on cash flows and on the value of the property in case of default. A small decrease in NOI can have a significant negative impact on the cash flow available to equity investors after meeting debt servicing obligations.

Note that leverage affects the returns on an investment in real estate, but has no impact on the value of the property itself. Also, if an investor finances a real estate investment entirely with her own equity there is no risk from financial leverage, but it does not mean

that she has eliminated her interest rate risk. This is because if interest rates rise, there is a risk of real estate values declining due to higher financing costs for buyers (who generally tend to finance part of their real estate investments with debt).
- Other risk factors: Other risk factors include unobserved physical defects in the property, natural disasters, and acts of terrorism.

Risk that can be identified in advance can be hedge away through insurance. Investors can mitigate property-specific risks through diversification and in certain cases transfer risks to other parties through contractual arrangements (e.g., raising rental rates in line with inflation).

Real Estate Risk and Return Relative to Stocks and Bonds

Real estate investments have both bond-like and stock-like characteristics.

- Lease agreements call for periodic rental payments, similar to periodic coupon payments on bonds.
- At the end of the lease term there is uncertainty regarding the renewal of lease and the rental rate, which depend on availability of competing space, the profitability of companies leasing the space and macroeconomic factors. These factors also affect stock prices.

Historically, real estate as an asset class has exhibited higher returns and risk than bonds, but lower returns and risk than stocks.

LESSON 2: TYPES OF COMMERCIAL REAL ESTATE AND AN INTRODUCTION TO VALUATION

LOS 43d: Describe commercial property types, including their distinctive investment characteristics. Vol 6, pp 19–22

Commercial Real Estate

Properties that are widely believed to be low-risk include offices, industrial and warehouse properties, retail properties, and multi-family (apartments). Hospitality properties (e.g., hotels) entail higher risk as their returns are highly correlated with the business cycle. For each type of property, location plays a vital role in determining value. Below we discuss the major economic value determinants for each of the different types of commercial real estate properties.

Office

The demand for office buildings is influenced by employment growth, especially in industries that are heavy users of office space, like finance and insurance. Lease lengths for office space vary globally, but are generally influenced by (1) the desirability of the property, (2) the financial strength of the tenant, and (3) other terms in the lease such as future rent changes and whether there is an option to extend the lease.

An important consideration in office leases is whether it is the owner or the tenant who bears the risk of operating expenses (e.g., utilities) increasing in the future. A lease may be structured as a net lease, where the *tenant* is responsible for paying operating expenses or as a gross lease, where the *owner* is responsible for paying operating expenses. Rent for a net lease is *lower* than rent for an equivalent gross lease because the tenant bears operating expenses and takes on the risk of operating expenses rising in the future.

Office leases may sometimes be structured such that the owner pays for operating expenses, but amount of annual operating expenses paid for by the owner is capped at the level of operating expenses in the first year. The tenant is responsible for paying any increases in operating expenses (as an expense reimbursement).

In a multi-tenant building, expenses are usually prorated among the tenants based on the amount of space they lease. While having multiple tenants may make it a bit tedious to manage the property, it reduces risk as a tenant's non-extension of a lease will not affect cash flows too significantly.

From the discussion above, you should realize that lease terms have a significant impact on the risk and return associated with investing in office buildings. Therefore, it is important for investors to analyze how leases are typically structured in a particular market, and to also stay informed regarding any changes in the typical structure.

Industrial and Warehouse

The demand for industrial and warehouse properties is heavily influenced by the strength of the overall economy, prospects for growth, and import and export activity. Leases for industrial and warehouse properties may also be structured as net leases, gross leases, or leases with expense reimbursements.

Retail

The demand for retail space is primarily influenced by consumers' willingness to spend, which in turn is influenced by the strength of the overall economy, job growth, population growth, and savings rates.

Lease terms for retail space are influenced by the quality of the property as well as by the size and importance of the tenant. Favorable lease terms are usually offered to larger tenants (e.g., a department store) to attract them to the property. Such tenants are referred to as anchor tenants as they attract other tenants.

A type of lease that is unique to retail properties is the percentage lease. Under this type of lease, tenants pay a *minimum* rent as long as their sales remain below a threshold level, but must pay *additional* rent once their sales surpass the threshold level.

For example, a lease may require a tenant to pay a minimum rent of $60 per square foot and an additional 15% of sales once sales exceed $400 per square foot. In this case, 15% of $400 equals the minimum rent of $60 so the $400 threshold is referred to as the natural breakpoint.

- If sales amount to $400 or less, the tenant will keep paying the minimum rent of $60.
- If sales *exceed* $400, let's say they amount to $450, the tenant will have to pay $67.5 [= 60 + 0.15 (450 − 400)].

Note that we will get the same answer if we simply multiply $450 by 15% ($67.5). This is only because $400 is the natural breakpoint. A lease may not always have a breakpoint at its natural level. In such a case, it is important that the lease clearly defines how the rent will be calculated.

Multi-Family

The demand for multi-family space depends on demographic factors such as population growth, relevant age segment for renters, and propensity to rent. Demand also depends on the cost of ownership relative to the cost of renting (i.e., the ratio of home prices to rents). If home prices rise, people will lean toward renting, and vice-versa. Home prices are also influenced by the level of interest rates. Higher mortgage rates make purchases more expensive to finance, so people shift toward renting.

Leases for multi-family properties usually range from 6 months to 2 years. The tenant may or may not be responsible for paying expenses such as utilities, but is usually responsible for cleaning the space rented and for insurance of personal property, while the owner is usually responsible for the upkeep of common property, insurance, and repair and maintenance of the property.

LOS 43e: Compare the income, cost, and sales comparison approaches to valuing real estate properties. Vol 6, pp 22–27

Appraisals and Value

Since real estate properties are traded relatively infrequently and are unique, appraisals (estimates of value) are important for performance measurement and evaluation. In most cases, appraisals aim to estimate the market value of a property, which can be defined as the amount a *typical* investor would be willing to pay for the property. Other definitions of value include:

- Investment value: This is the value that a *specific* investor places on the property. Investment value may be higher or lower than market value depending on the particular investor's motivations, how well the property fits into her portfolio, her tax circumstances, and so on.
- Value in use: This is the value to a particular investor of using the property (e.g., the value of a manufacturing plant to a company using the building as part of its business).
- Assessed value: This is the relevant value of a property for property tax purposes.
- Mortgage lending value: This is a more conservative value used by mortgage lenders to determine the value of collateral if the borrower defaults.

Introduction to Valuation Approaches

Appraisers typically use the following approaches to estimate value:

Cost approach: Under this approach, the value of a property is estimated as its **replacement cost** (i.e., the current cost to buy the land and construct a new, but similar, property on the site). Adjustments need to be made if:

- The subject property is older or not of a modern design,
- It is not feasible to construct a new property in the current market, or
- The location of the property is not ideal for its current use.

Sales comparison approach: Under this approach, the value of a property is estimated based on **recent transactions** involving similar or comparable properties. Adjustments need to be made for differences in size, age, location, and condition of the subject and comparable properties.

Income approach: Under this approach, the value of a property is calculated as the **present value of expected future income** from the property, including proceeds from resale at the end of the holding period. The discount rate is based on the expected rate of return that is commensurate with the risk inherent in the investment.

Highest and Best Use

This is an important concept in real estate appraisal. The highest and best use of a vacant site refers to the use that would result in the highest implied value for a property, irrespective of what it is currently being used for. Implied value equals the value of the property after construction less costs to construct the building.

- Value after construction refers to what the property would sell for once it is constructed and leased.
- The cost to construct the building includes profit to the developer for handling construction and getting the property leased.

For example, consider a piece of land which can be used for constructing an apartment building, office building, or a shopping mall. The following information is available:

	Office	Shopping Mall	Apartment
Value after construction	$6 million	$4 million	$5 million
Cost to construct building	$5.5 million	$2.5 million	$4 million
Implied land value	$0.5 million	$1.5 million	$1 million

From the table above, we can see that the highest and best use of the land is to build a shopping mall, as it would result in the highest implied land value ($1.5 million). This is the maximum price that an investor would be willing to pay for this piece of land.

You should also notice here that the highest and best use of the site is not the use that results in the highest total value once the project is completed (value after construction). Even though the office has the highest value if it is built, the relatively high cost to construct means that any investor who wants to develop an office project on the site would pay a maximum of $0.5 million for the land.

The value of a piece of land should be based on its highest and best use even if there is an existing building on the site. If there is an existing building that is not the highest and best use, then the value of the building will be lower, not the value of the land. For example, assume that a site with a warehouse would sell for $2 million (land plus building) and if vacant, the land would sell for $1.5 million. This means that the value of the warehouse (existing building) is $500,000. As long as the value under existing use exceeds the land value, the building should remain. However, if the value under existing use is less than the land value, the existing building should be demolished so that the building that represents the highest and best use can be constructed. For example, if the value as a warehouse (land plus building) were $1.2 million, the implied value of the building is negative $300,000. In this case, the building should be demolished if demolition costs are less than $300,000.

LESSON 3: THE INCOME APPROACH TO VALUATION

LOS 43f: Estimate and interpret the inputs (for example, net operating income, capitalization rate, and discount rate) to the direct capitalization and discounted cash flow valuation methods. Vol 6, pp 27–44

LOS 43g: Calculate the value of a property using the direct capitalization and discounted cash flow methods. Vol 6, pp 27–44

The Income Approach to Valuation

The direct capitalization method and discounted cash flow method are two income approaches used to estimate the value of commercial (income-producing) property. Both these methods focus on net operating income (NOI) as a measure of income and a proxy for cash flow.

Net Operating Income

The income approach focuses on net operating income (NOI) generated from a property to estimate its value. NOI may either be projected for the entire economic life of the property, or for a typical holding period with the assumption that the property will be sold at the end of the holding period. NOI is calculated as follows (see Example 3-1):

> Rental income at full occupancy
> + Other income (such as parking)
> = Potential gross income (PGI)
> − Vacancy and collection loss
> = Effective gross income (EGI)
> − Operating expenses (OE)
> = Net operating income (NOI)

It is very important for you to remember that:

- Operating expenses include items such as property taxes, insurance, maintenance, utilities, and repairs.
- NOI is a before-tax unleveraged measure of income. It is calculated before deducting financing costs and federal income taxes on income generated from the property.
- Sometimes leases may be structured such that *tenants* are responsible for paying operating expenses. In such cases, those operating expenses are not deducted from income when calculating NOI. In case they have been deducted, the additional income received from the tenants as expense reimbursements would be included in the calculation of NOI.

Example 3-1: Calculating Net Operating Income (NOI)

Consider the following information regarding an apartment building:

- Total number of units = 60
- Number of units rented = 50
- Rent = $1,200 per unit per month
- Other income = $800 per rented unit per year
- Operating expenses = 30% of effective gross income
- Property management fee = 15% of effective gross income
- Interest expense = $500,000
- Income tax rate = 40%

Calculate the NOI for the property.

Solution:

Rental income at full occupancy	60 × $1,200 × 12 =	$864,000
Other income	60 × $800 =	+48,000
Potential gross income		$912,000
Vacancy loss	10/60 × $912,000 =	−152,000
Effective gross income		$760,000
Operating expenses	30% × $760,000 =	−228,000
Property management fee	15% × $760,000 =	−114,000
NOI		$418,000

Note that income taxes and interest expense are not subtracted in the calculation of NOI.

The Direct Capitalization Method

Under this method, the value of a property is estimated by capitalizing its current NOI at a rate referred to as the **capitalization rate** (or **cap rate**).

The cap rate is closely linked to the discount rate, but they are not the same. The cap rate is applied to first-year NOI, while the discount rate is applied to current and future NOI. Generally, **when income and value are growing constantly at the same rate,** the relationship between the cap rate and discount rate can be expressed as:

$$\text{Cap rate} = \text{Discount rate} - \text{Growth rate}$$

From the formula above, you should recognize that the growth rate is implicit (included) in the cap rate. This point will become clearer in a little bit. The cap rate can be defined as the current yield on an investment:

$$\text{Capitalization rate} = \frac{NOI_1}{\text{Value}}$$

For the purpose of computing the cap rate, NOI is usually based on the amount expected during the current or first year of ownership of the property. The term going-in cap rate is sometimes used to clarify that the cap rate is based on the first year of ownership. The term terminal cap rate refers to the cap rate that is based on expected income for the year after the anticipated sale of the property.

Rearranging the above equation, we can estimate the value of a property by dividing its first-year NOI by the cap rate.

$$\text{Value} = \frac{\text{NOI}_1}{\text{Cap rate}}$$

An estimate of the appropriate cap rate for a property can be obtained from the selling price of similar or comparable properties.

$$\text{Cap rate} = \frac{\text{NOI}}{\text{Sale price of comparable property}}$$

We mentioned earlier that the growth rate is implicit in the cap rate. To understand this concept, note that the reciprocal of the cap rate (price / NOI) is somewhat similar to the price-earnings multiple for a stock. Just as a higher price-earnings multiple implies higher expected earnings growth, a higher ratio of price to current NOI (and hence a lower cap rate) implies greater income growth potential for a property. As a result, cap rates on comparable properties must still be adjusted to reflect differences in future income growth and risk.

Sometimes, adjustments may need to be made for specific lease terms and characteristics of a market. In the U.K. for example, when lease terms require the tenant to pay all operating expenses, the value of the property is estimated by applying a cap rate to rental payments rather than to NOI. The cap rate derived by dividing rent by recent sales prices of comparables is known as the all risks yield (ARY). The value of a property is then calculated as:

$$\text{Market value} = \frac{\text{Rent}_1}{\text{ARY}}$$

ARY is a capitalization rate and will differ from the required total return (discount rate) an investor might expect to earn through future growth in rents and value. See Example 3-2.

- If rents are expected to remain unchanged for the foreseeable future, then the ARY will equal the total return (discount rate).
- If rents are expected to increase after every rent review, the investor's expected return will be greater than the ARY.
- If rents are expected to increase at a constant compound rate, the investor's expected return will equal the ARY plus the growth rate.

Example 3-2: Calculating the Value of a Property

The NOI of a property for the first year equals $375,000. Given a capitalization rate on comparable properties of 10%, calculate the value of the property.

Solution:

$$\text{Value} = \frac{\text{NOI}_1}{\text{Cap rate}}$$

$$= \frac{\$375,000}{0.1} = \$3,750,000$$

If a rent review for the property reveals that rents are expected to increase every year by 5%, then the IRR of this property would approximately equal 5% + 10% = 15% (i.e., growth rate plus cap rate).

Stabilized NOI

When applying the cap rate to the first-year NOI for a property, it is implicitly assumed that first-year NOI is representative of the typical first-year NOI for comparable properties. However, sometimes actual first-year NOI for the subject property may *not* be representative of typical or expected first-year NOI (e.g., if the property has a higher-than-expected vacancy rate due to ongoing renovation work). In order to determine the value of the property once the renovation is complete, the appraiser must:

- Project a stabilized NOI, which reflects what NOI will be once the renovation work is complete.
  - Applying the cap rate to the lower (during renovation) NOI will understate the value of the property as it would assume that the lower NOI is expected to continue.
- Base the valuation on a cap rate from comparable properties that are not being renovated, as they represent the typical situation.

If the property is purchased before renovation is complete, a slightly lower price will be paid to reflect the fact that the purchaser would have to wait for a certain period until the property starts bringing in the after-completion or typical (higher) NOI. See Example 3-3.

Example 3-3: Calculating Value of a Property Based on Stabilized NOI

An investor plans to purchase a property that requires some renovation to be competitive with comparable properties. All renovations will be completed by the seller at the seller's expense. If the property were already renovated, it would have NOI of $12 million next year, which would increase by 4% every year thereafter. Because of the ongoing renovation, NOI will only be $5 million next year. Given that investors would normally require a rate of return (IRR) of 10% to purchase the property once it has been renovated, calculate the current value of the property.

Solution:

Given the required rate of return (discount rate) and the annual growth rate, the cap rate for property can be calculated as:

Cap rate = Discount rate − Growth rate = 10% − 4% = 6%.

The value of the property if it were already renovated is calculated as first-year NOI divided by the cap rate:

Value if renovated = $12 million / 0.06 = $200 million

However, due to the renovation, there is a loss in NOI amounting to $7 million (= $12 million − $5 million). The present value of this loss in income is calculated as:

PV of the loss in value = $7 million / 1.10 = 6,363,636.36

Therefore, the total value of the property is calculated as the value if renovated minus the PV of income lost during the renovation:

Value of the property = $200,000,000 − $6,363,636.36 = $193,636,363.64

Other Forms of the Income Approach

An alternative to using NOIs and cap rates is to use the gross income multiplier, which equals the ratio of the selling price to the gross income expected from the property in the first year after sale. The gross income multiplier is also usually derived from sales of comparable properties (just like cap rates).

$$\text{Gross income multiplier} = \frac{\text{Selling price}}{\text{Gross income}}$$

Once we obtain the gross income multiplier for comparable properties, we apply it to the subject property's expected gross income to estimate value:

$$\text{Value of subject property} = \text{Gross income multiplier} \times \text{Gross income of subject property}$$

A drawback of this approach is that it does not explicitly consider vacancy rates and operating expenses. If the subject property's vacancy rates and/or operating expenses are lower relative to comparable properties, its gross income multiplier (and hence value) should be higher.

The Discounted Cash Flow Method (DCF)

Under this method, the value of a property is estimated by projecting income beyond the first year and then discounting the income stream (using an appropriate discount rate).

From our earlier discussion, we know that the following relationship between the discount rate and the cap rate holds if income and value for a property are expected to change over time at the same rate:

Cap rate = Discount rate − Growth rate

Rearranging this formula, we get:

Discount rate = Cap rate + Growth rate

Therefore, we can say that the investor's total return (discount rate) comes from (1) the return on first-year income (cap rate) and (2) growth in income and value over time (growth rate). If NOI for the property is expected to grow at a constant rate, then the value of the property can be calculated as:

$$\text{Value} = \frac{NOI_1}{(r - g)}$$

If NOI is expected to remain constant (growth rate = 0) like a perpetuity, then the cap rate and discount rate will be the same. See Example 3-4.

> Notice that this equation is similar to the constant-growth dividend discount model (Gordon growth model) used to value stocks. r = Discount rate (required rate of return). g = Growth rate for NOI. Note that given the constant growth rate in income, value will also grow at the same rate. $r − g$ = Cap rate

Example 3-4: Appraisal Based on a Constant Growth Rate for NOI

A property's NOI for the first year is expected to be $300,000. NOI is expected to increase by 4% per year for the foreseeable future. The property's value is also expected to increase at a rate of 4% per year. Given that investors expect a rate of return of 10% given the level of risk in the investment, calculate the value of the property at the beginning of the year (today).

Solution:

$$\text{Value of the property} = \frac{NOI_1}{(r - g)}$$
$$= \frac{\$300,000}{(0.10 - 0.04)} = \$5,000,000$$

The Terminal Capitalization Rate

If the growth rate in NOI is not expected to remain constant, investors forecast (1) NOI for each year during a specific holding period and (2) a terminal value (estimated sale price) at the end of the holding period (instead of projecting NOI into infinity). The sum of the present values of these amounts (discounted at the required rate of return) is used as an estimate of the value of the property.

Terminal value is one of the most important inputs when valuing a property using DCF methodology. Theoretically, it represents the present value of income to be received by the *next* investor. Practically speaking however, it is very difficult to estimate NOI for another holding period beyond the initial one with great accuracy. Therefore, the direct capitalization method is used to estimate terminal value at the end of the holding period.

$$\text{Terminal value} = \frac{\text{NOI for the first year of ownership for the next investor}}{\text{Terminal cap rate}}$$

The terminal cap rate (also called residual cap rate) is selected at the time of valuation and refers to the cap rate that is applied to expected income for the first year after the anticipated sale of the property. The terminal cap rate may be the same, higher, or lower than the going-in cap rate. See Example 3-5.

It would help you to remember the formula, Cap rate = Discount rate – Growth rate, to understand these relationships.

- The terminal cap rate is usually higher than the going-in cap rate as it is applied to an income stream that is more uncertain. Other reasons for a higher terminal cap rate include higher expected future interest rates (discount rates) or lower growth in NOI.
- The terminal cap rate can be lower than the going-in cap rate if investors expect interest rates to be lower and/or growth in NOI to be higher in the future.

Example 3-5: Appraisal Based on Terminal Value

A property's NOI is expected to be $500,000 for the next 6 years because of existing leases. Starting in Year 7, NOI is expected to increase to $700,000 and grow at 2% annually thereafter. The value of the property is also expected to increase by 2% per year after Year 6. Given that investors require a rate of return of 10% and expect to hold the property for 6 years, calculate the current value of the property.

Solution:

The current value of the property equals the sum of the present value of NOI for Years 1–6 and the present value of the terminal value at the end of Year 6.

The present value of NOI for Years 1–6 can be calculated as:

$$N = 6; \ I / Y = 10; \ PMT = 500,000; \ FV = 0; \ CPT \, PV \rightarrow PV = \$2,177,630.35$$

The terminal value at the end of Year 6 is calculated as:

Since NOI and property value are both expected to grow at the same constant rate after Year 6, the terminal cap rate can be calculated as the discount rate minus the growth rate.

$$\text{Terminal value}_6 = NOI_7 \ / \ \text{Terminal cap rate}$$
$$= 700,000 \ / \ (10\% - 2\%) = \$8,750,000$$

The present value of the terminal value can be calculated as:

$$N = 6; \ I / Y = 10; \ PMT = 0; \ FV = 8,750,000; \ CPT \, PV \rightarrow PV = \$4,939,146.888$$

Therefore, the current value of the property is calculated as 2,177,630.35 + 4,939,146.888 = $7,116,777.24

Notice that in this example, the going-in cap rate is lower than the terminal cap rate.

- The going-in cap rate is calculated as NOI in the first year divided by the value of the property. The going-in cap rate equals \$500,000 / \$7,116,777.24 = 7.03%
- The terminal cap rate equals 8%.

In this case, the investor is willing to pay a higher price for current NOI because he knows that NOI will increase when the lease is renewed in 6 years. The expected increase in NOI when the lease is renewed is implicit in the cap rate.

Adopting to Different Lease Structures

Lease structures tend to vary across countries. In the U.K. for example all operating expenses are borne by the tenant, and the cap rate is known as the all risks yield (ARY). If the date of valuation falls between the initial letting (or the last rent review) and the next rent review, adjustments must be made in the valuation process to account for the fact that the current contract rent (also called the passing rent) does not equal the current market rent (also called the open market rent). If the contract rent is lower than the current market rent (which is typically the case), it is likely to be adjusted upwards in the next rent review. Such a property is said to have "reversionary potential" when the current lease term expires.

Two approaches for incorporating the anticipated change in rent into the valuation process are the term and reversion approach **and** the layer method.

1. Term and Reversion Approach

   This approach splits total value into two components (1) term rent and (2) reversion. See Example 3-6. The value of each component is appraised separately by applying different capitalization rates:
   - Term rent is the passing (current contract) rent from the date of appraisal to the next rent review. The discount rate applied to rental income over the current contract term, term rent is typically lower than the discount rate applied to value the reversion component because it is generally less risky. Receipt of income over the current contract term is relatively more secure as the property is already occupied and tenants are less likely to default because they are on leases with below-market rents.
   - Reversion is the estimated rental value (ERV). The capitalization rate used for appraising this ERV is derived from sales of comparable fully-let properties. Note that this value must be discounted (as it is a future value) from the time of rent review to the present. Convention dictates that the discount rate used to compute the present value of this future reversionary value be the same as the capitalization rate used to compute it (even though they need not be the same in practice).

Example 3-6: A Term and Reversion Valuation

A property was leased 4 years ago at £600,000 per year. The next rent review is in 2 years. The estimated rental value (ERV) in 2 years based on current market conditions is £800,000 per year and the all risks yield (cap rate) on comparable fully rented properties is 6%. A 5% discount rate is considered appropriate to discount the term rent as it is less risky than market rent. Estimate the value of the property.

Solution:

The present value of the term rent of £600,000 per year for 2 years is calculated as:

$$N = 2; \ I/Y = 5; \ PMT = 600,000; \ FV = 0; \ CPT \ PV \rightarrow PV = £1,115,646.26$$

The value of reversion to ERV (at the time of the rent review) is calculated as:

$$\text{Value of reversion to ERV} = NOI_1 / ARY = £800,000 / 6\% = £13,333,333.33$$

The present value of the reversion component of value is calculated as:

$$N = 2; \ I/Y = 6; \ PMT = 0; \ FV = 13,333,333.33; \ CPT \ PV \rightarrow PV = £11,866,619.2$$

Finally, the total value of the property is calculated as the sum of the PV of term rent and the PV of the reversion component.

$$\text{Total estimated value of the property} = 1,115,646.26 + 11,866,619.2 = £12,982,265.46$$

> According to convention, the cap rate (ARY) used to compute the reversionary value is also used to compute the present value of reversionary value.

Note that this example is very similar to Example 3-5, except for differences in terminology and the application of different cap rates for the term rent and the reversion to current market rents.

Figure 3-1: Assumed Cash Flows

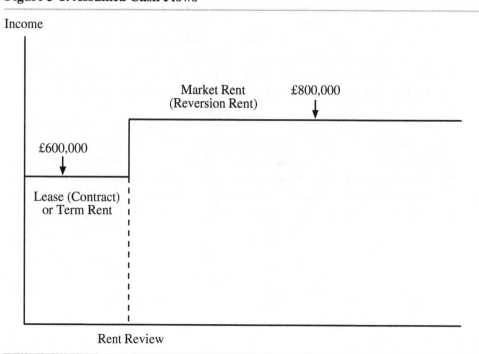

Income

Market Rent (Reversion Rent) £800,000

£600,000

Lease (Contract) or Term Rent

Rent Review

2. The Layer Method

This method assumes that one component of income is the current contract rent, which will continue indefinitely (like a perpetuity), and then adds a second component which comes from the value of the incremental rent expected to be received after the rent review. See Example 3.7.

- The cap rate applied to the contract rent is usually close to, or equal to the all risks yield (ARY) since this is relatively secure income (rental rates can only be revised upward in the U.K.).
- The cap rate applied to the additional income expected after the rent review is usually higher than the ARY as it is regarded as more risky. This is despite the fact that rents could increase even more after subsequent rent reviews (and as we know now, higher growth should theoretically lead to a lower cap rate).

Example 3-7: The Layer Method

Continuing from Example 3-6, suppose that the current contract (term) rent should be discounted at 6%, and any incremental rent should be discounted at 7%. Estimate the value of the property using the layer method.

Solution:

The present value of the term rent (bottom layer) into perpetuity is calculated as:

$$\text{Term rent} / \text{Term rent cap rate} = 600,000 / 6\% = £10,000,000$$

$$\text{Rent of top layer} = \text{Reversion to ERV} - \text{Term rent (Bottom layer)}$$
$$= £800,000 - £600,000 = £200,000$$

The value of the top layer into perpetuity as of the time of rent review (based on a cap rate of 7%) is calculated as:

$$\text{Value of top layer} = £200,000 / 7\% = £2,857,142.857$$

The present value of the value of the top layer is calculated as:

$$N = 2; I / Y = 7; PMT = 0; FV = 2,857,142.857; CPT \, PV \rightarrow PV = £2,495,539.22$$

The total estimated value of the property equals the sum of the present value of the bottom layer (term rent into perpetuity) and the present value of the top layer (additional income starting after 2 years into perpetuity).

$$\text{Total estimated value of the property} = £10,000,000 + £2,495,539.22 = £12,495,539.22$$

Figure 3-2: Assumed Cash Flows

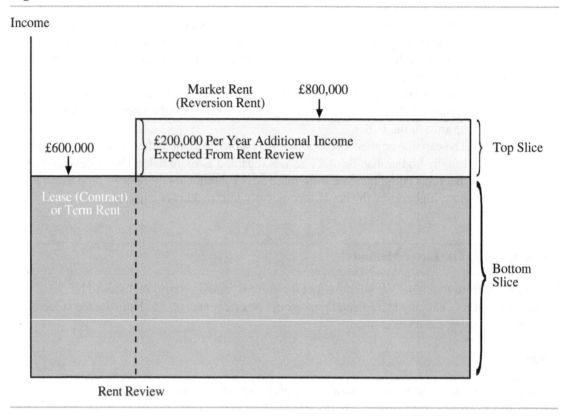

In the two approaches discussed above, we applied different cap rates to the two different sources of income (i.e., current contract rent and market rent). We can also compute the single discount rate that could be applied to both income streams and result in the same value of the property. This rate is called the equivalent yield. Note that the equivalent yield will not be the IRR unless we assume that there will be no increase in rents after the first rent review. Otherwise, it is an average of the two different cap rates (though not a simple mathematical average).

General Steps to a DCF Analysis

Project income from existing leases: This involves keeping track of the start and end dates for each individual lease as well as the various determinants of rent (e.g., base rent, projected increases and adjustments, and expense reimbursements).

Make assumptions about lease renewals: This requires estimating the probability that a lease will be renewed (renewal probability), what rental rate it will be renewed at, whether there will be any vacant days as the owner looks for a new tenant, and how much money would need to be spent on tenant improvements (to fix up the tenant space). These assumptions are important as they affect expected future cash flows from the property.

Make assumptions about operating expenses: Operating expenses include property taxes, insurance, maintenance, management, marketing, and utilities. They can be categorized as fixed, variable, or a hybrid of the two. Variable expenses depend on the level of occupancy, while fixed expenses do not vary with occupancy levels. However, fixed expenses may change over time (e.g., they may increase with inflation). See Example 3-8.

Make assumptions about capital expenditures: Capital expenditures (e.g., renovations or installation of new heating equipment) tend to be lumpy (i.e., there can be significant capital expenditures in certain years, and none at all in others). Rather than projecting capital expenditure for each year individually, analysts usually estimate an average annual amount of capital expenditure and deduct it from NOI to compute annual cash flows for DCF analysis.

Make assumptions about absorption of any vacant space: This refers to the length of the period a space will likely remain vacant until it is leased.

Estimate resale value (reversion): When performing DCF valuation, analysts should choose a holding period that extends beyond the term of existing leases. This makes it easier to estimate the resale price at the end of the holding period as all leases will reflect market rents.

Select discount rate to find PV of cash flows: It is important to use an appropriate discount rate which reflects the riskiness of the cash flows. The discount rate should be higher than the mortgage rate for a loan on the property because acquiring ownership of the property is more risky than making a collateralized loan. Analysts may sometimes apply different discount rates to cash flows expected from a property depending on their level of risk. For example, they might use a lower discount rate to estimate the present value of income from existing leases, and a higher discount rate for income from lease renewals and resale.

Example 3-8: Operating Expenses

Total operating expenses for an office building are assumed to be 20% fixed and 80% variable. If the 300,000-square-foot building was fully occupied, the utility expense would be $5 per square foot. Given that all utility expenses are allocated to occupied space, calculate the utility expense per occupied square foot if the building is 70% occupied.

Solution:

If the building were fully occupied, total operating expenses would amount to $5 × 300,000 = $1,500,000.

- Fixed operating expenses would amount to 0.2 × $1,500,000 = $300,000
- Variable operating expenses would amount to 0.8 × $1,500,000 = $1,200,000

Variable operating expenses per square foot can be calculated as $1,200,000 / 300,000 = $4/sq. ft.

Since the building is 70% occupied, variable operating expenses would amount to $4/sq. ft. × 300,000 × 0.7 = $840,000.
Total fixed operating expenses would remain the same ($300,000).

Therefore, total operating expenses would amount to $840,000 + $300,000 = $1,140,000.
Operating expense per occupied square foot would come to $1,140,000 / (0.7 × 300,000) = $5.43.

LOS 43h: Compare the direct capitalization and discounted cash flow valuation methods. Vol 6, pp 44–45

- Under the direct capitalization approach, a capitalization rate or income multiplier is applied to first-year NOI. Any growth in NOI is *implicit* in the capitalization rate. The higher the expected growth, the lower the capitalization rate, and the higher the value of the property.
- Under the DCF approach, the future income pattern, including the effects of growth, is *explicitly* considered. Further, DCF valuation can incorporate other cash flows that might occur in the future and are not reflected in NOI, such as capital expenditures.

The advantage of using an income approach, such as DCF analysis, is that it considers **all** the cash flows that investors are concerned with. Further, it is not dependent on current transactions from comparable sales as long as an appropriate discount rate is selected.

The disadvantage of the income approach is that it requires detailed information and assumptions regarding the growth rate of NOI, and detailed lease-by-lease analysis. Further, selecting an appropriate discount rate and terminal cap rate is critical to the valuation because slight changes in these assumptions have a significant impact on the property's estimated value.

Common errors made by analysts when making assumptions are listed below:

- The discount rate does not reflect the risk.
- Income growth is greater than expense growth.
- The terminal cap rate and the implied going-in cap rate are inconsistent.
- The terminal cap rate is applied to NOI that is not typical.
- The cyclical nature of real estate markets is not recognized.

LESSON 4: THE COST APPROACH

LOS 43i: Calculate the value of a property using the cost and sales comparison approaches. Vol 6, pp 46–52

Two other approaches commonly used to value properties include the cost approach and the sales comparison approach.

The Cost Approach

The cost approach is based on the view that a buyer would not pay more for a property than it would cost to purchase the land and construct a comparable building on it. This approach is generally used to value unique properties or those with a specialized use for which it is relatively difficult to obtain market comparables. Under the cost approach, the value of a property is estimated as the sum of:

- The value of the land, which is usually determined using the sales comparison approach; and
- The value of the building, which is based on adjusted replacement cost.

Replacement cost refers to the cost of constructing a brand new building today using current construction costs and standards. This replacement cost is then *adjusted* for different types of depreciation (loss in value) to arrive at adjusted or depreciated replacement cost. See Example 4-1. The different types of depreciation include:

- Physical deterioration: This refers to the physical wear and tear of the property as it ages over time. There are two types of physical deterioration:
  - *Curable physical deterioration* refers to a problem whose fixing/repairing will add at least as much to the value of the building as it costs to repair. For example, replacing a damaged roof would be expected to add more to the value of the building than it costs, so it would be classified as curable. The replacement cost estimate for the value of a property assumes that it has zero obsolescence (i.e., it is brand new) so the value estimate assumes that nothing needs to be cured. Therefore, the cost of fixing any curable deterioration must be deducted from the replacement cost estimate. A potential buyer would demand that curable items be fixed before purchasing a property or demand that the purchase price be adjusted for the cost of fixing them.
  - *Incurable physical deterioration* refers to a problem whose cost of repair would exceed the increase in value resulting from the repair, making it unfeasible to fix the problem. For example, there might be some structural problems with the foundation of a building, whose cost of fixing exceeds the increase in value it brings to the building. Since the costs of repairing such deterioration are not actually borne (since the problem is not repaired) analysts account for the effects of the property's age on its value through a depreciation charge. This depreciation charge is based on the effective age of the property relative to its economic life. Note that the effective age of a property may differ from its actual age depending on its amount of wear and tear. For example, if a property has an effective age of 15 years and its economic life is 60 years, then physical depreciation is assumed to be 25% (= 15 / 60). The loss from incurable physical deterioration (depreciation) is estimated by applying this percentage (25%) to the replacement cost *after* deducting the cost of curable physical deterioration.
- Functional obsolescence: This refers to the loss in the value of a building because its current design is not ideally suited for its intended use. Functional obsolescence can result in the building generating less NOI than it would otherwise due to higher operating expenses or lower rent. The cost of functional obsolescence is estimated by capitalizing the reduction in NOI.

> Functional obsolescence may also be categorized as curable and incurable.

- External obsolescence: This refers to the loss in the value of a building due to external factors, such as the location of the property or economic conditions.
  - *Locational obsolescence* occurs when the location of the building is no longer optimal for its intended use. For example, a developer may have constructed a luxury hotel on a piece of land 5 years ago when it was the land's highest and best use. Subsequently however, due to the development of a large manufacturing plant nearby, occupancy rates for the hotel have fallen such that its highest and best use is no longer a luxury hotel, but low-cost apartments for workers at the plant. Therefore, the value of the hotel would decline. Further, the value of the land may also decline as its current highest and best use may yield a lower implied land value. Analysts must be careful not to deduct this (decline in the value of land) portion of the decline in value of the property from replacement cost when adjusting for depreciation.

○ *Economic obsolescence* occurs when it is not feasible to construct a new building under current economic conditions. This can happen when rent levels are not high enough to generate a value for a newly-constructed property that is at least equal to development costs (including profit to the developer). As a result, the replacement cost of the new property exceeds the value of a new building if it were developed. In this case, even a new building would have a loss in value.

Example 4-1: Estimating Value Based on the Cost Approach

Consider the following information regarding an industrial property:

- The value of the land (based on recent selling prices of comparable pieces of vacant land) equals $6 million.
- The building was constructed 10 years ago, but based on its current condition, the appraiser estimates that its effective age is 12 years and that it has a remaining economic life of 48 years. Total economic life therefore equals 60 years.
- The building was built with higher ceilings than current standards. It would currently cost $53 million to reproduce a building with the same ceiling height and $48 million to construct a replacement property with the same utility but a normal ceiling height. These cost estimates include constructor's profit of $1 million but do not include developer's profit of $2 million.
- The building's roof needs to be replaced. This would cost $350,000. The building also requires other minor repairs which would cost $150,000. These expenses would increase the value of the building by at least $500,000.
- The poor design of the building leads to operating expenses being higher than they would be otherwise by $100,000.
- There is a design flaw with the building's elevators which would cost $300,000 to fix. Fixing the elevator would lead to an increase in the value of the building by at least this amount.
- Construction of a manufacturing plant nearby has reduced the NOI for the building by $200,000 per year.
- The appraiser has estimated a cap rate of 10% to value the property.

Based on the given information, estimate the value of the property using the cost approach.

Solution:

Replacement cost (built to current standards)[1]		$50,000,000
Curable physical deterioration		
Replacement of roof	$350,000	
Other minor repairs	$150,000	
	$500,000	
Incurable physical depreciation[2]	$9,900,000	
Curable functional obsolescence		
Fixing of elevators	$300,000	
Incurable functional obsolescence		
Capitalization of higher operating expenses[3]	$1,000,000	
Locational obsolescence		
Capitalization of lower NOI[4]	$2,000,000	
Total depreciation		$13,700,000
Depreciated cost		$36,300,000
Plus: Market value of the land		$6,000,000
Estimated value from the cost approach		$42,300,000

Notes:
1. When provided with reproduction costs and replacement cost, work with replacement cost as it creates a building with the same utility and in line with what is normally required. Both the constructor's and developer's profit must be included in the replacement cost estimate. The constructor's profit ($1m) is already included in the provided replacement cost estimate ($48m) but we must add the developer's profit ($2m).
2. Incurable physical deterioration (depreciation) is applied to replacement cost adjusted for curable physical deterioration ($50m − $0.5m = $49.5m). Ratio of effective age to total economic life = 12 / 60 = 20%. [= 20% × 49,500,000]
3. Higher operating expenses arise from the poor design of the building. These are capitalized at the cap rate. [= $100,000 / 10%]
4. Lower NOI comes from the adverse impact of the new manufacturing plant nearby. This loss is also capitalized at the cap rate. [= $200,000 / 10%]

The cost approach can be used to determine the upper limit on the value of a property, as an investor would never pay more for a property than it costs to purchase the land and construct a comparable building. However, analysts should consider that the development of another building would take time and effort and there may not be adequate demand for another building of the same type in the locality. Still, the approach has value in that a valuation higher than implied by the cost approach would have to be scrutinized in detail.

The main disadvantage of this approach is that it is difficult to estimate depreciation for a property that is older and/or has much obsolescence. Therefore, the cost approach is most appropriate for newer properties that have a relatively modern design in a stable market.

The Sales Comparison Approach

The sales comparison approach is based on the view that the value of a property depends on what investors are paying for similar properties in the current market. Since it is impossible to find a comparable property that (1) is exactly the same as the subject property in all respects and (2) is sold on the same date as the date of appraisal of the subject property. Adjustments must be made for differences between the subject property and comparable properties relating to size, age, location, property condition, and market conditions at the time of sale. The idea is to determine what comparable properties would have sold for if they were like the subject property. See Example 4-2.

Example 4-2: The Sales Comparison Approach

Consider the following information:

Variable	Subject Property	Comparables		
		1	2	3
Size (square feet)	20,000	30,000	25,000	35,000
Age (years)	15	10	5	20
Condition	Average	Poor	Good	Average
Location	Prime	Prime	Secondary	Secondary
Date of sale (months ago)		4	8	6
Sale price		7,500,000	5,000,000	3,500,000
Sale price per square foot		250.00	200.00	100.00

Other information:

- Each adjustment is based on the unadjusted sales price of the comparable.
- The properties depreciate at 2% per annum.
- Condition adjustment: Good, none; Average, –10%; Poor, –20%.
- Location adjustment: Prime, none; Secondary; –15%.
- Over the last 12 months, the market has been rising by 1.5% per month.

Solution:

We illustrate the adjustments for Property 1 in detail below:

- Depreciation is 2% per annum. Since the subject property is 5 years older than Property 1, we will need to apply a further 5 years worth of depreciation on it to make it comparable to the subject property. This implies a downward adjustment of 10% (= 2.0% × 5).
- Since Property 1 is in poor condition while the subject property is in average condition, we will need to adjust Property 1's value upward by 10% to make it comparable to the subject property.
- The value of Property 1 does not need to be adjusted for location because it is in a prime location (like the subject property).
- The market has been rising by 1.5% per month. Since Property 1 was sold 4 months ago, an upward adjustment worth 6% (=1.5% × 4) must be made to its value since the subject property is being valued today.

The adjustments for all three properties are summarized in the table below:

| Adjustments | Comparables | | |
	1	2	3
Age (years)	−10%	−20%	10%
Condition	10%	−10%	0%
Location	0%	15%	15%
Date of sale (months ago)	6%	12%	9%

The price of the subject property is estimated by computing the average adjusted price per square foot for the comparable properties and then multiplying that average price per square foot by the actual size of the subject property:

| Adjustments | Subject Property | Comparables | | |
		1	2	3
Sale price per square foot		250	200	100
Age (years)		−25	−40	10
Condition		25	−20	0
Location		0	30	15
Date of sale (months ago)		15	24	9
Adjusted price per square foot		265	194	134
Average price per square foot	197.67			
Size of subject property (square feet)	20,000			
Appraised value	**$3,953,333.33**			

The calculations for Property 1 are given below. Note that the question states that all adjustments are based on the unadjusted sales price of the comparable.

Age adjustment: $-10\% \times 250 = -\$25$
Condition adjustment: $10\% \times 250 = \$25$
Location adjustment: None required
Time elapsed since date of sale adjustment: $6\% \times 250 = \$15$

The quality of the value estimate from the sales comparison approach depends on the number of recent transactions involving comparable properties. Application of this approach is relatively easy when the market is active, but difficult when the market is weak. Even in an active market, it might be difficult to find comparable sales for some properties (e.g., regional malls and special purpose properties).

Further, the sales comparison approach assumes that purchasers behave rationally i.e., the prices they pay reflect current market values. However, this may not always be the case as the investment value of a property to a particular investor may exceed its market value. Further, in times of exuberance when real estate markets are in a "bubble," the sales comparison approach can lead to inflated valuations, especially when considered in light of values in more "normal" market conditions.

The sales comparison approach is generally used to value single-family homes for which income is not relevant and there is availability of sales data for reasonable comparables.

Reconciliation

The three approaches to valuation (income approach, cost approach, and sales comparison approach) are likely to result in different estimates of value due to differences in their assumptions and sources of data. In order to arrive at a final estimate of value, appraisers must reconcile the differences in value estimates.

An appraiser might give more weight to a particular approach depending on the type of property and market conditions. For example, in an active market with lots of transactions, the appraiser might give more weight to the sales comparison approach. On the other hand, if the market is weak and the building is old (making it difficult to estimate depreciation) she may attach a higher weight to the income approach.

LESSON 5: DUE DILIGENCE IN PRIVATE REAL ESTATE INVESTMENT, INDICES, AND PRIVATE MARKET REAL ESTATE DEBT

LOS 43j: Describe due diligence in private equity real estate investment.
Vol 6, pp 54–55

Both private debt and equity real estate investors normally perform due diligence to verify the facts and conditions that might affect the value of the property. Due diligence usually includes the following:

- Review of the lease and history of rental payments.
- Review of operating expenses by obtaining copies of bills (e.g., utility bills).
- Review of cash flow statements of the previous owner.
- An environmental inspection to ensure that there are no contaminant materials on the site.
- A physical/engineering inspection to ensure that there are no structural issues with the property and to check the condition of the building systems, structures, foundation, and adequacy of utilities.
- Review of ownership history to ensure that there are no issues related to the seller's ability to transfer free and clear title that is not subject to any previously unidentified liens.
- Review of service and maintenance agreements.
- A property survey to ensure that any physical improvements are within boundary lines and to identify any easements that may affect value.
- Verification that the property is compliant with zoning, environmental regulations, parking ratios, and so on.
- Verification of payment of property taxes, insurance, special assessments, and so on.

Investors interested in acquiring commercial real estate usually sign a contract or "letter of intent" which states their intent to acquire the property at a specified price, but subject to due diligence. If problems are identified during the due diligence process, the investor may try to renegotiate the price or back out of the deal. While due diligence can be costly, it lowers the risk of unidentified legal and physical problems.

LOS 43k: Discuss private equity real estate investment indices, including their construction and potential biases. Vol 6, pp 57–61

There are a variety of indices that investors may use to track the performance of real estate. These include appraisal-based indices and transaction-based indices. Investors should be aware of how these indices are constructed and their associated limitations.

Appraisal-Based Indices

These indices rely on appraisals of value (rather than prices from actual transactions) to estimate changes in the value because real estate transactions involving a specific property occur relatively infrequently. Appraisal-based indices combine valuation information from individual properties to provide a measure of market movements.

A well-known appraisal-based index in the United States is the NCREIF Property Index (NPI). Members of NCREIF submit relevant information including appraised value, NOI, and capital expenditures every quarter. The return for all the properties is then calculated as follows:

$$\text{Return} = \frac{\text{NOI} - \text{Capital expenditures} + (\text{Ending market value} - \text{Beginning market value})}{\text{Beginning market value}}$$

- Beginning and ending market values are based on appraisals of the properties.
- The return computed from the formula is the holding period return or the single-period IRR.

The returns on all the properties in the index are then value-weighted to get the index return.

The above formula for computing the return can be divided into two components.

- NOI divided by the beginning market value equals the cap rate. This is also known as the income return for the property.
- The remaining component, that is, [(Ending market value – Beginning market value – Capital expenditures) / Beginning market value], is referred to as the capital return. In order to have a positive capital return, the increase in market value must exceed capital expenditures during the period.

Appraisal-based indices allow investors to compare the performance of real estate relative to other asset classes such as stocks and bonds. Further, the quarterly returns can be used to measure risk (standard deviation). Investors may also use appraisal-based indices to benchmark returns on their real estate portfolios.

One of the disadvantages associated with appraisal-based indices is the appraisal lag as appraised values tend to lag transaction prices when there are sudden shifts in the market. In a bull market, transactions prices start to rise first, and then as these prices are reflected in comparable sales and investor surveys, they begin to be captured in appraised values. As a result, appraisal-based indices may not reflect changes in transaction prices until much later.

Another issue related to the appraisal lag is that the lag tends to smoothen returns on the index, (i.e., the index exhibits less volatility). Therefore, appraisal-based indices tend to underestimate the volatility of real estate returns. Finally, the lag in appraisal-based indices tends to result in the index return exhibiting a lower correlation with other asset classes. This can lead to a higher-than-appropriate allocation to real estate in a well-diversified portfolio.

The appraisal lag may be adjusted by "unsmoothing" the index or using a transaction-based index.

Transaction-Based Indices

These indices are based on actual transactions rather than appraised values. However, the fact that the same property does not sell very frequently still needs to be controlled for. This can be done by either creating a repeat sales index or a hedonic index.

- A repeat sales index relies on the repeat sales of the same property. The idea is that if a specific property is sold twice in a given period, its change in value between the two sale dates indicates how market conditions have changed over time. Regression analysis is then used to allocate the change in value to each quarter.
- A hedonic index requires only one sale (instead of repeat sales of the same property). In order to account for the fact that different properties are being sold each quarter, it includes (independent) variables in the regression that control for differences in the characteristics of each property, such as size, age, quality of construction, and location. The unexplained variation in the regression reflects the impact of changes in overall market conditions on values.

Transaction-based indices are considered better than appraisal-based indices. However, the need to use statistical techniques to estimate the index can lead to random elements in the observations (noise).

LOS 43m: Calculate and interpret financial ratios used to analyze and evaluate private real estate investments. Vol 6, pp 61–64

The amount of debt an investor can obtain to finance the purchase of commercial real estate is usually limited by (1) the loan to value ratio (LTV ratio) or (2) the debt service coverage ratio (DSCR), depending on which measure results in a lower loan amount.

The LTV ratio is calculated as follows:

$$\text{LTV ratio} = \frac{\text{Loan amount}}{\text{Appraised value}}$$

The DSCR is calculated as follows:

$$\text{DSCR} = \frac{\text{NOI}}{\text{Debt service}}$$

Debt service (also referred to as the loan payment) includes both interest payments and principal payments (if required). Principal payments (e.g., on a mortgage) lead to a reduction in the outstanding loan balance. An "interest-only" loan does not have any principal payments during the term of the loan, so the loan balance remains constant over time. See Example 5-1.

Example 5-1: Loan on Real Estate

A property that has recently been valued at $6 million has an NOI of $500,000. A real estate lender is willing to make a 10% interest-only loan as long as the LTV ratio does not exceed 80% and the DSCR is at least 1.25. Calculate the maximum loan amount.

Solution:

Based on the loan-to-value ratio, the loan amount can be calculated as 80% of $6 million, which equals $4.8 million.

Given a DSCR of 1.25, the maximum debt service can be calculated as:

Debt service = NOI / DSCR

Debt service = 500,000 / 1.25 = $400,000

$400,000 is the debt service payment that would result in a DSCR of 1.25 for the loan.

Given that this is an interest-only loan, the loan amount can be simply calculated by dividing the debt service payment by the interest rate.

Loan amount = 400,000 / 0.10 = $4 million

Since the DSCR methodology results in a lower loan amount, $4 million is the maximum amount that can be borrowed.

When investors use debt to finance the purchase of a property, they often calculate the equity dividend rate to measure how much cash flow they are getting as a percentage of their equity investment. This is also referred to as the cash-on-cash return. See Example 5-2.

$$\text{Equity dividend rate} = \frac{\text{First year cash flow}}{\text{Equity investment}}$$

Example 5-2: Equity Dividend Rate

Continuing from Example 5-1, calculate the equity dividend rate given that the property is purchased at its appraised value.

Solution:

First-year cash flow equals NOI minus debt service.

First year cash flow = $500,000 − $400,000 = $100,000

The amount of equity investment equals the purchase price minus the loan amount.

Equity investment = $6 million − $4 million = $2 million

Therefore, the equity dividend rate equals $100,000 / $2,000,000 = 5%

Example 5-3: Leveraged IRR

Continuing from Examples 5-1 and Example 5-2, given that the property is sold after 5 years for $8 million, calculate the IRR that the equity investor will earn on her investment.

Solution:

At the end of the holding period, the entire loan amount of $4 million is outstanding. The cash flow received by the equity investor upon sale equals the difference between the selling price and the loan amount.

Cash flow received by the equity investor = $8 million − $4 million = $4 million

Further, the investor receives an annual cash flow of $100,000 (difference between NOI and debt service payment) during the holding period.

Therefore, leveraged IRR can be calculated as:

$N = 5$; $PV = -2,000,000$; $PMT = 100,000$; $FV = 4,000,000$; $CPT\,I/Y \rightarrow I/Y = 18.77\%$

Example 5-4: Unleveraged IRR

Using the information from Examples 5-1, 5-2, and Example 5-3 calculate the IRR if the property were purchased on an all-cash basis.

Solution:

In this case, the investor will receive the entire proceeds from sale ($8 million) as well as annual NOI of $500,000 during the holding period. Note, that the initial investment equals $6 million.

Therefore, unleveraged IRR can be calculated as:

$N = 5$; $PV = -6,000,000$; $PMT = 500,000$; $FV = 8,000,000$; $CPT\,I/Y \rightarrow I/Y = 13.43\%$

READING 44: PUBLICLY TRADED REAL ESTATE SECURITIES

LESSON 1: TYPES OF PUBLICLY TRADED REAL ESTATE SECURITIES

LOS 44a: Describe types of publicly traded real estate securities. Vol 6, pp 80–82

Types of Publicly Traded Real Estate Securities

Publicly traded real estate securities can be classified into two broad categories: (1) equity investments in properties (ownership) and (2) debt investments.

Equity

Equity REITs (Real Estate Investment Trusts) are entities that own, operate, and (to a very limited extent) develop income-producing real estate. REITs enjoy a tax advantage as they are allowed to deduct dividends paid for tax purposes, which effectively makes them exempt from income taxes at the corporate/trust level. REITs generate cash primarily in the form of recurring lease or rental income.

REOCs (Real Estate Operating Companies) are ordinary taxable companies that own real estate. Businesses are organized as REOCs if they are located in countries that do not recognize the (tax-advantaged) REIT structure, or when they rely primarily on sales of developed or improved properties for cash generation (rather than lease and rental income which is the case with REITs).

Debt

Mortgage-Backed Securities (MBS) are securitized debt obligations that represent rights to receive cash flows from portfolios of mortgage loans. Real estate debt securities are discussed in great detail in the fixed-income section.

Mortgage REITs make loans secured by real estate. They invest most of their assets in interest-bearing mortgages, mortgage securities, or short-term loans secured by real estate.

Note that the market capitalization of the publicly traded real estate debt securities market is much larger than that of the publicly traded real estate equity securities market. Further, in addition to publicly traded real estate securities, there are also privately held real estate securities that include private REITs and REOCs, privately held mortgages, private debt issues, and bank debt. Finally, there is another class of REITs known as hybrid REITs that invest in income-producing real estate, and in mortgages as well.

Publicly traded real estate equity securities usually retain some of the characteristics of direct ownership of income-producing real estate. Income-producing real estate generally provides a predictable and stable stream of contractual rental income under the terms of lease agreements. Further, they may also increase in value over the long term (leading to income from capital appreciation). Due to the relative stability of income from income-producing real estate, investors are able to use significant financial leverage, which can enhance returns on equity capital (if the rate of return on an after-tax basis exceeds the interest rate on debt financing). However, greater financial leverage also entails greater risk.

LOS 44b: Explain advantages and disadvantages of investing in real estate through publicly traded securities. Vol 6, pp 82–91

LOS 44c: Explain economic value determinants, investment characteristics, principal risks, and due diligence considerations for real estate investment trust (REIT) shares. Vol 6, pp 94–96

LOS 44d: Describe types of REITs. Vol 6, pp 91–94

Most REITs are equity REITs that take ownership positions in income-producing real estate. Equity REITs aim to (1) generate cash flows from owned real estate, (2) expand ownership by investing in additional properties, and (3) selectively develop, improve, or redevelop properties.

REIT Structure

REITs are usually structured in a manner designed to avoid the recognition of taxable income if a property that has appreciated in value is transferred to the REIT. Two popular REIT structures (where partnerships hold REIT properties) are Umbrella partnership REITs (UPREITs) and DOWNREITs:

- In an UPREIT, the REIT has a controlling interest in the partnership and is also the general partner in the partnership that owns and operates the properties. UPREITs are the most common REIT structure in the United States.
- In a DOWNREIT, the REIT has an ownership interest in more than one partnership, and may own properties at both the REIT level and the partnership level.

Investment Characteristics

Exemption from income taxes: REITs are typically exempt from income taxes at the corporate/trust level if (1) a specified majority of their income and assets relate to income-producing property and (2) they distribute all their potentially taxable income to shareholders.

High income distributions: Due to the fact that REITs must distribute virtually all their income to shareholders in order to qualify for income tax exemption, they typically offer higher dividend yields than most publicly traded equities.

Relatively low volatility of reported income: Due to the fact that they must generate most of the earnings from income-producing property (rental income) to qualify for income tax exemption, REITs typically use conservative, rental-property focused business models, which result in relatively stable revenue streams (except in the case of hotel REITs).

More frequent secondary equity offerings compared with industrial companies: Due to the distribution requirement, REITs are not able to retain earnings to finance growth. Therefore, they rely on new equity issues to finance property acquisitions.

Advantages of Publicly Traded Equity Real Estate Securities

Publicly traded equity real estate securities (both equity REITs and REOCs) have the following advantages over private real estate assets:

Greater liquidity: Shares in REITs and REOCs trade on stock exchanges so they offer more flexibility in the timing of sale and realization of cash. Direct investments in real estate and real estate partnerships are less liquid and entail higher transaction costs. This is because property transactions are relatively large, involve unique properties, and require negotiations and due diligence.

Lower investment requirements: Shares in REITs and REOCs represent fractional interests in the underlying properties, so they can be purchased with a much lower investment than an entire commercial property.

Limited liability: Just like shareholders of other publicly listed companies, shareholders of REITs are not liable for the obligations of the REIT beyond the amount originally invested. Note that limited partnerships do offer limited liability, but other types of real estate investments (e.g., general partnership interests) do expose investors to liabilities that can potentially exceed the amount originally invested.

Access to superior quality properties and a range of properties: For some investors it is difficult to directly invest in prestigious properties like super-regional shopping malls and landmark buildings because their attractive location, architecture, and/or construction can result in extremely high prices. Investors can acquire ownership interests in these properties by purchasing shares of REITs that own them.

Active professional management: Direct investments in real estate require investment expertise and property management skills. Investors in REITs and REOCs do not need to have these expertise as REITs and REOCs employ professional management to choose attractive investments, maximize rental rates and occupancy rates, and minimize operating costs.

Diversification: By investing in REITs, investors can diversify their real estate portfolios by geography and property type. Such diversification is difficult to attain with direct real estate investments due to the high cost of purchasing (entire) properties.

Protection: As is the case with other public companies, REITs and REOCs are also subject to regulatory, financial reporting, disclosure, and governance requirements. Public investors monitor the performance of management and the board of directors to ensure that the REIT is run in an efficient manner.

Advantages of Investing in REITs as Opposed to Publicly Traded REOCs

Exemption from taxes: As mentioned earlier, REITs are exempted from income taxes at the corporate level as long as certain conditions are met. Further, distributions/dividends received by REIT shareholders are divided into (1) ordinary taxable income, (2) capital gains, and (3) return of capital. While, taxable income and capital gains are taxed at their respective rates, the classification of a portion of distributions as return of capital generally tends to be favorable for investors.

Earnings predictability: Since rental income (which is fixed by contracts) is the primary source of income for REITs, their earnings tend to be more predictable than those of most industrial and natural resource companies.

High income payout ratios and yields: Their typically high payout ratios result in higher dividend yields for REITs compared to other publicly traded equities.

Advantage of Investing in REOCs as Opposed to REITs

Operating flexibility: REOCs are free to invest in any kind of real estate or related activity, and are only subject to limitations imposed by their articles of incorporation and/or the market. This allows them to allocate more resources to development activity, which has the potential to deliver higher returns. They can also retain more of their income than REITs, which enables them to take advantage of lucrative investment opportunities to increase shareholder wealth. Finally, REOCs can typically take on greater financial leverage than REITs.

Disadvantages of Publicly Traded Equity Real Estate Securities

Taxation: In some countries, investors that make direct investments in real estate are allowed to (1) deduct losses on real estate from taxable income and (2) defer taxes on gains if they replace one property for another property (known as a "like-kind exchange" in the United States). Investors in REITs and REOCs are not offered these benefits.

Control: Compared with direct property owners, minority shareholders in publicly traded REITs have little control over property-level investment decisions.

Costs: The maintenance of a publicly traded REIT structure is costly. These costs may not be worth it for investors if the REIT does have not sufficient economies of scale or if management does not add significant value.

Stock market determined pricing: Shares of REITs are traded continuously on the stock market, while the value of the underlying real estate portfolio is determined periodically based on appraisals of the properties. As a result, direct investments in real estate appear to be less risky (as prices do not fluctuate as much as stock market prices of REITs). It is important to note however, that appraised values are backward-looking by nature and may not reflect recent changes in market trends. As a result, net asset values based on appraised values tend to underestimate volatility.

Structural conflicts: UPREIT and DOWNREIT structures can lead to conflicts of interest between the partnership and REIT shareholders. For example, when it comes to selling properties or taking on additional debt, the tax implications for the general partner can be different from implications for shareholders, which may cause the general partner to act in self-interest (as opposed to in the best interest of all stakeholders).

Moderate income growth potential: The income growth potential for REITs is relatively low because of their low earning retention ratios. This can result in stock market values of REIT shares becoming depressed, especially if the market places a high value on growth companies.

Potential for forced equity issuance at disadvantaged pricing: REITs typically use financial leverage and regularly go to the debt markets to refinance maturing debt. If funds to repay mature debt must be raised in times when credit is difficult to obtain, a REIT may have to raise funds by issuing equity at dilutive prices.

Considerations in Analysis and Due Diligence

Remaining lease term: Lease renewals present an opportunity for rental rates to be brought in line with current market rental rates. If the remaining lease term is short, and the economy and/ or rental market are expanding (contracting), it would be looked upon favorably (unfavorably) by investors. Hotels and multi-family residential properties tend to have relatively short lease terms, while shopping centres, offices and industrial buildings typically have longer lease terms.

Inflation protection: Leases that contain pre-set periodic increases in rent over the course of the lease term provide a degree of inflation protection for investors.

Market rent analysis: If existing tenants are paying lower (higher) rents compared to current market rents, then there is upside (downside) potential in cash flows upon lease renegotiation. Further, properties that are rented out at higher-than-market rents entail greater risk as the tenant may leave, resulting in reduction in cash flow.

Cost of re-leasing space: Costs typically incurred to lease out a space when the lease term expires include brokerage commissions, allowances for improvements to the space, free rent, and downtime between leases.

Tenant concentration: Attention should be paid to the financial strength of tenants who rent a significant proportion of the space and account for a high percentage of total rents collected. If a big tenant leaves or fails to make rental payments on time, cash flows from the property can suffer significantly.

Availability of new competitive supply: New buildings under construction or planned by other developers should be examined as greater supply can affect the profitability of the REIT's existing properties.

Balance sheet/leverage analysis: The REIT's financial position should be examined and particular attention should be given to leverage levels, cost of debt, and debt maturity.

Management: There should be a review of the backgrounds, skill sets, and track records of members of the REIT's senior management.

Equity Reits: Property Subtypes

Shopping Center/Retail REITs

These usually invest in regional shopping malls and community/neighborhood shopping centers. They may sometimes also invest in premium retail space in larger cities.

- Regional shopping malls are large enclosed spaces retailing higher-priced discretionary goods.
  - Lease terms are typically for 3 to 10 years and usually require tenants to pay the greater of the fixed minimum rental rate and a percentage of sales.
  - Anchor retailers have very long-term, fixed-rent leases, or they may own their premises.
- Community shopping centers usually consist of stores linked by open-air walkways or parking lots. They generally provide basic necessity goods and services, such as food, groceries, home furnishings, and so on. Lease maturities for all tenants are similar, and rents tend to be non-participatory but subject to periodic increases.

When evaluating shopping center REITs, analysts usually focus on rental rates and sales per square foot/meter for the rental property portfolio.

Office REITs

These usually invest in multi-tenanted office properties.

- Lease terms are typically long with fixed rents that are adjusted upward periodically.
- Apart from rent, tenants also pay their proportionate share of operating expenses, common area costs, and property taxes.
- Rental income tends to be relatively stable over the short term.
- There is often a demand-supply mismatch and vacancy rates and rental rates tend to vary over the economic cycle. This is because construction of new office towers is usually initiated during periods of strong economic growth, but since it takes a long time to construct office towers, projects may be completed at a time when the economy is relatively weak.
- When analyzing office REITs, analysts usually focus on new space under construction in the REIT's local market, site location and access to public transportation, and business conditions of the REIT's principal tenants. Factors such as quality of the REIT's office space (age and durability of the building) are also important.

Industrial REITs

These usually invest in single-tenant or multi-tenant industrial properties that are used as warehouses, distribution centers, and light manufacturing facilities.

- These tend to be less cyclical than other property/REIT types because of (1) longer lease terms, (2) shorter time periods required to construct industrial buildings, and (3) the ability to build and prelease.
- When evaluating industrial REITs, analysts usually focus on changes in tenants' requirements and their impact on the desirability of the space. Property location and availability of transport links (airports, seaports, and roads) are other important considerations.

Multi-Family/Residential REITs

These usually invest in rental apartments that are leased to individual tenants typically on 1-year leases.

- The demand for rental apartments tends to be relatively stable. However, rental income may fluctuate due to competition from condominium construction, tenant (move-in) inducements, regional economic strengths and weaknesses, effects of inflation on operating costs, and taxes and maintenance costs (as apartment leases are typically structured as gross leases).
- When evaluating residential REITs, analysts usually focus on local demographics and income trends, age and competitive appeal, move-in inducements offered, cost and availability of home ownership in local markets, and the degree of government control of local residential units (rent control). Fuel and energy costs are also important considerations as landlords are usually required to pay for part or all of operating costs.

Storage REITs

These usually own and operate self-storage properties (also referred to as mini-warehouse facilities).

- Leases are typically structured as gross leases. Space is rented out on a monthly basis to individuals and small businesses.
- Since the business is relatively easy to enter, there have been periods of excess supply of self-storage properties.
- When evaluating storage REITs, analysts usually focus on construction of new competitive facilities, trends in housing sales activity that can have an impact on demand for temporary storage, local demographic trends, new business start-up activity, and seasonal trends in storage demand.

Health Care REITs

These usually invest in nursing homes, assisted living, and independent residential facilities for retired persons, hospitals, medical office buildings, and rehabilitation centers.

- In several countries, REITs are not allowed to operate these facilities themselves if they want to maintain their exemption from paying income tax at the corporate/trust level. They are required to lease them to health care providers.
- Leases are usually structured as net leases.
- While they are relatively immune to the effects of slowdowns in the overall economy, health care REITs are exposed to the effects of population demographics, government funding programs for health care, construction cycles, financial conditions of health care facility operators/lessees, and costs arising from litigation by residents.
- When evaluating health care REITs, analysts usually focus on operating trends in facilities, government funding, litigation settlements, and insurance costs. The number of new facilities under construction, prospective demand, and prospects for acquisitions are other important considerations.

Hotel REITs

These usually invest in hotel properties.

- Similar to health care REITs, in many countries REITs are not allowed to operate these facilities themselves if they want to maintain their tax-advantaged REIT status. As a result, the properties are usually leased to taxable REIT subsidiaries (or other third-party lessees) who operate them, and the REIT receives passive rental income.
- This rental income represents the major portion of the hotel's net operating cash flow. However, a minor portion of operating cash flow is subject to income taxes.
- The hotel sector is exposed to the business-cycle driven short-term changes in regional, national, and international business and leisure travel.
- When evaluating hotel REITs, analysts usually focus on trends in occupancies, average room rates, and operating profit margins by hotel type and geographic location. Further, they keep a close eye on trends in hotel room bookings by category (individual, corporate, group, convention), in food and beverage sales, and in margins. Finally, analysts also consider expenditures required to maintain and improve the property, and rates of new room construction and completion in the local market.
- A widely-monitored barometer of the hotel business is revenue per available room (RevPAR), which is the product of average room rates and average occupancy.

Diversified REITs

These own and operate more than one type of property.

- Investors may favor them due to their lower risk and the wider opportunities that come with diversification.
- When evaluating diversified REITs, analysts usually focus on management's experience with each property type and degree of local market presence.

Economic Value Determinants of REITs

The major economic factors that affect REITs, along with their relative importance to the different types of equity REITs, are listed in Table 1-1.

Table 1-1: Importance of Factors Affecting Economic Value for Various Property Types[1]

	National GDP Growth	Job Creation	Retail Sales Growth	Population Growth	New Space Supply vs. Demand
Retail	1	3	2	4	4
Office	1	2	5	4	3
Industrial	1	5	2	3	4
Multi-family	1	2	5	2	4
Storage	1	3	5	2	4
Health care	1	4	5	2	3
Hotels	1	2	5	4	3

Notes: 1 = most important, 5 = least important.

1 - Exhibit 6, Vol 5, CFA Program Curriculum 2018.

The largest driver of economic value for all REIT types is growth in the overall economy or national GDP. Economic growth leads to the creation of more jobs, which leads to higher demand for office space. Economic growth also leads to more disposable income, higher demand for multi-family accommodation, hotel rooms, storage space, and retail space.

Principal Risks of REITs

Risks tend to be highest for REITs that concentrate on properties (1) where demand for rental space can fluctuate widely in the short term (especially hotels) and (2) in which dislocations between demand and supply are likely to happen (especially offices, hotels, and healthcare). Further, a REIT's risk profile is also determined by the quality and location of the properties it holds, and their leasing and financing status.

Real Estate Operating Companies (REOCs)

As mentioned earlier, these are ordinary taxable companies that primarily generate cash from sales of developed or improved properties rather than from recurring lease or rental income.

The risks faced by REOCs and REITs are similar to those faced by private real estate investments. These include leasing, operating, financing, market, and economic risks. Although REOCs enjoy more operating flexibility, most investors prefer REITs because of their tax advantages, high-income distributions, and rigorous operating and financial requirements. As a result, in most countries, REOCs generally tend to have less access to equity capital and lower market valuations (higher cost of equity) compared to REITs.

REOCs may elect to convert to REIT status if they satisfy the general requirements, but they must consider potential tax consequences on themselves and their investors.

LESSON 2: VALUATION

LOS 44e: Justify the use of net asset value per share (NAVPS) in REIT valuation and estimate NAVPS based on forecasted cash net operating income. Vol 6, pp 97–103

LOS 44g: Compare the net asset value, relative value (price-to- FFO and price-to-AFFO), and discounted cash flow approaches to REIT valuation. Vol 6, pp 103–109

Valuation: Net Asset Value Approach

Analysts generally use net asset value per share (NAVPS) for valuing REITs and REOCs. NAVPS is the amount (on a per share basis) by which the current market value of a company's assets exceeds the current market value of its liabilities. Stock market prices of REITs and REOCs are compared with their NAVPS to determine whether they are under- or over-valued in the market.

> Note that the NAVPS calculation uses current market values, not accounting book values.

In cases where reliable appraisals are not available, analysts estimate the value of operating real estate by capitalizing net operating income (NOI). This first requires the determination of a capitalization rate (cap rate), which represents the market required rate. The cap rate is estimated based on recent comparable transactions.

$$\text{Capitalization rate} = \frac{\text{NOI of a comparable property}}{\text{Total value of comparable property}}$$

Once the cap rate is determined, it is used to capitalize expected NOI for the coming year of the subject property. In order to compute expected NOI for the coming year, the following adjustments must be performed on current year actual NOI:

- Non-cash rents should be deducted from current period NOI. Non-cash rents result from the accounting practice of "straight-lining" rental revenue from long-term leases. The amount of the deduction equals the difference between the average contractual rent over the leases' terms and the cash rent actually paid for the year.
- Current-year NOI must also be increased to reflect a full year's rent for properties acquired during the year.
- An expected growth rate may then be applied to estimate NOI for the coming year.

Once next year's expected NOI is capitalized at the appropriate cap rate to compute the value of the REIT's operating real estate, the value of other tangible assets (e.g., prepaid expenses, cash, accounts receivable, land for future development, etc.) is added, and the value of liabilities subtracted, to compute the REITs total net asset value. This total net asset value is then divided by the total number of shares outstanding to calculate NAVPS (see Example 2-1). Note that:

- Land is sometimes taken at market value if it can be determined reliably. Typically however, analysts tend to use book values.
- Goodwill, deferred financing expenses, and deferred tax assets are not included in total assets.
- Deferred tax liabilities are not included in total liabilities. Further, liabilities are adjusted to replace the face value of debt with market values if they are significantly different.

Example 2-1: Calculating Net Asset Value per Share (NAVPS)

Consider the following information regarding XYZ REIT:

	$ '000
Last 12 months real estate NOI	584,960
Non-cash rents	9,885
Full year impact of acquisitions	5,279
Cash and cash equivalents	74,388
Land for future development	27,874
Accounts receivable	36,912
Other assets excluding intangible assets	18,375
Total debt	1,625,370
Other liabilities (excluding deferred taxes)	342,579

The REIT has 70,285,000 shares outstanding and the appropriate cap rate is 10%. Given that NOI is expected to grow at a rate of 1.6% next year, estimate NAVPS for XYZ REIT.

Solution:

	$ '000
Last 12 months real estate NOI	584,960
Less: Non-cash rents	9,885
Add: Adjustment for full year impact of acquisitions	5,279
Pro-forma cash NOI for last 12 months	580,354
Add: Next 12 months growth in NOI (=0.016 × 580,354)	9,286
Estimated next 12 months cash NOI	589,640
Assumed cap rate	10%
Estimated value of operating real estate	5,896,397
Add: Cash and cash equivalents	74,388
Add: Land held for future development	27,874
Add: Accounts receivable	36,912
Add: Other assets	18,375
Estimated gross asset value	6,053,946
Less: Total debt	1,625,370
Less: Other liabilities	342,579
Net asset value	**4,085,997**
Shares outstanding	70,285
NAVPS	**$58.13**

Important Considerations in a NAV-Based Approach to Valuing REITs

The NAV approach to valuation is generally used by sector-focused real estate investors and value-oriented investors. It also gains importance when there is significant leveraged buyout activity in the broader market. Investors should consider the following points when using the NAV approach:

- The discount rate used by a private owner/operator of commercial real estate may be different from the discount rate used by investors purchasing shares of REITs. NAV reflects the value of the REIT's assets to a private market buyer, which is usually different from the value that public equity investors ascribe to the business. As a result, there have historically been significant differences between NAV estimates and actual market prices of REIT shares.
- NAV implicitly treats a company as an individual asset or as a static pool of assets. This treatment is not consistent with the going-concern assumption.
- NAV estimates can be quite subjective in times when property markets are illiquid and/or there are few comparable transactions.

LOS 44f: Describe the use of funds from operations (FFO) and adjusted funds from operations (AFFO) in REIT valuation. Vol 6, pp 104–108

Valuation: Relative Valuation (Price Multiple) Approach

Analysts commonly use (1) the price to funds from operations ratio, (2) the price to adjusted funds from operations ratio, and (3) enterprise value to EBITDA ratio to value shares of REITs and REOCs.

Funds from operations (FFO) is calculated as:

> Accounting net earnings
> Add: Depreciation charges on real estate
> Add: Deferred tax charges
> Add (Less): Losses (gains) from sales of property and debt restructuring
> **Funds from operations**

- Depreciation is added back to net income because investors believe that real estate maintains its value to a greater extent than other business assets, and often appreciates in value. Depreciation deductions for real estate under accounting standards therefore do not represent economic reality.
- Deferred tax liabilities and associated deferred tax charges are also added back as they may not be paid for many years, if at all.
- Gains and losses from sales of property and debt restructuring are excluded as they do not represent sustainable, normal income.

Adjusted funds from operations (AFFO) (also referred to as funds available for distribution or cash available for distribution) is considered a more accurate measure of current economic income. It is calculated as:

> Funds from operations
> Less: Non-cash rent
> Less: Maintenance-type capital expenditures and leasing costs
> **Adjusted funds from operations**

- Under IFRS and U.S. GAAP, the average contractual rent over the lease term (known as straight line rent) is recognized as revenue. The difference between this amount and actual rent paid out during the period is known as non-cash rent or straight-line rent adjustment.
- Maintenance-type capital expenditures and leasing costs (including leasing agents' commissions and tenants' improvement allowances) are deducted to reflect costs that must be incurred to maintain the value of the properties.

AFFO is preferred over FFO as it takes into account the capital expenditures necessary to maintain the economic income of a property portfolio. Practically however, FFO is more commonly used because AFFO is subject to more variation and error in estimation.

The EV/EBITDA ratio is discussed in more detail in the Equity section. For a REIT, EBITDA can be computed as NOI minus general and administrative (G&A) expenses.

There are three main drivers behind the P/FFO, P/AFFO, and EV/EBITDA multiples for most REITs and REOCs:

1. Expectations for growth in FFO/AFFO. The higher the expected growth, the higher the multiple for relative valuation.
2. Risk associated with the underlying real estate. For example, hotels entail greater risk than apartments, so apartment-focused REITs tend to trade at higher multiples.
3. Risk associated with the company's capital structures and access to capital. As financial leverage increases, the value of these multiples falls as required return increases due to greater risk.

P/FFO and P/AFFO multiples: Advantages and Drawbacks

Advantages:
- Earnings multiples are widely accepted in evaluating shares across global stock markets and industries.
- They enable portfolio managers to put the valuation of REITs and REOCs into context with other investment alternatives.
- Estimates for FFO are readily available through market data providers.
- They can be used in conjunction with expected growth and leverage levels to deepen the relative analysis among REITs and REOCs.

Drawbacks:
- They may not capture the intrinsic value of all real estate assets (e.g., land parcels and empty buildings that are currently not producing any income) held by the REIT or REOC.
- P/FFO does not adjust for the impact of recurring capital expenditures needed to keep properties operating smoothly.
- New revenue recognition rules and increased levels of one-time gains and accounting charges in recent times have made P/FFO and P/AFFO more difficult to calculate and compare across companies.

Valuation: Discounted Cash Flow Approach

REITs and REOCs return a significant portion of their income to their investors in the form of dividends, which makes dividend discount models appropriate for valuing their shares. Investors usually use two- or three-step dividend discount models with specific assumptions for the near-term, intermediate-term, and/or long-term growth.

> Dividend discount models are discussed in more detail in the Equity section.

The following factors should be considered when forecasting long-term growth rates:

- Internal growth potential resulting from rent increases over time.
- Impact of investment activities (e.g., acquisitions and new development) on the long-term growth rate.
- Impact of changes in capital structure on growth.
- Contribution of retaining and reinvesting a portion of free cash flow on the growth rate.

LOS 44h: Calculate the value of a REIT share using net asset value, price-to-FFO and price-to-AFFO, and discounted cash flow approaches. Vol 6, pp 103–109

We demonstrate the valuation of a REIT using the three approaches to valuation in Example 2-2.

Example 2-2: Calculating the Value of REIT Share

An analyst gathers the following information:

	$ '000
Estimated next 12 months (2013) cash NOI	480,255
Non-cash rents	21,645
Cash and cash equivalents	65,280
Accounts receivable	31,285
Total debt	1,125,468
Other liabilities	215,380
Accounting net earnings	365,295
Depreciation expense	24,415
Deferred tax expense	31,905
Gain on sale of property	64,684
Recurring maintenance-type capital expenditures	38,295

Other information:	
Shares outstanding	100,000
Next year's (2013) expected annual dividend ($)	3
Dividend growth rate for the years 2014 and 2015	3.00%
Dividend growth rate from 2016 into perpetuity	1.50%
Assumed cap rate	10%
Average P/FFO multiple in the industry	10
Average P/AFFO multiple in the industry	12
Cost of equity capital	13%
Risk-free rate	5%

Based on the given information, estimate the value of the property using the following approaches:

1. Net asset value
2. Price-to-FFO
3. Price-to-AFFO
4. Discounted cash flow

Solutions:

1. **Computation of Net Asset Value per Share**

Net Asset Value Approach

	$ '000
Estimated next 12 months cash NOI	480,255
Assumed cap rate	10.00%
Estimated value of operating real estate	4,802,550
Add: Cash and cash equivalents	65,280
Add: Accounts receivable	31,285
Estimated gross asset value	4,899,115
Less: Total debt	1,125,468
Less: Other liabilities	215,380
Net asset value	3,558,267
Shares outstanding	100,000
NAVPS ($)	**35.58**

Note:

- Estimated next 12 months cash NOI is computed after making all required adjustments to current year NOI (including deduction of non-cash rents).

2. **Relative Valuation Using P/FFO**

P/FFO Multiple Approach

	$ '000
Accounting net earnings	365,295
Add: Depreciation expense	24,415
Add: Deferred tax expense	31,905
Less: Gain on sale of property	64,684
Funds from operations (FFO)	356,931
Shares outstanding	100,000
FFO/Share	3.569
Market P/FFO multiple	10
Value per share ($)	**35.69**

3. **Relative Valuation Using P/AFFO**

P/AFFO Multiple Approach

	$ '000
Funds from operations (FFO)	356,931
Less: Non-cash rents	21,645
Less: Recurring maintenance-type capital expenditures	38,295
Adjusted funds from operations (AFFO)	296,991
Shares outstanding	100,000
AFFO/Share	2.97
Market P/FFO multiple	12
Value per share ($)	**35.64**

4. **Valuation Using DCF Analysis**

Discounted Cash Flow Approach

	2012	2013	2014	2015	2016
Dividends per share ($)		3.00	3.09	3.18	3.23
Terminal value at the end of 2015				28.09	
Present values		2.65	2.42	21.67	
Net present value	**26.75**				

Note:

- Terminal value at the end of 2015 = $3.23/(0.13 - 0.015) = 28.09$

READING 45: PRIVATE EQUITY VALUATION

LESSON 1: INTRODUCTION TO VALUATION TECHNIQUES IN PRIVATE EQUITY TRANSACTIONS

There are two perspectives on private equity valuation. In the earlier part of this reading we take the perspective of the private equity (PE) firm that performs valuations of potential investments (portfolio companies). Later in this reading, we take the perspective of outside investors (PE investors) who must evaluate the costs and risks of investing in private equity funds set up by PE firms.

Figure 1-1: Relating PE Investors, PE Firms, and Portfolio Companies

	Partnership Interest		Ownership Stake	
Private Equity Investor	←	Private Equity Fund	←	Portfolio Company
	Investment		Investment	

It is also important to distinguish between the price paid for a private equity stake and its value. Price is determined through negotiations between the buyer and seller, who may assign a different value to the same private equity stake. Unlike public companies, whose value equals market capitalization, valuation of private firms requires the use of complex models. The application of these models is largely dependent on the stage of development of the target company. Further, value also depends on the motives and interests of the counterparties.

LOS 45a: Explain sources of value creation in private equity. Vol 6, pp 141–143

The private equity governance model offers some economic advantages that give PE firms an edge in creating value relative to public companies. These potential advantages are described below:

The Ability to Re-engineer Companies to Generate Superior Returns

Many PE firms hire seasoned industry veterans, including former CEOs and senior advisors, to develop effective high-end re-engineering, reorganization, and consulting capabilities to add value to portfolio companies.

The Ability to Access Credit Markets on Favorable Terms

In the corporate finance section, under the Modigliani-Miller propositions, we learned that taking on more debt increases the value of a firm (due to the interest tax shield) until the company reaches a point where interest tax shield benefits of adding more leverage to the capital structure are offset by higher costs of financial distress.

PE firms are able to raise higher levels of debt compared to public companies due to their:

- Direct control over management; and
- Reputation for having raised and successfully repaid such high levels of debt in previous transactions.

The effect of leverage on the performance of PE firms can also be examined through Jensen's free cash flow hypothesis. Companies generating high cash flows and large capital budgets tend to invest in projects with negative NPVs (that end up destroying value) instead of distributing excess cash to shareholders. High levels of debt in PE transactions may generate value as:

- They keep managers "on their toes" as they have to ensure that they meet payment obligations on debt; and
- They limit manager's discretionary use of cash.

> CDOs and CLOs are described in detail in the Fixed Income section.

PE firms typically raise funds from the syndicated loan market, but frequently repackage those loans via structure products such as collateralized loan obligations (CLOs). Sometimes PE firms issue high yield bonds, which are sold to firms that create collateralized debt obligations (CDOs). CLOs and CDOs result in a transfer of risk from PE firms to the credit market. However, with the credit crisis of 2008, PE firms have found it increasingly difficult to obtain financing for large buyouts.

A Better Alignment of Interests

Studies have shown that managers of private companies are able to undertake higher value-added projects over a longer time frame compared to managers of public companies, who feel pressured to focus on short-term performance due to the emphasis placed by shareholders, the analyst community and the board of directors on quarterly earnings targets.

LOS 45b: Explain how private equity firms align their interests with those of the managers of portfolio companies. Vol 6, pp 143–144

PE firms are able to align the interests of managers of the companies they control with their own (as owners) more effectively than public companies. This is primarily the result of an effective structuring of investment terms in the term sheet to include:

- Results-driven management pay packages and other contractual clauses that ensure that management is properly incentivized to achieve targets.
- Contractual provisions (e.g., tag-along, drag-along rights) that enable management to participate in the upside in value from a successful exit from the portfolio company.
- Provisions that ensure that the PE firm attains control through board representation if the company experiences a major corporate event (e.g., takeover, restructuring, IPO, bankruptcy, or liquidation).
- Noncompete clauses that restrict founders of portfolio companies from launching competing companies for a predefined period of time.
- Clauses that entitle the PE firm to preference dividends, and guarantee the PE firm a multiple of its original investment in the company before other shareholders receive any returns.
- Clauses that make certain important matters (e.g., changes in business plan, acquisitions, and divestitures) subject to approval or veto by the PE firm.
- Mechanisms (known as earn-outs) that link the acquisition price paid by the PE firm to the portfolio company's future financial performance.

In short, there are significant uncertainties regarding the future performance of portfolio companies. Effective contractual structuring can allow the PE firm to significantly increase its level of control in the company over time in case the company fails to achieve pre-specified goals.

LESSON 2: CONTRASTING VALUATION IN VENTURE CAPITAL AND BUYOUT SETTINGS

LOS 45c: Distinguish between the characteristics of buyout and venture capital investments. Vol 6, pp 144–145

Buyout and venture capital (VC) are the two main categories of PE investments.

- VC firms typically have a specialized industry focus (e.g., technology). They aim to invest in new companies with new technologies and focus on revenue growth.
- Buyout firms typically invest in portfolios of larger, more established companies with more predictable cash flows. Their focus is more on EBIT and EBITDA growth.

The following table summarizes the characteristics of buyout and venture capital investments:

Table 2-1: Characteristics of Buyout and Venture Capital Investments[1]

Buyout Investments:	Venture Capital Investments:
Steady and predictable cash flows	Low cash flow predictability, cash flow projections may not be realistic
Excellent market position (can be a niche player)	Lack of market history, new market, and possibly unproven future market (early stage venture)
Significant asset base (may serve as basis for collateral lending)	Weak asset base
Strong and experienced management team	Newly formed management team with strong individual track record as entrepreneurs
Extensive use of leverage consisting of a large proportion of senior debt and significant layer of junior and/or mezzanine debt	Primarily equity funded. Use of leverage is rare and very limited
Risk is measurable (mature businesses, long operating history)	Assessment of risk is difficult because of new technologies, new markets, lack of operating history
Predictable exit (secondary buyout, sale to a strategic buyer, IPO)	Exit difficult to anticipate (IPO, trade sale, secondary venture sale)
Established products	Technological breakthrough but route to market yet to be proven
Potential for restructuring and cost reduction	Significant cash burn rate required to ensure company development and commercial viability
Low working capital requirement	Expanding capital requirement if in the growth phase

1 - Exhibit 3, Volume 5, CFA Program Curriculum 2018

Table 2-1 (*continued*)

Buyout Investments:	Venture Capital Investments:
• Buyout firm typically conducts full blown due diligence approach before investing in the target firm (financial, strategic, commercial, legal, tax, environmental)	• Venture capital firm tends to conduct primarily a technology and commercial due diligence before investing; financial due diligence is limited as portfolio companies have no or very little operating history
• Buyout firm monitors cash flow management, strategic, and business planning	• Venture capital firm monitors achievement of milestones defined in business plan and growth management
• Returns of investment portfolios are generally characterized by lower variance across returns from underlying investments; bankruptcies are rare events	• Returns of investment portfolios are generally characterized by very high returns from a limited number of highly successful investments and a significant number of write-offs from low performing investments or failures
• Large buyout firms are generally significant players in capital markets	• Venture capital firms tend to be much less active in capital markets
• Most transactions are auctions, involving multiple potential acquirers	• Many transactions are "proprietary," being the result of relationships between venture capitalists and entrepreneurs
• Strong performing buyout firms tend to have a better ability to raise larger funds after they have successfully raised their first funds	• Venture capital firms tend to be less scalable relative to buyout firms; the increase in size of subsequent funds tend to be less significant
• Variable revenue to the general partner (GP) at buyout firms generally comprise the following three sources: carried interest, transaction fees, and monitoring fees	• Carried interest (participation in profits) is generally the main source of variable revenue to the general partner at venture capital firms; transaction and monitoring fees are rare in practice

LESSON 3: VALUATION ISSUES IN BUYOUT AND VENTURE CAPITAL TRANSACTIONS AND EXIT ROUTES

LOS 45d: Describe valuation issues in buyout and venture capital transactions. Vol 6, pp 145–149

Private Equity Valuation Techniques

There are six techniques that are generally used to value private equity portfolio companies.

- The income approach (discounted cash flows) is generally applied to companies with sufficient operating history (typically expansion to mature stage companies).
- Relative valuation (using earnings multiples) is generally applied to companies with significant operating history and a predictable stream of cash flows.

- Real option valuation is applied in situations where management/shareholders have significant flexibility in decisionmaking. It is generally applied to companies in the seed or startup phase.
- Replacement cost is applied to earlystage companies that are in the development stage and are currently generating negative cash flow. It rarely applies to mature companies.
- The venture capital method and the leveraged buyout model are discussed later in this reading.

Using Market Data in Valuation

In relative valuation, prices of comparable public companies and recent acquisition prices of comparable companies are used to determine multiples that are then applied to subject company fundamentals to estimate value. When applying price or acquisition multiples, it is very important to adjust those multiples for differences in stages of development, lines of business, capital structure, and risk between benchmark companies and the subject company. Sometimes it can be difficult to find any comparable companies/transactions, especially if the subject company operates in a niche sector or is a pioneer in terms of its product.

When applying the income approach, market data is used in estimating the appropriate discount rate. Recall that in the pureplay method, betas for private companies are estimated by adjusting betas of comparable public companies for differences in leverage. Factors that must be considered in estimating private company valuation parameters from comparable public company data include:

- To what extent are the benchmark public companies comparable to the subject private company?
- What is the target capital structure for the private company?
- What comparable public companies should be used if the private company operates in several lines of business?

Finally, terminal values in DCF analysis can be estimated by either applying the perpetual growth assumption or a trading multiple.

- Changes in the assumed growth rate (input in the perpetual growth model) have a significant impact on the terminal value estimate.
- The average trading multiple for comparable public companies may require adjustments (as described above).

Other Challenges in Private Equity Valuation
- Forecasting the company's future profitability and cash flows based on expectations of exogenous factors (e.g., interest rates, exchange rates, etc.) and value drivers for the business (sales margins, etc.)
- Incorporating ways through which the PE firm can enhance financing, operations, management, and marketing of the portfolio company into those forecasts.
- Determining the appropriate (1) premium for control, (2) lack of liquidity discount (as investments in portfolio companies are typically not readily convertible into cash), and (3) lack of marketability discount (as investors usually face restrictions on the sale of shares).
- Estimating the country risk premium (when valuing companies in emerging markets).

Valuation Issues in Buyout Transactions

A buyout (as the name suggests) is a private equity transaction where the buyer acquires a controlling interest in the target company. Buyouts include management buyouts (MBOs), leveraged buyouts (LBOs), and takeovers. In this reading, our focus is on LBOs, in which borrowed funds are used to finance a significant portion of the acquisition price.

LBOs are typically financed with equity capital, senior debt, high yield bonds, and mezzanine finance. Mezzanine finance is a bridge between equity and debt that can be tailored to meet the requirements of each transaction.

The LBO Model

Strictly speaking, the LBO model is not a valuation technique. It is simply a technique that allows a PE firm to assess the impact of capital structure, purchase price, and various other factors on its expected return from an investment. The LBO model has three main inputs:

1. Forecasted cash flows of the target company.
   - Cash flow forecasts are provided by the target's management and must be carefully scrutinized by the PE firm.
2. Expected return to the providers of financing.
3. The amount of financing available for the transaction.

On the basis of these parameters, a PE firm would use the LBO model to determine the maximum price that it should pay to acquire a company given the returns required by the providers of financing. Analysts also vary the timeofexit assumption to evaluate its impact on expected returns. The exit value is typically estimated using the market approach (using the EVEBITDA multiple of comparables).

Total exit value can be broken down into the following four components:

1. This initial amount invested in the company.
2. Earnings growth resulting from operational improvements and enhanced corporate governance.
3. Multiple expansion from diminishing uncertainty around the company as it nears a successful exit.
4. Utilizing operating cash flows for debt reduction before exit.

Exit value = Initial cost + Earnings growth + Multiple expansion + Debt reduction

Each component of value creation (earnings growth, multiple expansion, and debt reduction) should be carefully considered and examined through lengthy due diligence and scenario analysis to develop a range of estimates for possible value creation from a private equity investment. See Example 3-1.

Example 3-1: Applying the LBO Model to Compute the IRR for a PE Firm

A PE firm is considering the purchase of a company that is valued at $1,500 million. The following information is also available:

- The acquisition will be financed with 65% debt and 35% equity.
- The PE firm expects to exit the investment in 4 years at a projected value of 1.60 times the initial cost.
- The equity investment of $525 million is composed of:
  - $325 million in preference shares. These shares belong to the PE firm and offer an annual dividend of 12% (compounded annually and payable upon exit).
  - $200m in equity. The PE firm holds $175 million of equity while management holds the remaining $25 million.
- The PE firm will receive 87.5% of the company's residual value (after accounting for payments to creditors and preference shareholders) at exit, while management (as part of the management equity program, MEP) will receive the remaining 12.5%.
- By exit, the company expects to pay off $500 million of the initial $975 million in debt by utilizing operating cash flow.

1. Calculate the payoff to the each of the company's providers of capital.
2. Calculate the payoff multiple and IRR for the providers of equity (the PE firm and management).

Solution:

Calculating payoffs to all providers of capital

First we compute the exit value:

$$\text{Exit value} = 1,500m \times 1.6 = \$2,400m$$

Then we compute the payoffs to each of the company's providers of capital:

Debt holders receive the amount outstanding after accounting for the $500m that were paid off using operating cash flows before exit.

$$\text{Payment to debt holders} = 975m - 500m = \$475m$$

Preferred shareholders receive the face value of their investment plus preferred dividends compounded over 4 years at 12%.

$$\text{Payment to preferred shareholders} = \$325m \times (1.12)^4 = \$511.39m$$

Equity holders receive the residual value of the firm after all creditors and preferred shareholders have been paid off:

Payments to equity holders:
Private equity firm: $(2,400 - 475 - 511.39) \times 0.875 = \$1,236.91m$
Management: $(2,400 - 475 - 511.39) \times 0.125 = \$176.70m$

Calculating the payoff multiple for equity holders:

The total payoff to the PE firm equals the sum of the payoffs on its preference shares and equity stake in the company.

Total payoff for PE firm = 511.39 + 1,236.91 = $1,748.3m

Payoff multiple for PE firm = 1,748.3/(325 + 175) = 3.5 times

The total payoff to management equals its pro rata share of the company's residual value.

Total payoff for management = 176.70 million

Payoff multiple for management = 176.70/25 = 7.07 times

Calculating IRRs for the equity holders:

IRR for PE firm:

PV = − $500; FV = $1,748.3; N = 4; CPT I/Y I/Y = 36.75%

IRR for management:

PV = − $25; FV = $176.7; N = 4; CPT I/Y I/Y = 63.05%

Note that:

- The return on the equity owned by management and the return on equity held by the PE firm are most sensitive to changes in the exit value.
  - The larger the exit multiple, the greater the return earned by management and the PE firm on their respective equity interests in the company.
- Senior debt in LBO transactions is typically amortizing. In our example, over the 4 years, debt outstanding fell from an initial level of $975m to $475m at exit.
  - The use of debt magnifies returns available to shareholders.
  - However, higher leverage also exposes the company to greater risk (e.g., of going into bankruptcy).
- Typically, a number of scenarios with varying assumptions regarding exit value, time of exit, growth rates, debt levels, etc. are examined in the LBO model.

Note that LBOs can also be valued using other incomebased valuation approaches (e.g., discounted cash flows and adjusted present value) because future cash flows are fairly predictable (as long as the declining financial leverage is appropriately built into projections). Relative valuation techniques are also often used to corroborate the results of the income approach.

Valuation Issues in Venture Capital Transactions

There are two fundamental concepts in venture capital (VC) transactions:

- Premoney valuation (PRE) refers to the agreed value of the company prior to a round of investment (I).
- Postmoney valuation (POST) refers to the value of the company after a round of investment.

$$POST = PRE + I \quad \text{... (Equation 1)}$$

The proportionate ownership of the VC investor is calculated as: I / POST. See Example 3-2.

Example 3-2: Investment and Ownership Interest of a VC Firm

A VC firm invested $6m in a company currently valued at $9 million. Calculate the postmoney value and the ownership proportion of the VC firm.

Solution:

Postmoney value = Premoney value + Investment

$\qquad$ = 9 million + 6 million = $15 million

Ownership proportion of the VC firm = 6 million / 15 million = 40%

Factors that must be considered in Venture Capital Valuation

- Negotiations between the VC firm and the founder(s) of the portfolio company determine the premoney valuation and the amount of venture capital investment. The VC firm must bear in mind that its ownership stake in the company will be diluted if (1) the company requires subsequent rounds of financing, (2) convertible securities are converted into equity in the future, and/or (3) stock options are issued to management.
- It is fairly difficult to apply the discounted cash flow model to value venture capital investments due to the uncertainty involved in estimating its future cash flows.
- The relative value approach is also difficult to apply, as startups generally have unique features and it is generally not easy to find comparable public companies in the same field.
- As a result, alternative valuation methodologies, including the real option methodology and venture capital approach (described later in this reading) are used to determine value.
- Generally speaking, the premoney valuation is based on the value of the company's intangible assets, including the founder's knowhow, experience, patents, and an assessment of the potential market for the company's product(s).

LOS 45e: Explain alternative exit routes in private equity and their impact on value. Vol 6, pp 149–151

As illustrated in Example 3-1, the exit value and timing of exit are important determinants of the total return on a private equity investment. PE firms consider exit options very carefully before deciding to make an investment in a particular company. They generally have access to the following four exit routes:

Initial public offerings (IPOs) involve taking the company public. IPOs generally result in higher valuation multiples as they result in greater liquidity of company shares, enable the company to access large amounts of capital and make it possible for the company to attract highercaliber managers. On the downside, the process of taking a company public can be quite cumbersome, entails significant costs, and leaves the company with less flexibility.

An IPO is an appropriate exit route for large, established companies with excellent growth prospects. However, the timing of the IPO is very important. After the internet bubble burst in 2000, the number of successful IPOs diminished, forcing PE firms to seek alternative routes to exit their investments.

A secondary market sale involves the sale of an ownership stake in the company held by a financial investor to other financial or strategic investors. Given the segmented nature of private equity, secondary market transactions usually occur within segments. For example, buyout firms tend to sell to other buyout firms (secondary buyouts) and venture firms tend to sell to other venture firms (secondary venture capital transactions). Venture capital exits via buyouts are not common because buyout firms are reluctant to use significant amounts of leverage to finance early stage companies.

A secondary market sale typically results in highest valuation for a company outside of an IPO. Further, the segmented nature of the market results in PE firms specializing in particular areas, (e.g., restructuring, merger, new market) and add substantial value to portfolio companies.

A management buyout (MBO) involves the takeover of a company by its management using significant amounts of leverage to finance the acquisition. Although this method results in the best alignment of interests, the company suffers from reduced flexibility as a result of its significant financial leverage.

Liquidation involves an outright sale of the company's assets. It results in the lowest value for the company. Further, liquidation may result in negative publicity for the PE firm due to its obvious failure to add value to the company or if a large number of employees are displaced.

It is very important for a PE firm to time the exit and to take the optimal exit route. Exits during exuberant market conditions obviously result in higher valuation multiples. Also note that if a PE firm plans to exit an investment in the next year or two, use of multiples extracted from comparable public companies is appropriate. However, if exit is anticipated after a much longer period of time, current valuations multiples are less relevant. Stress tests must then be conducted using a wider range of values to determine the anticipated exit multiple.

LESSON 4: PRIVATE EQUITY FUND STRUCTURES, DUE DILIGENCE, AND VALUATION

LOS 45f: Explain private equity fund structures, terms, valuation, and due diligence in the context of an analysis of private equity fund returns. Vol 6, pp 151–161

We now move on and look at private equity investments from the perspective of an investor in a PE fund. It is very important for investors in PE funds (that are managed by PE firms) to gain a good understanding of the PE fund's structure, terms of investment, and PE fund valuation.

Private Equity Fund Structures

The most common form of private equity fund structures is the limited partnership. It consists of:

- Limited partners (LPs), who are the providers of funds that are invested in target companies. They have limited liability and are not actively involved in the management of portfolio companies.
- A general partner (GP), who manages the fund and is jointly liable for all the firm's debts.

An alternative to the limited partnership structure is a company limited by shares, which works in the same way as a limited partnership, but offers better legal protection to the partners.

Note that most of these fund structures are closed-end. Investors cannot redeem their shares during the life of the fund, and new investors can only enter the fund at pre-specified times at the discretion of the GP.

Private equity firms operate in two businesses, (1) raising funds and (2) managing the investments financed with those funds. PE firms typically spend a year or two raising funds and once the target fund size is reached, they draw on those funds to invest them in portfolio companies. PE funds usually have duration of 10 to 12 years, which may be extended for an additional 2 to 3 years. Figure 4-1 illustrates the different stages of a typical PE fund.

Figure 4-1: Funding Stages for a PE Fund[2]

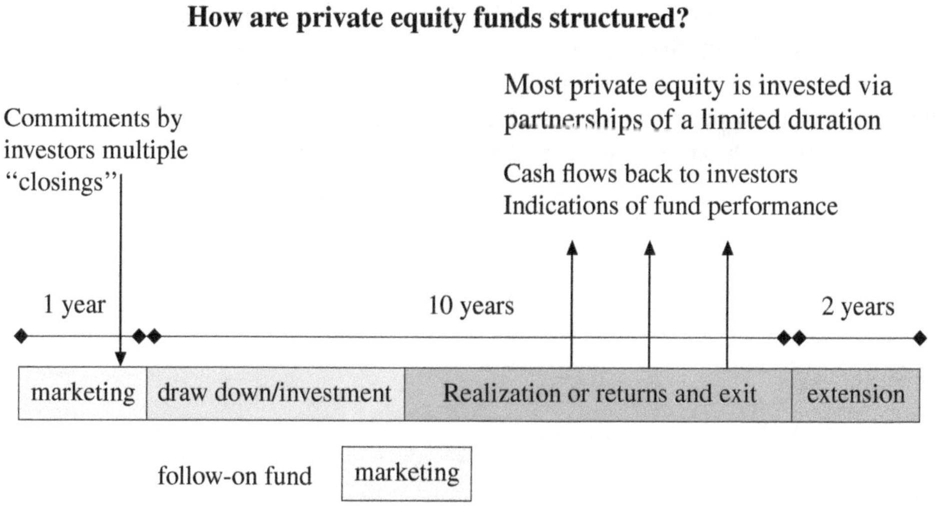

How are private equity funds structured?

2 - Exhibit 6, Volume 5, CFA Program Curriculum 2018

Private Equity Fund Terms

The terms of a PE fund are defined in the fund prospectus or the limited partnership agreement. The terms (1) ensure that the interests of GPs and LPs are aligned and (2) define GP compensation (transaction fees, profit shares, etc.).

The terms of the fund are negotiated by the GP and LPs. These days, the balance of negotiating power tends to be in favor of the GPs, especially for oversubscribed funds.

The terms of a PE fund may be classified broadly as economic terms and corporate governance terms.

Economic Terms

- Management fees are paid annually to the GP over the lifetime of the fund. They are typically calculated as a percentage of committed capital (usually 1.5 to 2.5%), but may sometimes be based on invested capital or net asset value.
    - Committed capital refers to the amount of funds promised by LPs to the PE fund.
    - Paid-in or invested capital refers to the amount of funds actually received from investors and invested in portfolio companies by the PE fund.
    - Net asset value is described later in the reading.
- Transaction fees are paid to the GP as compensation for investment banking services (e.g., M&A advisory) for transactions for the fund. These fees are usually evenly split between the LPs and the GP and, when paid, are deducted from management fees.
- Carried interest is the GP's share of profits generated by the fund. Carried interest is typically around 20% of the fund's profits (net of management fees).
- Ratchet is a mechanism that determines the allocation of equity between the PE firm and the management of the target company. Ratchets enable target company management to increase its equity interest in the company based on its actual future performance, and on the return earned by the PE firm.
- Hurdle rate is the IRR that the private equity fund must achieve before the GP can receive any carried interest. The hurdle rate is typically in the range of 7 to 10%. It serves to align the interests of the GP with those of LPs by incentivizing the GP.
- Target fund size refers to the total size of the private equity fund stated in the fund prospectus or information memorandum. The target fund size gives an indication to investors about the size of the portfolio that the GP is comfortable managing. If the PE firm is unable to raise the targeted amount of funds, PE investors would construe it as a negative signal about the PE firm's abilities.
- Vintage year is the year in which the fund was launched. References to vintage years facilitate comparisons of performance of different funds.
- Term of the fund is the duration of the fund (typically 10 years).

Corporate Governance Terms

- A key man clause names key executives who are expected to play an active role in the management of the PE fund. In case a key man leaves the PE fund, or does not spend an adequate amount of time on its management, the GP may be prohibited from making any new investments until a new key executive is brought in.
- A disclosure and confidentiality term specifies what fund-performance information can be disclosed by investors in the fund to their shareholders. While performance-related disclosures are permitted, information relating to portfolio companies cannot typically be disclosed.
- A clawback provision ensures that the distribution of profits between the GP and LPs is in line with the agreed profit split. For example, if the fund exits from a highly profitable investment relatively early in its lifetime, but subsequent exits are less profitable, the GP would be required by the clawback provision to return fees, expenses, and capital contributions to LPs so that the overall profit sharing ratio conforms to the agreed profit split. Clawbacks are typically due on fund termination, but can sometimes be reconciled annually (referred to as a true-up). See Example 4-2.
- A distribution waterfall outlines the mechanism for distribution of profits to LPs and the GP (see Example 4-1). Two distinct types of distribution methods are:
  - Deal-by-deal waterfalls, in which the GP receives carried interest after each individual deal. Deal-by-deal waterfalls result in earlier distributions to the GP.
  - Total return method, in which carried interest is calculated on profits earned by the entire portfolio. Total return waterfalls result in earlier distributions to LPs. There are two alternatives under the total return method.
    - In the first alternative, the GP receives carried interest only after the fund has returned the entire **committed capital** to LPs.
    - In the second alternative, the GP receives carried interest on all distributions once the value of the investment portfolio exceeds a certain threshold above **invested capital**.
- Tag-along, drag-along rights ensure that any acquisition offers are extended to all shareholders, including management; not just to the controlling interest in the company.
- A no-fault divorce clause allows for the removal of the GP (without cause) if a super majority (generally above 75%) votes in favor of the removal.
- Removal for "cause" is a clause that allows for the removal of the GP, or the termination of the fund, given a "cause." Such "cause" may include gross negligence of the GP, a "key person" event, a felony conviction of a key management person, bankruptcy of the GP, or a material breach of the fund prospectus.
- Investment restrictions impose requirements for a minimum level of diversification in the fund's investment portfolio, limits on borrowing, and so on.

- Co-investment. LPs are granted the first right to invest in other funds of the GP. LPs benefit from lower (or no) management fees on coinvested capital, and GPs obtain access to another source of funds. The GP is prohibited from using capital from different funds to invest in the same portfolio company as this would give rise to a conflict of interest. The PE firm would be tempted to use capital from a newer fund to invest in a troubled company that had previously received capital from another fund.

Example 4-1: Carried Interest and Distribution Waterfalls

Alpha Equity Fund has committed capital of $250 million. The GP is entitled to receive carried interest of 20%. The following three investments were made by the fund at the beginning of 2011 and exited at the end of 2011:

Portfolio Company	Amount Invested	Proceeds Upon Exit
A	$60 million	$85 million
B	$80 million	$75 million
C	$20 million	$40 million

Calculate the amount of carried interest paid to the GP for 2011 assuming that:

1. Carried interest is paid on a deal-by-deal basis with a hurdle rate of 50%.
2. Carried interest is based on the first alternative of the total return method (i.e., if the value of the investment portfolio exceeds committed capital).
3. Carried interest is based on the second alternative of the total return method (i.e., if the value of the investment portfolio exceeds the value of invested capital by 20%).

Solutions:

1. Theoretical carried interest on investment in Company A = $(85 - 60) \times 20\% = \$5$ million
   IRR of investment in Company A = $(85 / 60) - 1 = 41.67\%$
   Since the IRR of the investment in Company A (41.67%) is lower than the hurdle rate (50%), no carried interest will be paid on this deal.

   No carried interest will be paid on the investment in Company B as it resulted in a loss of 6.25%.

   Theoretical carried interest on investment in Company C = $(40 - 20) \times 20\% = \$4$ million
   IRR of investment in Company C = $(40 / 20) - 1 = 100\%$

   Since the IRR of the investment in Company C (100%) is greater than the hurdle rate (50%), carried interest amounting to $4m [= 20% of (40 − 20)] will be paid to the GP.

2. Under the first alternative of the total return method, carried interest is paid to the GP only when the value of the portfolio exceeds **committed capital**.

Total committed capital = $250 million

Ending value of the portfolio = $85m + $75m + $40m = $200 million

Since the value of the portfolio is less than committed capital, no carried interest will be paid to the GP.

3. Under this alternative of the total return method, carried interest is paid to the GP only when the value of the portfolio exceeds **invested capital** by 20%.

Invested capital = $60m + $80m + $20m = $160 million

Carried interest will only be paid if the value of the portfolio exceeds $192m (= 160 × 1.2). Since the value of the portfolio is $200m, carried interest will be paid.

Carried interest = $(200 - 160) \times 20\% = \$8$ million

Example 4-2: Clawback Provision

Mega Equity Fund has committed capital of $200 million. At the end of the first year, the fund exited one of its investments and earned a profit of $20 million. However, the following year, the fund incurred a loss of $8 million when it exited one of its other investments.

Given that the GP is entitled to 20% carried interest on a deal-by-deal basis, and that a clawback provision with an annual true-up applies, determine the amount of carried interest received by the GP in Year 1 and whether the GP should return any profits to the LPs in the following year.

Solution:

Carried interest paid in the first year = $20m × 0.2 = $4 million

With a subsequent loss of $8 million, the GP would have to pay back 20% of the loss to LPs under the clawback provision with an annual true-up.

Amount to be paid back to LPs = $8m × 0.2 = $1.6 million

Due Diligence Investigations by Potential Investors

Prior to investing in a private equity fund, prospective investors generally conduct a thorough due diligence of the fund because of the following reasons:

- PE investments are locked in for the long term and are relatively illiquid. However, note that investors' funds are not generally locked in for the lifetime of the fund. If there are successful exits in the interim, cash is returned to investors immediately.
- Returns of PE funds usually tend to persist over time (i.e., top-performing funds typically continue to outperform, while poor-performing funds continue to underperform and eventually go out of business).
- The difference in returns between top-performing funds and poor-performing funds is very large. Therefore, a thorough examination of the past performance of a PE firm's funds is important in choosing which PE firm to invest in.

Private Equity Fund Valuation

Because there is no secondary market for private equity investments, the description of private equity valuation in a fund's prospectus is typically related to the fund's net asset value (NAV), which equals the value of the fund's assets less liabilities (accrued fund expenses). The assets of the fund are usually valued by the GP in one of the following six ways:

1. At cost with significant adjustments for subsequent financing events or deterioration.
2. At lower of cost or market value.
3. By revaluing a portfolio company whenever a new financing round involving new investors takes place.
4. At cost with no interim adjustment until exit.
5. With a discount for restricted securities.
6. Marked to market by reference to a peer group of public comparables and applying illiquidity discounts. This method is not used too often.

Issues in Calculating NAV for a PE Fund

- If the NAV is only adjusted when a new round of financing occurs, reported NAV will be outdated if there is an extended period with no financing round.
- The value of investments in portfolio companies cannot be calculated with certainty before exit as there is no active market for them.
- LPs are legally obligated to meet capital calls for funds that have been committed by them, but not yet called for and invested by the GP. These funds are not included in the NAV calculation. Further, the value of these undrawn LP capital commitments depends on the future cash flows they generate when they are invested by the GP. If new investments earn high returns, they will increase the NAV and total return to investors.
- Funds with different investment strategies may use different valuation policies. For example, an early-stage venture capital firm may carry its investments at cost, while a late-stage development fund may value its holdings based on public market comparables. Asset price bubbles would inflate NAVs based on market multiples.
- Valuations are usually performed by GPs. However, note that there is increasing pressure from LPs to have appraisals performed by independent third parties.

LESSON 5: RISKS AND COSTS OF INVESTING IN PRIVATE EQUITY AND EVALUATING FUND PERFORMANCE

LOS 45g: Explain risks and costs of investing in private equity. Vol 6, pp 161–164

Differences between investing in public equities and private equity firms include the following:

- Unlike public firms, whose shares are available for purchase to the general public, private equity investments are only available to qualified investors (institutions and high-net-worth individuals who meet certain wealth criteria).
- In public market investing, investors gain ownership of shares in the company at the time that a trade is settled (at the same time that they put up the money for the purchase). On the other hand, in private equity, investors initially only commit to investing a certain amount of capital which is then drawn down by the PE firm as it deploys funds in portfolio companies.
- Private equity returns typically follow a "J-curve" pattern. Low or negative returns are reported in the early years of the fund, followed by increased returns as portfolio companies near exit. Returns on investments in public companies do not follow any such pattern.

Aside from investment strategy specific risk factors (buyout, venture capital, and mezzanine), industry specific risk factors, investment vehicle specific risk factors, and (sometimes) regional or emerging market risks, there are some general private equity risk factors that include:

- Illiquidity of investments. PE investors are not able to liquidate their investments whenever they desire as there is no active secondary market.
- Unquoted investments. Investing in unquoted securities is more risky than investing in securities that are quoted on a regulated securities exchange.
- Competition for attractive investment opportunities. Competition to find lucrative investment opportunities on reasonable terms may be high.
- Reliance on the management of investee companies (agency risk). Managers of portfolio companies may not prioritize the interests of the PE firm. This risk is particularly high in early stage deals, where management may retain a controlling stake in the company and abuse this control to maximize personal benefits at the expense of other shareholders.
- Loss of capital. Investors may withdraw capital in times of high business and financial risk.
- Adverse impact of government regulations. Changes in regulations may adversely impact the company's business.
- Taxation risk. Changes in the tax treatment of capital gains, dividends, or limited partnerships can affect investor appetite for PE investments.
- Valuation of investments. Valuations of private investments are difficult to perform, and may be biased unless performed by an independent third party.
- Lack of investment capital. Portfolio companies may struggle to raise funds in subsequent rounds of financing.
- Lack of diversification. Investment portfolios may be highly concentrated, which can lead to significant losses. PE investors should ideally invest in a mix of PE funds with different vintages, different strategies (buyout, VC, restructuring, mezzanine, etc.) and different stages of development for underlying companies (early stage, late stage, etc.)
- Market risk. Changes in general market conditions (interest rate, currency exchange rates, etc.) may have an adverse impact on PE investments. Note that short term fluctuations are not very relevant given the long-term horizon of PE investments.

The costs associated with private equity investments are much more significant than the cost of investing in public companies. Costs of investing in private equity can be broken down into:

- Transaction fees. These include costs of due diligence, bank financing costs, and legal fees for acquisition and sale transactions in portfolio companies.
- Investment vehicle fund setup costs. These include legal costs of setting up the investment vehicle (e.g., limited partnership, company limited by shares) and are amortized over the vehicle's life.
- Administrative costs include custodian, transfer agent, and accounting costs and are usually charged as a percentage of the fund's net asset value.
- Audit costs are fixed annual charges.
- Management and performance fees for PE funds are typically higher than that for plain investment funds. In the private equity industry management and performance fees are around 2% and 20% respectively.
- Dilution. Shareholders suffer dilution of their equity interests in portfolio companies from additional rounds of financing and from stock options granted to management.
- Placement fees. These are charged by placement agents who raise funds for PE firms. Placement fees may be charged upfront (usually 2%), or as trailer fees that are charged annually as a fraction of the amount invested by limited partners, as long as the amount remains invested.

LOS 45h: Interpret and compare financial performance of private equity funds from the perspective of an investor. Vol 6, pp 161–164

Evaluating Fund Performance

The performance of a private equity fund may be evaluated using either the internal rate of return (IRR) or a multiples-based approach.

Internal Rate of Return (IRR)

IRR is a cash-weighted (or money-weighted) return measure that accounts for the time value of money. IRR is the recommended measure of private equity performance according to the Global Investment Performance Standards (GIPS) and other venture capital and private equity standards. However, in a private equity setting, the IRR should be interpreted with care because it assumes that interim cash flows are reinvested at the IRR, whereas NAV is primarily illiquid for most of a PE fund's life. IRR may be calculated gross or net of fees (management fees, carried interest, etc).

- Gross IRR relates cash flows between the private equity fund and its portfolio companies. It is therefore, a relevant measure for evaluating the PE firm's ability to create value.
- Net IRR relates cash flows between the private equity fund and LPs and is therefore, a relevant measure of return to investors.

Multiples

Multiples simply measure the total return to investors relative to the total amount invested. Although they ignore the time value of money, multiples are popular among the LPs because of their simplicity and ability to distinguish between realized returns (proceeds from actual successful exits) and unrealized returns (based on the GP's estimates of NAV).

Quantitative Measures of Return

The most commonly used multiples are:

- PIC (paid-in capital): Ratio of paid-in capital to date to committed capital.
  - This ratio measures the proportion of committed capital called by the GP thus far.
- DPI (distributed to paid-in) or cash-on-cash return: Value of cumulative distributions paid to LPs as a proportion of cumulative invested capital.
  - It is a measure of the fund's **realized** return on investment.
  - DPI is typically presented net of management fees and carried interest.
- RVPI (residual value to paid-in): Value of LPs' shareholdings held with the fund as a proportion of cumulative invested capital.
  - It is a measure of the PE fund's **unrealized** return on investment.
  - The value of portfolio holdings is determined by the GP.
  - RVPI is also typically presented net of management fees and carried interest.
- TVPI (total value to paid-in): Value of portfolio companies' distributed (realized) and undistributed (unrealized) value as a proportion of cumulative invested capital.
  - TVPI equals the sum of DPI and RVPI.
  - It is also typically presented net of management fees and carried interest.

Qualitative Measures

In addition to the quantitative measures of return, the following qualitative aspects should also be analyzed:

- Investments realized since inception. All successes and failures should be evaluated.
- Unrealized investments. Troubled portfolio companies should be identified and the expected time to exit should be estimated for each portfolio company.
- Cash flow forecasts for each portfolio company and for the overall portfolio.
- Portfolio valuation, NAV, and audited financial statements.

For example, consider a fund that follows a venture capital strategy in tech companies. This fund had a vintage year of 1999 and a term of 10 years. Five years into its life (midlife) the fund had a DPI of 5% and a RVPI of 52%.

The TVPI of 57% indicates that the J-curve for this fund will probably be extended. The fund is half-way into its life and LPs' total return (realized and unrealized) is still well short of committed capital. Further, the bulk of the return is unrealized (as RVPI is significantly greater than DPI) which suggests that the fund has been unable to harvest many of its investments. Given that the fund was formed just before the Internet bubble burst in 2000, we can infer that exit opportunities must have diminished and the fund may have had to write off some investments.

In this situation, the LPs should carefully evaluate existing companies in the fund's portfolio and carefully scrutinize the GP's valuations of those companies to ensure that they are not inflated given the bleak outlook for the technology sector. See Example 5-1.

Example 5-1: Comparing Private Equity Fund Performance

An analyst gathered the following information regarding two private equity funds:

Fund	Gross IRR	Net IRR	DPI	RVPI	TVPI	Performance quartile	Maturity of fund
Fund A	18.4%	12.1%	1.21	1.35	2.56	1	7 years
Fund B	2.1%	−0.2%	0.26	1.08	1.34	2	3 years

Compare the performance of the two private equity funds.

Solution:

Based on the information given, we can infer the following regarding the two funds:

Fund A:
- It has so far returned $1.21 to LPs for every $1 of capital drawn down.
- Its RVPI of 1.35 indicates that the fund is expected to offer a substantial return at termination when it harvests its investments.
- The gross IRR of 18.4% and net IRR of 12.1% after 7 years also represent good performance.
- The fund ranks in the first quartile, which implies that it belongs to the best performing funds of that category and vintage year.

Fund B:
- It is a less mature fund than Fund A.
- Its gross IRR of 2.1% and net IRR of −0.2% indicate that it is still experiencing the J-curve effect.
- A DPI of 0.26 indicates that the fund's realized returns are not yet substantial. However, the RVPI of 1.08 indicates that despite the fact that it is only 3 years old, the fund has made some fairly profitable investments.

Benchmarks

The IRR of a particular PE fund should be compared with the median IRR for the peer group of comparable PE funds that have a similar investment strategy and vintage year. This is because PE returns follow clear trends over time, with some vintage years performing much better than others.

Analysts must also be careful when comparing the performance of private equity to that of other asset classes. This is because PE funds are usually measured using the IRR (which is a money-weighted return measure), while the performance of most other asset classes is measured in terms of time-weighted rates of return. One solution is to calculate the money-weighted rate of return for benchmark equity indices using the cash flow patterns of PE funds. Unfortunately however, this technique suffers from significant limitations.

LOS 45i: Calculate management fees, carried interest, net asset value, distributed to paid in (DPI), residual value to paid in (RVPI), and total value to paid in (TVPI) of a private equity fund. Vol 6, pp 161–164

Example 5-2: Calculating Performance Measures

Gamma Fund has committed capital of $250 million. The general partner (GP) of the fund is paid carried interest of 20% if the fund's NAV before distributions exceeds committed capital. Further, the fund charges a management fee of 3% of paid-in capital. The following table provides information regarding the fund's capital calls and performance for the first 7 years of its life.

Year	Capital Called Down	Operating Results	Distributions
1	70	−30	
2	50	−20	
3	30	5	
4	20	70	
5	20	80	40
6	10	100	80
7	10	155	120

1. Calculate paid-in capital, management fees, NAV before distributions, carried interest, and NAV after distributions for each of the 7 years.
2. Calculate the fund's DPI, RVPI, and TVPI at the end of 7 years.

Solution:

Years	Capital Called Down	Paid-in Capital	Management Fees	Operating Results	NAV before Distributions	Carried Interest	Distributions	NAV after Distributions
1	70	70	2.1	−30	37.9	0.0		37.9
2	50	120	3.6	−20	64.3	0.0		64.3
3	30	150	4.5	5	94.8	0.0		94.8
4	20	170	5.1	70	179.7	0.0		179.7
5	20	190	5.7	80	274.0	4.8	40	229.2
6	10	200	6.0	100	333.2	11.8	80	241.4
7	10	210	6.3	155	400.1	13.4	120	266.7

1. **Paid-in capital (PIC)** simply equals the cumulative amount called-down. For example:

    PIC (Year 6) = 70 + 50 + 30 + 20 + 20 + 10 = $200m

    Management fees for each year are calculated as 3% of PIC. For example:

    Management fee (Year 6) = 200 × 3% = $6m

NAV before distributions = Prior year's NAV after distributions + Capital called down − Management fees + Operating results

NAV before distributions (Year 6) = 229.2 + 10 − 6 + 100 = $333.2m

The GP starts earning **carried interest** once the fund's NAV exceeds committed capital ($250m). This occurs in Year 5, when the fund's NAV before distributions equals $274m. Therefore, carried interest will be paid as 20% of the excess.

Carried interest (Year 5) = (274 − 250) × 20% = $4.8m

Carried interest in each subsequent year will be paid on the increase in NAV before distributions over the year.

Carried interest (Year 6) = (333.2 − 274) × 20% = $11.8m

NAV after distributions = NAV before distributions − Carried interest − Distributions

NAV after distributions (Year 6) = 333.2 − 11.8 − 80 = $241.4m

2. DPI is the value of cumulative distributions paid to LPs as a proportion of cumulative invested capital.

DPI = Cumulative distributions / PIC
DPI = (40 + 80 + 120) / 210 = 1.1429

A DPI greater than 1.0 indicates that LPs' realized return already exceeds the amount they invested in the fund.

RVPI equals the value of LPs' shareholdings held with the fund as a proportion of cumulative invested capital.

RVPI = NAV after distributions / PIC
RVPI = 266.7 / 210 = 1.27

TVPI equals the sum of DPI and RVPI.

TVPI = DPI + RVPI = 2.4129

The TVPI indicates that when realized and unrealized returns are combined, LPs should expect to earn almost 2.5 times their investment in the fund once all the fund's investments have been harvested.

LESSON 6: VALUATION OF VENTURE CAPITAL DEALS

LOS 45j: Calculate pre-money valuation, post-money valuation, ownership fraction, and price per share applying the venture capital method 1) with single and multiple financing rounds and 2) in terms of IRR. Vol 6, pp 166–176

The Basic Venture Capital Method (in Terms of NPV)

The basic venture capital method using the NPV framework requires the following steps. The calculations and the rationale behind them are illustrated in Example 6-1.

Step 1: Determine the post-money valuation.

Step 2: Determine the pre-money valuation.

Step 3: Calculate the ownership percentage of the VC investor.

Step 4: Calculate the number of shares to be issued to the VC investor.

Step 5: Calculate the price of shares.

Example 6-1: Applying the Basic Venture Capital Method with a Single Round of Financing

The entrepreneur founders of Tiara Ltd. believe that in 5 years they will be able to sell the company for $60 million. However, they are currently in desperate need of $7 million. A VC firm that is interested in investing in Tiara estimates that the discount rate commensurate with the relatively high risk inherent in the firm is 45%. Given that current shareholders hold 1 million shares and that the venture capital firm makes an investment of $7 million in the company, calculate the following:

1. Post-money value
2. Pre-money value
3. Ownership proportion of the VC firm
4. The number of shares that must be issued to the VC firm
5. Share price after the VC firm invests $7 million in the company

Solutions:

1. After receiving the $7 million, Tiara is expected to be worth $60 million in 5 years. Therefore, the post-money value of the company equals the present value of the anticipated exit value.

$$\text{Post-money value} = \frac{\text{Exit value}}{(1 + \text{Required rate of return})^{\text{Number of years to exit}}}$$

$$= \frac{60}{1.45^5} = \$9.3608\text{m}$$

---

2. The pre-money value is calculated as the post-money value minus the VC firm's investment.

   Pre-money value = Post-money value – Investment
   $$= 9.3608 - 7 = \$2.3608 \text{ million}$$

3. The VC firm is investing $7 million in a company that will be worth $9.3608 million. Therefore, the ownership stake of the VC firm is calculated as:

   $$\text{Ownership proportion of VC investor} = \frac{\text{Investment}}{\text{Post-money value}}$$
   $$= 7/9.3608 = 74.78\%$$

4. The current shareholders own 1m shares and they have a 25.22% (= 100 – 74.8%) equity interest in Tiara. The number of shares that must be issued to the VC firm such that it has a 74.78% ownership stake is calculated as:

   $$\text{Shares to be issued} = \frac{\text{Proportion of venture capitalist investment} \times \text{Shares held by company founders}}{\text{Proportion of investment of company founders}}$$
   $$= \frac{0.7478 \times 1 \text{ million}}{(1 - 0.7478)} = 2{,}965{,}143$$

5. The price per share is then calculated as:

   $$\text{Price per share} = \frac{\text{Amount of venture capital investment}}{\text{Number of shares issued to venture capital investment}}$$
   $$= 7{,}000{,}000 / 2{,}965{,}143 = \$2.36 \text{ per share}$$

Venture Capital Method in Terms of the IRR

The venture capital method can also be explained in terms of the IRR. Whether based on NPV or IRR, the venture capital method gives exactly the same answer. The IRR method involves the following steps. The calculations and the rationale behind them are illustrated in Example 6-2.

Step 1: Calculate the future wealth required by the VC investor to achieve its desired IRR.

Step 2: Calculate the ownership percentage of venture capital investor.

Step 3: Calculate the number of shares to be issued to the venture capital investor.

Step 4: Calculate the price of shares.

Step 5: Determine the post-money valuation.

Step 6: Determine the pre-money valuation.

Example 6-2: Applying the IRR-Based Venture Capital Method

Work with the information from Example 6-1 (regarding Tiara Ltd.) and calculate the following using the IRR-based venture capital method.

1. The future wealth required by the VC to attain its desired IRR
2. Ownership percentage of the VC firm
3. The number of shares that must be issued to the VC firm
4. Stock price per share
5. Post-money value
6. Pre-money value

Solutions:

1. First we need to determine the amount of wealth the VC needs to accumulate over the 5 years to achieve the desired return of 45% on its $7m investment in Tiara.

$$\text{Required wealth} = \text{Investment} \times (1 + \text{IRR})^{\text{Number of years to exit}}$$

$$= 7m \times (1 + 0.45)^5 = \$44.868m$$

2. The percentage ownership that the VC firm requires to achieve its desired 45% return on a $7 million investment is calculated by dividing the required wealth by the expected value of the company at exit:

$$\text{Ownership proportion} = \text{Required wealth} / \text{Exit value}$$

$$= 44.868m / 60m = 74.78\%$$

3. The current shareholders of Tiara hold 1m shares in the company and have an equity stake of 25.22% = (100% − 74.78%). The number of shares that must be issued to the VC firm so that it owns 74.78% of Tiara is calculated as:

$$\text{Shares to be issued} = \frac{\text{Proportion of venture capitalist investment} \times \text{Shares held by company founders}}{\text{Proportion of investment of company founders}}$$

$$= \frac{0.7478 \times 1 \text{ million}}{(1 - 0.7478)} = 2,965,143$$

4. Given that the VC firm is investing $7m in Tiara, the price of a share is calculated as:

$$\text{Price per share} = \frac{\text{Amount of venture capital investment}}{\text{Number of shares issued to venture capital investment}}$$

$$= 7,000,000 / 2,965,143 = \$2.36 \text{ per share}$$

> 5. The post-money value can be calculated in two ways:
>
>> An investment of $7 million gives the VC firm a 74.78% equity interest in Tiara. Therefore, the post-money valuation of the company is calculated as 7m / 0.7478 = $9.3608m (allowing for rounding error).
>>
>> Alternatively, there are 3,965,143 (= 1,000,000 + 2,965,143) shares in the company that are each worth $2.36. Therefore, the value of the company equals 2.36 × 3,965,143 = $9.3608m (allowing for rounding error).
>
> 6. The pre-money value can also be calculated in two ways:
>
>> The pre-money value can be calculated as the post-money value minus the amount invested by the VC: $9.3608m − 7m = $2.3608m.
>>
>> Alternatively, we can multiply the number of shares held by the current shareholders by the price per share: 1m × 2.36 = $2.3608m (allowing for rounding error).

Venture Capital Method with Multiple Rounds of Financing

When there are 2 rounds of financing, the venture capital method requires the following steps (see Example 6-3):

Step 1: Define appropriate compound interest rates between each financing round.

Step 2: Determine the post-money valuation after the second round.

Step 3: Determine the pre-money valuation after the second round.

Step 4: Determine the post-money valuation after the first round.

Step 5: Determine the pre-money valuation after the first round.

Step 6: Determine the required ownership percentage for second round investors.

Step 7: Determine the required ownership percentage for first round investors. Note that this is not their final ownership percentage as their equity interest will be diluted in the second round.

Step 8: Determine the number of shares that must be issued to first round investors for them to attain their desired ownership percentage.

Step 9: Determine price per share in the first round.

Step 10: Determine the number of shares at the time of the second round.

Step 11: Determine the number of shares that must be issued to second round investors for them to attain their desired ownership percentage.

Step 12: Determine price per share in the second round.

Example 6-3: Applying the Basic Venture Capital Method with Multiple Rounds of Financing

Suppose Tiara Ltd. actually intended to raise $10 million. However, doing so in a single round of financing would not have been feasible as it would have led to a pre-money valuation of –$0.639 million. Therefore, the company decided to undertake an initial financing round worth $7 million and to follow that up with another financing round worth $3 million after 4 years. The entrepreneur founders still believe the company's exit value will be $60 million at the end of 5 years. Given that investors in the second financing round feel that a discount rate of 25% is appropriate, calculate the price per share after the second round of financing.

Solution:

First we compute the compound discount rates:

Between first and second round $= (1.45)^4 = 4.4205$

Between second round and exit $= (1.25)^1 = 1.25$

Then we calculate the post-money value after the second round by discounting the terminal value for 1 year at 25%.

$POST_2 = 60 / 1.25 = \$48$ million

Then we compute the pre-money value at the time of the second round by deducting the amount of second round investment from $POST_2$.

$PRE_2 = POST_2 - Investment_2$

$= 48m - 3m = \$45m$

Then we compute the post-money value after the first round by discounting the pre-money valuation at the time of the second round at 45% for 4 years.

$POST_1 = PRE_1 / (1 + r1)^t$

$= 45m / 4.4205 = \$10.18m$

Then we compute the pre-money value at the time of the first round by deducting the first round investment amount from $POST_1$.

$PRE_1 = POST_1 - Investment_1$

$= 10.18m - 7m = \$3.18m$

Then we determine the required ownership percentage for second round investors who will contribute $3 million to a company that will be worth $48 million after they make the investment.

$F_2 = Investment_2 / POST_2$

$= 3 / 48 = 6.25\%$

> This implies that after the second round, the entrepreneurs and first round investors would hold a combined 93.75% stake in the company. This stake is worth 0.9375 × 48m = 45m, which is also the pre-money valuation at the time of the second round.

> **The final ownership stake (after second round dilution) of first round investors equals $0.9375 \times 0.6876 = 64.47\%$.**

Then we determine the required ownership percentage for first round investors. First round investors put $7 million into a company that will be worth 10.18 million after they make the investment. Note that this is not their final ownership percentage as their equity interest will be diluted by a factor of $(1 - F_2)$ in the second round.

$$F_1 = \text{Investment}_1 / \text{POST}_1$$
$$= 7 / 10.18m = 68.76\%$$

Then we determine the number of shares that must be issued to first round investors for them to attain their desired ownership percentage and the price per share in the first round.

$$\text{Number of new shares issued}_1 = 1m \times [0.6876 / (1 - 0.6876)] = 2{,}201{,}376$$

$$\text{Price per share}_1 = 7{,}000{,}000 / 2{,}201{,}376 = \$3.18 \text{ per share}$$

Then we determine the number of shares that must be issued to second round investors for them to attain their desired ownership percentage and the price per share in the second round. The important thing to note here is that the existing number of shares at the time of the second round equals the 1m shares held by the entrepreneurs plus the 2,201,376 shares issued to first round investors. This is why we must work from the earliest financing round to determine the number of shares and price per share.

$$\text{Number of new shares issued} = 0.0625 \times [(1m + 2.201m) / (1 - 0.0625)] = 213{,}425$$

$$\text{Price per share} = 3{,}000{,}000 / 213{,}425 = \$14.06 \text{ per share}$$

For more than two rounds of financing, the procedure is an extension of the one described above:

- First define the compound discount rates between all rounds.
- Then find the post- and pre-money valuation by working backward from the terminal value to the first round. For each round, discount the pre-money valuation of the subsequent round to get the post-money valuation of the round.
- Given the post-money valuations for each round calculate the required ownership percentages.
- Finally, compute the number of shares to be issued and price per share starting from the first round.

Estimating the Terminal Value

Multiples-based approaches for estimating terminal value have the following drawbacks when it comes to venture capital/private equity:

- It is difficult to come up with a good estimate of earnings (in order to apply an earnings multiple) particularly in new or emerging industries.
- It may be easier to estimate sales or assets, but then it can be difficult to find truly comparable companies/transactions to extract benchmark multiples from.
- Multiples extracted from similar transactions in the industry may be inflated if those transactions occurred in an over-exuberant market.

For the NPV, CAPM, APT, and other equilibrium valuation models, it is difficult to come up with reasonable cash flow forecasts so valuations obtained from these models are as likely to be inaccurate as those estimated by applying multiples.

LOS 45k: Demonstrate alternative methods to account for risk in venture capital. Vol 6, pp 171–172

Venture capitalists typically apply very high discount rates when evaluating target companies for the following reasons:

- VC firms must be compensated for the significant nondiversifiable risk inherent in portfolio companies.
- Estimates of terminal value do not necessarily reflect *expected earnings*. They reflect future earnings in some kind of *success scenario*.

There are two ways of dealing with this:

- Adjusting the discount rate so that it reflects (1) the risk of failure and (2) lack of diversification (see Example 6-4).

    ○ Adjusted discount rate = $\dfrac{1+r}{1-q} - 1$

    ○ r = Discount rate unadjusted for probability of failure.
    ○ q = Probability of failure.
- Adjusting the terminal value using scenario analysis (see Example 6-5).

Example 6-4: Accounting for Risk by Adjusting the Discount Rate

A venture capital firm is considering investing in a private company involved in generating power through alternative sources of energy. The discount rate after accounting for systematic risk is 35%. However, the venture capital firm believes that the founders of the private company are too optimistic and that the chance of the company failing in any given year is 20%.

Calculate the adjusted discount rate that incorporates the company's probability of failure.

Solution:

$$\text{Adjusted discount rate} = \frac{1+r}{1-q} - 1$$

$$= \frac{1+0.35}{1-0.2} - 1 = 68.75\%$$

Example 6-5: Accounting for Risk by Adjusting the Terminal Value Using Scenario Analysis

Compute the terminal value estimate for Blue Horizons Pvt. Ltd. given the following scenarios and their probability of occurrence:

1. The company's earnings in Year 5 are $13 million and the appropriate exit price-to-earnings multiple is 8. The probability of occurrence of this scenario is 65%.
2. The company's earnings in Year 5 are $6 million and the appropriate exit price-to-earnings multiple is 5. The probability of occurrence of this scenario is 25%.
3. The company fails to achieve its goals and has to liquidate its assets in Year 5 for $5 million. The probability of occurrence of this scenario is 10%.

Solution:

Terminal value in scenario 1 = 13m × 8 = $104 million

Terminal value in scenario 2 = 6m × 5 = $30 million

Terminal value in scenario 3 = $5 million

Expected terminal value = (104m × 0.65) + (30m × 0.25) + (5m × 0.1) = $75.6 million

Some final notes:

- The results of any method of valuation depend on the assumptions employed.
- Our purpose here is not really to determine the true value of the company, but to establish a ballpark figure that can be used by venture capitalists and entrepreneurs in negotiations over how the returns of the venture should be split.
- The actual split depends primarily on the relative bargaining power of the parties.

LESSON 1: COMMODITY SECTORS

LOS 46a: Compare characteristics of commodity sectors. Vol 6, pp 187–192

Commodity Sectors

As an asset class, commodities represent a different type of ownership than traditional financial securities in that their value directly depends on their appeal to consumers or to their usefulness as part of the production process. Commodities are unique because they are susceptible to a loss in value through spoilage, theft, leakage, and even death. In addition, they must be transported. Unlike stocks and bonds, commodities do not generate any cash flows. In fact, the cost of maintaining the value of the commodity often results in a negative intermediate cash flow. Commodities historically offer low correlations with other asset classes and, as such, have their own particular exposures that provide both opportunities and obstacles for investors.

The following sections represent commodity sectors.

Energy: Crude Oil, Natural Gas, and Refined Products

Energy has a high economic value as businesses, governments, and local and national economies use energy in some form regularly. Every developed nation creates and manages an energy policy that outlines production, use, safety, national security issues, and that impacts its economic policies.

Crude Oil
Crude oil has natural storage space under the ground and will be extracted only if the marginal cost of extraction is less than the marginal benefit of selling it. Crude oil enjoys a natural high demand because it is used as an energy source in automobiles, planes, and ships, as well as in the manufacturing process. It must also be transported and refined. There are different qualities of crude oil, which means each type will have its own price, return, and risk.

For example, light crude oil typically sells for a premium over heavier oils. Light crude oil is low in density, flows freely at room temperature, is more efficiently refined into diesel fuel and gasoline, and is therefore more valuable. Crude oil from the Middle East, Nigeria, the southern part of the United States, and the North Sea are considered to be light. Oil from Mexico, in contrast, tends to be heavier and often sells at a steep discount to light crude because it is more expensive to refine and transport.

Technological advances in oil production through the use of shale oil extraction during the 2010s have led to an increase in supply. Oil located deeper in the earth and around tight rock formations was previously too costly to extract. The new techniques, however, have made extraction much more productive at a lower marginal cost, and the result has been falling oil prices. In addition, oil prices depend on the technical efficiency of refineries. Improvements in the process to refine oil can lead to greater supply and availability for use in transportation vehicles. Competition from renewable resources such as the sun and wind will impact the price of oil, as will minimum gas mileage requirements for automobiles. Crude oil prices are functions of global supply and demand, with expanding economies using more crude oil than contracting economies. Advances in technology, such as shale oil production, conflicts between and among oil-producing countries, and environmental concerns will affect returns to commodity investments in crude oil. The price of oil is also considered a form of consumption tax because individuals will spend higher percentages of their income on oil-related products when it rises. This has important economic consequences, as individuals spend less on other consumption goods when faced with rising energy prices.

Political uncertainty is among the most important factors in determining the price of crude oil. Historical geopolitical conflicts in the Middle East have had great impacts on the availability of oil and have caused major spikes in oil prices at discrete random intervals. Political instability can cause significant reductions in the supply of oil for two reasons: Oil cannot be extracted during these conflicts, and transportation routes become unreliable. As a result, oil prices become highly volatile during periods of high political uncertainty.

Successful oil investors will have a strategic plan to manage the risks of oil price volatility. Factors that tend to increase oil prices include political conflicts, competition from alternative energy sources, and restrictions on the construction of new refineries. Factors that tend to reduce prices include technical advances, the resolution of geopolitical conflicts, and more efficient transportation vehicles.

Natural Gas

Natural gas is an energy source that comes in the form of a gas that can be used directly for transportation, for electrical generation, and in the chemical production process. Transportation and storage costs tend to be higher for natural gas than for other commodities.

Key determinants of supply and demand include the weather, the technology in the electrical generation process, greenhouse gas emission concerns, and general economic conditions.

Refined Products

Refined products are end-use fuels that include propane, gasoline, and heating oil. These fuels are the main power sources for personal and commercial transportation as well as chemical production. Refined products have shelf lives that are typically measured in days, which places significant importance on the ability of the refinery to store quickly and ship efficiently to the end consumer. It also means that refineries are in almost continuous operation and are located near major bodies of water to have the opportunity to ship the refined products on cargo ships or planes.

The supply and demand for refined products depend on the weather, in terms of both major events like hurricanes and also extreme heat or cold that will increase demand. Supply conditions depend on technology to extract, store, and transport these products, while greenhouse gas emission concerns can lessen demand.

Grains

Grain commodities include corn, wheat, and soybeans. The largest grain producers are the United States, China, and Brazil. Grains are global commodities because they are consumed in all parts of the world not only by humans but by animals as well. They are traded on international exchanges.

The supply and demand for grains depend on weather, disease, pests, and the technology to store and transport the grain. Grain prices, especially corn, can be influenced by government policies that require their use as an input for fuel manufacturing (e.g., ethanol).

Industrial Metals

Industrial metals are processed mined ore that is converted to copper, nickel, lead, tin, and other useful metals, which are used in manufacturing, construction, and industrial production.

The supply of mined ore depends on the technology used in the extraction process, and demand depends primarily on economic growth. Industrial metals have long-term storage capability, which makes weather less important in affecting supply. Weather will affect demand, however, as construction slows in poor conditions. Government policies have considerable influence on supply and demand by limiting production because of environmental concerns, and labor costs can be high due to the ability of workers to strike.

Livestock

Livestock consists of animals such as cattle, poultry, and hogs, typically raised on farms from conception to slaughter.

Economic growth is critical in determining supply and demand as emerging market countries move their consuming habits from sustenance foods like rice to chicken and beef. Both supply and demand depend on grain market activity and gross domestic product. Expanding economies with significant grain production tend to have large livestock supplies. Livestock storage costs depend on grain prices necessary to keep the animals healthy and growing.

Livestock prices may fall over the short term when grain prices are high, and may rise when grain prices are low. This occurs when farms decide to slaughter the animals early to avoid the high input costs or when they increase their grain inventory to take advantage of falling grain prices.

Once the animals are slaughtered, the meat can be frozen for extended periods. Weather and disease affect the health of any herd and can significantly change prices.

Precious Metals

Gold, silver, and platinum are precious metals that have value to individuals as a direct investment but also to producers of jewelry, electronics, and the manufacturing of industrial products. Historically, South Africa has led the mining of precious metals, but China has recently emerged as the industry leader in mining. Investors tend to buy precious metals as hedges against inflation. Precious metals also tend to perform well in times of national government deficits.

Precious metals can be stored almost indefinitely. The demand for these metals has little do with weather and mostly depends on inflation expectations, fund flows, and commercial production. Technology is very important on the demand side, especially for platinum as it used in a variety of production processes. The total supply of these metals is fixed, and geologists have a reasonable estimate of how much remains underground. Available supply, then, depends on the willingness of mining firms to extract the metals.

Cash Crops

Soft commodities such as coffee and sugar are considered cash crops because they are grown and sold for income rather than consumed for subsistence. The majority of cash crops are grown near the earth's equator in South America and Africa.

Storage costs can be high because cash crops lose value as their freshness fades. Global economic growth influences demand and supply, as do weather, disease, and the popularity of consumption.

LOS 46b: Compare the life cycle of commodity sectors from production through trading or consumption. Vol 6, pp 192–199

Sector Life Cycles

Commodity life cycles are different for each commodity sector. Commodities with short life cycles can handle major events better than those commodities with long life cycles. Each commodity market will have a unique reaction to economic, technical, and industry events, which makes the ability to forecast returns quite challenging. Analysts with a more complete understanding of life cycles for each commodity will tend to make better investment decisions.

Energy Life Cycle

Energy commodities go through six stages from production through consumption:

1. Extraction takes between 50 and 100 days.
2. Transportation takes between 1 and 10 days. Trains, ships, planes, trucks, and pipes are used to transport both crude oil and natural gas.
3. Storage occurs over a few days to months. Oil and natural gas can be stored almost anywhere in the world.
4. Trading occurs only with natural gas at this point because it is ready to be consumed at this stage.
5. Refining takes between 3 and 5 days as crude oil is converted to gasoline, propane, and heating oil.
6. Additional transportation and trading take between 5 and 20 days to move the refined products to their ultimate consumption destination.

The total energy life cycle can range from roughly two to four months. The time depends on companies and governments willing to make huge investments in refineries and pipelines, which can cost many billions of dollars.

Precious and Industrial Metal Life Cycle

Metal life cycles go through eight stages from production to consumption, as evidenced by the example of the copper purification process:

1. Extracting the ore from a mine or pit.
2. Grinding the ore into powder.
3. Concentrating and enriching the ore.
4. Roasting the powdered and enriched ore.
5. Smelting the enriched ore as it is heated even more than during the roasting stage.
6. Converting continues the purification process by blowing air into the smelted ore.
7. Electro refining reshapes the copper.
8. Storage and logistics: The copper is held in warehouses until it can be shipped to the ultimate consumption destination.

The metals in this commodity sector go through similar life cycles. The processing plants require significant investments to make the steps more efficient. Firms in this industry will perform better during economic expansions because the increased demand helps cover their huge costs. During recessions, however, these firms are particularly susceptible to losses in cash flow because it is not easy for them to reduce or shut down operations.

Livestock Life Cycle

The time to maturity for livestock depends on the type of animal, with poultry maturing in weeks and hogs maturing in months, while it takes cattle several years to mature. Their availability for slaughter depends on the weather and the quality and quantity of their food.

Once slaughtered, there is high concern for spoilage, even as firms have developed efficient freezing systems. The increases in technology have allowed the transportation of frozen meat globally, which has increased the global demand for the final product.

Grains Life Cycle

Grains typically follow these steps:

1. Planting
2. Growth
3. Pod, head, or ear formation
4. Harvest

Soft Commodity Life Cycle

Coffee, an example of a soft commodity, is grown and harvested throughout the year and is consumed daily by individuals globally. The following steps are relevant for the coffee life cycle:

1. Planting of coffee trees, which take about three to four years to bear fruit.
2. Harvesting, which occurs by hand as only the ripe fruit is taken.
3. Removal of husk and fruit, leaving the dry bean.
4. Bagging for final market consumption.
5. Transportation to buyers, who then complete the process by roasting to their own tastes.
6. Delivery to retailers or other outlets such as coffeehouses.

Summary of Life Cycle Types

1. Constant yearlong global production of coffee.
2. Seasonal planting and harvesting of grains.
3. Natural gas characterized by straight-through process from extraction to consumption.
4. Crude oil and refined energy products moving from inputs to refined outputs.

LOS 46c: Contrast the valuation of commodities with the valuation of equities and bonds. Vol 6, pp 199–201

Commodity Valuation and Markets

Valuation of Equities

Corporate equity ownership results from an exchange of capital provided by shareholders for a promise made by the firm's executives to make wealth-maximizing investments. The value of a share of stock therefore depends on the quality of these investments. For example, watch manufacturing firms lost value in the early 2000s as consumers replaced watches with smart phones as the primary source of time. As such, equity values change over time as the quality of the investments changes. Frequently used stock pricing models value shares of stock as the present value of an infinite dividend stream plus the present value of expected capital gains. The dividend discount model is one such method to estimate stock price.

Valuation of Bonds

Bondholders provide capital in exchange for a promise by the issuer to make regular coupon payments and a final principal payment. Issuing firms use the proceeds to make wealth-increasing investments, while issuing governments use the proceeds to finance budget deficits. The value of any bond depends on the probability that the issuer will make all those payments. Various bond pricing models show that the value of a bond is the present value of the promised payment stream.

Valuation of Commodities

Commodity ownership, on the other hand, is quite different from debt or equity ownership in that there are no such cash flow promises made. The value of a commodity is instead derived from its purchase and sale. Commodities in general are physical items that are consumed by individuals or businesses.

Commodity markets offer current delivery of the asset, known as the spot market, or a future delivery of the asset, known as a forward or futures market.

The spot value of a commodity depends on supply and demand conditions. Commodity values change when there are inventory surpluses or deficits, which are dependent on variables such as technology, weather, and government regulations. Consequently, spot pricing is a function of macroeconomic and microeconomic variables. For example, a shortage of orange production in Florida because of poor weather conditions will surely cause a rise in the prices of oranges and consumer products such as orange juice.

Commodities have an inherent value that depends on their economic use. For example, an ounce of gold is worth more than an ounce of oil because gold has more valuable uses.

The value of a commodity in a derivative forward or futures market depends mostly on its spot value, but also on expected supply and demand conditions in addition to its price volatility. For example, a hurricane that destroys oil rigs built in the ocean will reduce the future supply of oil, causing prices in the oil futures market to rise. This is true even if there is ample current supply. The derivative contracts are legal commitments to buy or sell a commodity at a specified price on a specified date. For example, a manufacturing firm that uses natural gas to heat its factories is likely to benefit from using a futures contract to lock in the future price of its energy costs.

Another unique aspect of commodity ownership is the necessity of incurring storage and transportation costs. Higher costs translate into higher forward and futures contract prices. The spot price can be either greater than or less than the price in the derivatives market. The natural relationship is for the futures price to exceed the spot price, as the long position is willing to pay the producer to store and transport the commodity. Under certain market conditions, however, this natural relationship might not hold.

Example 1-1

Consider a farmer who raises cattle and grows peaches. This farmer also owns a share of stock in a conglomerate firm that pays a dividend, and he owns a municipal bond that pays semiannual interest coupons for the next 10 years.

Discuss the expectations the farmer is most likely to have regarding ownership in each asset.

Define the risks to which the farmer is exposed with ownership in each asset.

Solution:

The farmer expects to recover all of his operating costs of raising cattle and growing peaches by selling the commodities for a profit. The operating costs might include storage costs for the peaches and transporting the cattle. The farmer expects to receive dividend payments from the share of stock as well as the possibility of a capital gain when selling the share. Finally, the farmer expects to receive periodic interest payments for 10 years as well as a final principal payment from the issuing municipality.

The farmer is exposed to commodity price risk by raising cattle and growing peaches, as well as other operating risks such as disease, death, and theft. The share of stock exposes the farmer to systematic risk if he has a well-diversified equity portfolio and both interest rate and default risk as the owner of the municipal bond.

Example 1-2

Identify the use of the spot and futures market by an airline firm.

Describe the value of the commodity in each market.

Solution:

An airline firm is naturally short in the spot market for oil because it benefits when prices fall. If it believes the price of oil will fall, it will purchase most if not all of its oil in the spot market. When those expectations change, however, the airline will take the long position in an oil futures contract to protect itself against rising prices. The airline will choose a percentage of its position to hedge. Very few firms would hedge 100% of their energy needs, because oil prices are so volatile.

The value of oil in the spot market will depend on supply and demand conditions in the energy market. Prices will fall when there is a surplus of oil and will rise when there is a shortage. Government bodies, like the Organization of Petroleum Exporting Countries (OPEC), will influence the spot price of oil with their policies. The futures price of oil will depend on the spot price in addition to expectations about future demand and supply conditions.

LESSON 2: COMMODITY FUTURES MARKETS AND PARTICIPANTS

LOS 46d: Describe types of participants in commodity futures markets.
Vol 6, pp 201–204

Futures Market Participants

There is great demand for a market in which buyers and sellers agree to trade a commodity at some time in the future at an agreed-upon price.

Historically, forward markets operated to provide buyers and sellers with unique contract terms tailored to their own needs. For example, a farmer operating in the United States in the 1820s might agree to sell 56,000 bushels of corn during the third week in August at a specified price. The problem with forward contracts was the frequency of default when either the farmer or the counterparty was unable to deliver the crop or the cash.

Consequently, futures markets, with standardized contracts and daily settlements requirements, became popular and significantly reduced default risk. Trading in rice futures contracts began in Japan in 1710, in agriculture commodity futures contracts in Chicago in 1865, and in copper futures contracts in London in 1877. Today, there are many global futures markets that provide financial services to a broad range of clients.

There are at least five types of participants in futures markets: hedgers, traders and investors, commodity exchanges, commodity market analysts, and regulators.

Hedgers

Hedgers are those who have natural spot positions in the commodity and use futures contracts to remove price uncertainty from a future trade. For example, a firm that produces breakfast products that use corn as an input is short in the corn spot market, as it benefits when corn prices drop and its input costs fall. Consequently, the firm will take the (opposite) long position in a futures market to hedge the commodity price risk. On the other hand, a mining company is long in the spot precious metals market and will hedge by taking the short position in a specific metals futures contract.

Note that, by definition, hedgers use futures contracts in effect to bet against themselves. If hedgers are long in the spot market, they will take the short in the futures, thus locking in a future trading price.

Hedgers tend to be fairly knowledgeable market participants, but generally not more accurate than other traders in predicting future demand and supply conditions. Hedgers take positions in the futures market only if they expect prices to move against their natural position in the spot market.

Example 2-1

An energy company drills for oil and natural gas. It uses in-house economists to collect information on the natural gas market. The economists collectively predict a 5% to 7% rise in prices over the coming six months. The energy company typically hedges between 50% and 75% of its spot position in natural gas.

Describe the energy company's most likely six-month futures position.

> **Solution:**
>
> Since the energy company believes prices will rise, the market value of its inventory of natural gas will also rise. At first glance, it might seem appropriate for the firm not to hedge the commodity price risk. In reality, however, even economists know their predictions are not always accurate. In this case, it would be appropriate to hedge a small proportion of the exposed position. The hedged position might be between 10% and 25% of the spot position, just in case the economists are wrong. This percentage is not likely to be determined by a precise formula; rather, it will be chosen by the energy company as a way to manage commodity price risk.

Speculators are investors who have strong opinions on future commodity prices. Speculators often take the opposite position from hedgers and can be long or short, depending on their expectations.

The difference between hedging and speculating is illustrated in the following examples.

Hedging is often done by firms with natural positions in the spot market that then take the opposite position in the futures market. For example, farmers are naturally long in the spot market because they benefit when the prices of their crops rise.

Hedgers taking the long position in a commodity futures contract include:

- A jewelry company that uses gold and silver in the process to manufacture wedding bands.
- A food company that uses wheat and corn in the production of breakfast foods.

Hedgers taking the short position in a commodity futures contract include:

- A mining firm concerned about falling gold and silver prices.
- A diversified farm concerned about falling wheat, corn, cattle, and hog prices.

Speculators, on the other hand, have no natural position in the spot market. Rather, they trade on expectations of future commodity prices. For example, a college endowment fund might take the long position in an orange juice futures contract if it is permitted by the policy statement, if the analysts perform due diligence on the orange juice market, and if there is a compelling expectation that the price of orange juice will rise dramatically over the short term.

Speculators taking the long position in a commodity futures contract include:

- An institution performing research in the copper industry that strongly believes the price of copper will rise over the next three months.
- A hedge fund that researches the soft commodity industry and strongly believes the price of coffee will rise significantly over the next two months.

Speculators taking the short position in a commodity futures contract include:

- A retired farmer who predicts a shortage of cattle by the end of the current year due to an infectious disease spreading in his area.
- An endowment fund betting on falling natural gas prices due to significant advances in technology.

> **Example 2-2**
>
> A high-net-worth investor owns several Florida citrus groves and typically hedges about 50% of his spot position in orange juice futures contracts. This investor grew up on his family farm and planted, maintained, and harvested oranges most of his life. He remains an expert in orange juice production even though he has retired from actively managing any of the farms. He possesses compelling evidence that the price of oranges will rise in the next six months.
>
> Describe the futures contract position for this investor.
>
> **Solution:**
>
> As the citrus grove owner, this investor is naturally long in the spot market because he benefits when the price of oranges increases. He typically takes a 50% short position in the futures contract to hedge against falling prices. In this case, however, he believes the price of oranges will rise. He has two choices essentially: He can avoid the futures market entirely and will benefit when he sells his oranges at the higher future price. Alternatively, he can take a long position in a futures contract, thus benefiting twice when the price of oranges increases: first when he sells the oranges at a higher price and second when he settles his long position in the futures contract. In this case, the hedger has become a speculator.

Traders and Investors

Commodity traders and investors are typically grouped as informed investors, liquidity providers, or arbitrageurs.

Informed investors are hedgers or speculators who believe they possess superior knowledge about commodity prices. Speculators tend to believe in their superiority over hedgers because they have the flexibility to take either long or short positions in the futures market. Also included in this group are institutional investors and index managers.

Liquidity providers know that producers and consumers cannot possibly exercise perfect market timing, and are able to offer liquidity when it is most needed. Of course, liquidity providers charge a premium for providing capital to the futures market and do so whenever producers or consumers experience a rush to buy or to sell.

Arbitrageurs generally have access to physical storage or transportation systems and are able to manage inventory to generate an arbitrage profit. This scenario might occur when the cost of storage might be less than the futures price, so an arbitrageur can lock in a risk-free profit.

Commodity Exchanges

Futures exchanges provide financial services to international businesses and offer the support system to enable futures trading to operate efficiently. They provide clearinghouses to improve the integrity of the market, and they provide an outlet for commodity price discovery. Examples are the CME Group, which includes Chicago Mercantile Exchange, the Chicago Board of Trade, and the New York Mercantile Exchange; the London Metals Exchange; the Tokyo Commodity Exchange; and the Australian Securities Exchange.

Commodity Market Analysts

Researchers provide a valuable service to all investors by using fundamental and technical analysis on price information, volatility, and supply and demand conditions in futures markets.

The studies are financed by academic institutions, governments, or industry leaders. For example, commodity prices are excellent inflation indicators throughout he world, and investors in all markets are willing to pay for high-quality inflation research. In addition, government leaders, who determine monetary and fiscal policies, follow research provided by the analysts.

Regulators

Government bodies attempt to improve the quality of markets through development of rules and regulations. Agencies in the United States (Commodity Futures Trading Commission), China (China Securities Regulation Commission), and Europe (European Securities and Markets Authority) monitor all market participants to create an environment of efficiency and fairness.

LESSON 3: SPOT AND FUTURES PRICING

LOS 46e: Analyze the relationship between spot prices and expected futures prices in markets in contango and markets in backwardation. Vol 6, pp 204–209

Spot and Futures Pricing

Spot and Futures Prices

The spot price of a commodity is simply its market value designated for current delivery. In the spot market, buyers must either travel to a specific location to take delivery of the commodity or arrange for transportation from that location. Spot prices tend to be highly localized and dependent on local or regional economic conditions.

The futures price of a commodity, however, is the market value designated for future delivery. Futures prices are global, however, mostly the result of standardization of contract terms and the ability to cash settle daily. These futures market features allow speculators and arbitrageurs who have no interest in owning the underlying asset to participate actively in the price discovery process.

In both spot and futures markets, a defined quantity and quality of the commodity is traded.

The basis of a commodity is the difference between the spot and futures prices. Contango occurs when the futures price exceeds the spot price, and backwardation occurs when the spot price exceeds the futures price.

Historically, it was thought that contango occurred when the buyer of a commodity paid the seller a premium to defer delivery, as compensation for the storage costs the seller would incur. In a backward market, however, the premium would flow from the seller to the buyer to motivate the buyer to take delivery immediately. Although contango and backwardation occur in most markets, they do not persist, and many markets oscillate between contango and backwardation during the life of the contract.

Example 3-1

An oil futures contract trader observes the price of a barrel of oil to be USD 50 per barrel in the spot market while a six-month oil futures contract is priced at USD 55 per barrel.

Compute the basis of oil.

Identify the pricing condition in the oil market.

Solution:

The basis of any commodity is the futures price minus the spot price. In this case, the basis is USD 55 – USD 50 = USD 5 per barrel.

Since the futures price exceeds the spot price, the oil market is said to be in contango.

Example 3-2

The spot price of corn is USD 3 per bushel. The three-month futures price of corn is USD 3.15 per bushel. Over the next week, a drought hits the United States and reduces the expected harvest of corn over the next several weeks until farmers can plant more.

State whether the corn market is in contango or backwardation, and discuss market expectations for corn prices in the near future.

Solution:

The futures price exceeds the spot price, so the market is in contango. With a perceived reduction in the supply of corn, both spot and futures prices will rise, although spot prices will likely rise faster than futures prices as the economic shock tends to be felt more strongly in the short term than in the longer term, especially since corn has a relatively short growing season.

LESSON 4: THREE THEORIES OF FUTURES RETURNS

Overview

LOS 46f: Compare theories of commodity futures returns. Vol 6, pp 209–215

Futures Returns

Commodity futures contracts can be valuable additions to well-diversified portfolios for investors who can tolerate the specific risks inherent in futures markets. There are diversification benefits because of the low correlations between commodities and other asset classes. In addition, many investors use futures markets to enhance returns.

Three theories have been advanced to explain the return possibilities as they relate to the futures price curve.

Insurance Theory

Proposed by John Maynard Keynes in 1930 to explain the risk management behavior of farmers, the insurance theory suggests that producers of commodities desire to lock in the future selling prices of their crops. Farmers take short positions in the futures market to make their future cash inflows less volatile and therefore more predictable.

The insurance theory is also known as normal backwardation because farmers would repeatedly take short positions to sell their commodities at some future date. The consistent selling by farmers in the futures market would drive down futures prices below spot prices. Thus, a speculator would take the long position opposite farmers only if the futures price is less than the spot price, providing speculators with a form of insurance premium for guaranteeing the future value of the commodity.

Therefore, the insurance theory predicts that speculators will earn positive returns when the spot price exceeds the futures price because the two prices must converge at maturity. Convergence is an arbitrage condition, because at maturity there is no difference between spot and futures market prices, as they both provide immediate delivery.

Academic and professional research does not typically offer support for this theory, however, as several studies show that backwardation in markets does not lead to statistically significant positive returns or that contango leads to negative returns.

Example 4-1

The spot price of corn is USD 4 per bushel and the three-month futures price is USD 3.50. An investor agrees to take delivery from the farmer in the futures market in three months.

Describe the profit made by the investor if spot prices remain stable.

Solution:

The investor agrees to buy the corn from the farmer, which implies the long position in the futures contract. Essentially, the investor agrees to buy the corn for USD 3.50. If spot prices remain at USD 4, the futures price will rise to that same USD 4 on the maturity date of the contract.

Two events could occur at maturity.

The investor could take physical delivery of the corn and pay the farmer USD 3.50, and then immediately sell the corn in the spot market for USD 4, making a USD 0.50 per bushel profit. On the other hand, the investor is not required to take physical delivery and can simply settle in cash. The investor would settle the contract with the futures market clearinghouse and receive a profit of USD 0.50.

Either way, the investor makes a profit of USD 0.50.

Hedging Pressure Hypothesis

Futures prices are determined by the quantity of hedgers in both the short side and the long side of futures contracts. Commodity producers use futures contracts to lock in a future selling price of their commodity, while commodity consumers seek to lock in a future buying price. When the trading pressure from both sets of hedgers is equal, then spot and futures prices tend to be identical, producing a flat commodity curve.

The hedging pressure hypothesis suggests that the market will be in contango if consumers have greater demand for hedging than producers. Thus, futures prices will be greater than spot prices as consumers bid up the prices of futures contracts. Therefore, speculators will be drawn to the market, as they will be able to short the contract at higher prices and be provided with a better opportunity to generate a profit.

The hedging pressure hypothesis suggests that the market will be in backwardation if producers have greater demand for hedging than consumers. Thus, futures prices will be less than spot prices as producers bid down the prices of futures contracts. Therefore, speculators will be drawn to the market, as they will be able to take the long position at lower prices and have a better opportunity for profit.

For example, if an oil refinery (consumer) believes oil prices will rise more than oil drillers (producers) believe prices will fall, the oil market will be in contango.

Theory of Storage

Commodity inventory levels determine the shape of the futures price curve, according to the storage theory.

If storage costs are high, the market will likely be in contango, as the producers transfer these costs to consumers who desire future delivery. Therefore, commodity markets in contango are either the result of a commodity with naturally high storage costs or the result of consumers willing to pay those storage costs for certain commodities to defer consumption. Contango implies that supply dominates demand.

On the other hand, some commodities can be consumed as part of an efficient transportation or delivery system, which results in a market in backwardation. If storage costs can be avoided, then demand dominates supply and the spot price exceeds the futures price.

The theory of storage also considers the level of available inventory as a key component of futures prices. Sometimes, consumers hold inventory, and possibly incur storage costs, to have the added convenience of an extra supply in case of a shortage. Consumers take delivery of the commodity in the spot market instead of holding long positions in the futures market, which tends to place downward pressure on futures prices. This makes the convenience yield high when the inventory of the commodity is low.

The convenience yield is the value earned from owning the commodity rather than being long in the futures market. Consider the following example: Davis's neighbor offers to purchase his snowblower today for USD 500 and then sell it back to Davis in three months for USD 450 (with no credit risk or damage to the machine possible). If this offer occurs during the summer months, Davis would surely accept the offer because it is very unlikely to snow over the time period, which means he will not need the asset. If the offer occurs at the beginning of winter, however, Davis might reject the offer because he believes he will need the use of the snowblower during that time. Davis is willing to forgo a capital gain because he anticipates it will be worth at least USD 50 to him for the convenience of using his asset when it snows. This is the convenience yield, which explains the existence of backwardation and is applied even when there are storage costs to be considered.

The convenience yield cannot be directly calculated; rather, it is a plug number in the following equation:

$$\text{Futures price} = \text{Spot price} + \text{Storage costs} - \text{Convenience yield}$$

Example 4-2

A firm makes frozen breakfast foods such as waffles, pancakes, and toaster products and uses wheat daily in its production process. The firm believes wheat is going to experience a reduction in supply over the next six months due to changes in consumer habits. Consequently, the firm increases its wheat purchases in the spot market. Other wheat consumers agree with this belief.

Describe the relevance of the convenience yield to this firm.

Explain the convenience yield's effect on futures prices.

Solution:

If wheat is expected to be in short supply, companies that use wheat in their production process can earn a positive convenience yield if they hold an inventory of wheat. This firm will likely enjoy a high convenience yield over the next few months because spot prices will rise and it will not have to pay that higher price for its production input of wheat. If the spot price rose high enough under severe shortage conditions, the firm could even decide to sell the wheat instead of consuming it.

As the shortage continues, the spot price of wheat will rise (as will futures prices, but not as high as spot prices), and the market will be in backwardation until enough farmers can plant more wheat to increase future supply.

Example 4-3

An oil refinery stores an average of 500,000 barrels of oil monthly. The spot price of oil is USD 40 per barrel and the nine-month oil futures contract is priced at USD 44 per barrel. Over the next several weeks, the company expects to temporarily experience a reduction in supply, so it begins buying more oil in the spot market. Other firms follow and the spot price rises to USD 42. The company incurs insurance costs of USD 2.60 per barrel, inspection costs of USD 0.10 per barrel, and rent costs of USD 0.30 per barrel.

Compute the convenience yield.

Solution:

$$\text{Futures price} = \text{Spot price} + \text{Storage costs} - \text{Convenience yield}$$

Total storage costs are USD 3 (direct costs of insurance, inspection, and rent)

$$\text{USD } 44 = \text{USD } 42 + \text{USD } 3 - \text{CY}$$
$$\text{CY} = \text{USD } 1 \text{ per barrel}$$

LESSON 5: COMPONENTS OF FUTURES RETURNS

LOS 46g: Describe, calculate, and interpret the components of total return for a fully collateralized commodity futures contract. Vol 6, pp 215–219

Total Returns

Total commodity investment returns are computed and interpreted in a slightly different manner than traditional financial securities. There are three components of total commodity return:

1. Price return is the percentage change in futures contract prices, typically measured using the nearest-term contract.
2. Roll return is the percentage change in the value of futures contracts as they are rolled over to continue exposure beyond the maturity date of the maturing contract.
3. Collateral return is the yield on bonds used as the margin requirement to enter the futures contract. Yields on money market funds can also be used as the collateral return.

Example 5-1

A meatpacking firm uses cattle futures contracts to hedge its commodity price risk. The firm typically rolls over its futures position quarterly to maintain its desired exposure to cattle. It has experienced an annualized 1.8% price return and a 0.4% annualized roll return. The firm uses its portfolio of Treasury notes yielding 1.4% to fulfill the margin requirements.

Compute the total commodity return for this firm.

Solution:

Total return is the sum of the three return components:

$$\text{Total return} = 1.8\% + 0.4\% + 1.4\% = 3.6\%$$

Example 5-2

A German candy manufacturing firm uses white sugar futures contracts to hedge commodity price risk. A one-month contract has a price of EUR 6.06 per pound, while the two-month contract is priced at EUR 5.67 per pound. The firm uses a 10-day rolling period to adjust its exposure to sugar.

Compute the roll return for this firm.

Solution:

The roll return is the percentage change from rolling one contract into another. Since the candy maker is long in the futures contract (it is naturally short in the spot market because it benefits when the price of sugar falls), it will sell the first contract for 6.06 and the buy the second contract for 5.67. The roll return can be computed as:

[(Near-term futures price − Far-term futures price) ÷ (Near-term futures price)] ×
Percent of position rolled

$$[(6.06 - 5.67)/6.06] \times 0.10 = 0.00644$$

The percentage change in futures price must be adjusted as if the contract were rolled daily. The firm rolls every 10 days, which is 10% per day (1/10).

The distinction between gross roll return and net roll return is critical. In Example 5.2, the net roll return is 0.00644. The gross roll return is simply the percentage change in prices: (6.06 − 5.67)/6.06 or 0.0644.

Roll returns can be high for some commodities, but their volatility is also high, making them fairly unpredictable over extended periods. The energy futures market, however, has a reasonable statistical possibility of generating a positive roll return. In addition, roll returns tend to be sector dependent.

LOS 46h: Contrast roll return in markets in contango and markets in backwardation. Vol 6, pp 219–221

Roll Return

A market in contango is one in which the futures price exceeds the spot price, which implies that nearer-term contracts will have lower prices than longer-term contracts.

Those hedgers holding long positions in contango markets will sell the maturing contract for a lower price than what they will be paying for the new longer-term contract. The roll return will be negative.

Those hedgers holding long positions in backwardation markets will sell the maturing contract for a higher price than what they will be paying for the new longer-term contract. The roll return will be positive.

It is important to remember that the roll return is not simply the price differential of trading on the roll day. Rather, it is the cumulative effect of changes in spot prices and futures prices in contango and backward markets as futures and spot prices converge on the maturity date.

Example 5-3

A speculator has a total long position of USD 150 in corn futures contracts. The contracts are nearing maturity, so the speculator must roll over her investment. The maturing contracts are valued at USD 5 per pound, implying an investment in 30 contracts (150/5).

Determine the number of new contracts required to roll over the corn position if the far-term contract is priced at USD 4.50.

Determine the number of new contracts required to roll over the corn position if the far-term contract is priced at USD 5.50.

Explain the difference in roll returns for the two scenarios.

Solution:

If the futures price of corn for the new contract is USD 4.50, the speculator must take a position in 33 contracts to maintain her position (150/4.50).

If the futures price of corn for the new contract is USD 5.50, the speculator must take a position in 27 contracts to maintain her position (150/5.50).

If the market is in backwardation, the speculator will have to take a position in more futures contracts than she currently has. There will be a positive roll yield when the market is in backwardation, because the speculator will sell the maturing contracts for USD 5, but be able to reinvest in far-term contracts for only USD 4.50. Of course, the speculator will have to purchase 3 more contracts than the original 30 to maintain constant corn exposure.

If the market is in contango, the speculator will have to take a position in fewer futures contracts than she currently has. There will be a negative roll yield when the market is in contango, because the speculator will sell the maturing contracts for USD 5, but will have to purchase far-term contracts for USD 5.50. The good news is that the number of contracts required is less than the original 30.

Example 5-4

An institutional investor is long USD 25,000 worth of oil futures contracts that mature tomorrow. This contract trades at USD 50 per barrel. The institution intends to roll over the position tomorrow and maintain current exposure. The far-term contract trades at USD 47.62 per barrel.

Describe the transactions necessary for the institution to complete the roll.

Solution:

The institution will close out the current position by selling 500 contracts (25,000/50) and taking the long position in 525 new far-term contracts (25,000/47.62). These two trades will maintain the current USD 25,000 exposure to oil.

It is insightful to observe actual commodity returns to determine the relative importance of each commodity component return. Using the S&P Goldman Sachs Commodity Index over a 44-year period ending in 2014, the returns to the index show a geometric average of 8.1%. Most of this return can be explained by the level of interest rates or the collateral return. Less than half the index return can be attributed to the spot yield, and less than 10% is derived from the roll yield. Even more interesting is that the volatility of index returns and the correlations among the three components are derived mostly from changes in the spot yield.

Index returns will also include a measure to reflect the changing of the index's weights, known as the rebalancing return.

LESSON 6: COMMODITY SWAPS

LOS 46i: Describe how commodity swaps are used to obtain or modify exposure to commodities. Vol 6, pp 222–225

Commodity Swaps and Commodity Indexes

Simple Commodity Swaps

Swap contracts are derivative securities in which two parties agree to exchange cash flows at regular intervals. The simplest example involves two bondholders, one who owns a floating-rate bond and the other who owns a fixed-rate bond. They agree to swap coupon payments on the coupon payment dates. The same fixed-for-floating principle can be applied to commodity swaps.

Example 6-1

An oil company suffers a reduction in cash flow when the price of oil drops. The economists at the oil company expect oil prices to begin a downward trend that could last for several years. The company wants to hedge its commodity price risk over an extended period of time beyond that of available futures contract maturities.

Show how a swap can be arranged for the oil company.

Discuss conditions under which the hedge is beneficial to the oil company.

Solution:

The oil company would agree to receive a fixed price per barrel of oil. The fixed price can be negotiated between the two parties but will very likely be approximately equal to the current price. The company agrees to pay the floating price per barrel on specific dates in the future. The contract could be arranged to swap payments monthly.

If the price of oil drops, the company is guaranteed to receive the fixed price per barrel, thus providing hedging support in downward-trending markets. The fixed price effectively establishes a minimum price at which it can sell oil. If the price of oil rises, however, the company loses on the swap contract and will not be able to participate in the upward trend in prices.

The advantage of using swaps instead of futures contracts is that the daily settlement process can be avoided, as managing a significant number of futures contracts can be cumbersome. Swaps provide the opportunity for both a transfer of risk as well as additional ways to manage risk. Swaps can be tailored to meet almost any investor needs. Finally, swaps offer greater flexibility because they are typically cash settled.

Example 6-2

An oil refinery agrees to swap barrels of oil in which it will pay a fixed price per barrel and receive a floating price. The swap notional is 1 million barrels and the fixed price is USD 50. Assume the floating prices are USD 52, USD 47, and USD 59 over the next three months (these are unknown at the time of the swap initiation). Show the net payments (in millions USD) to the refinery.

Solution:

Month	Fixed Payment	Floating Payment	Net Payment
1	−USD 50	+USD 52	+USD 2
2	−USD 50	+USD 47	−USD 3
3	−USD 50	+USD 59	+USD 9

Note the refinery benefits in the swap when the price of oil rises, thus acting as a hedge against its loss incurred in the spot market when it is forced to pay the higher price.

Types of Commodity Swaps

Excess Return Swap

In an excess return swap, two parties agree to exchange payments above a reference rate or price. An oil company might agree to exchange a constant premium for a payment equal to the difference between the current market price of oil and a specified price (fixed).

Example 6-3

An oil company agrees to receive USD 5 per barrel of oil in exchange for a promise to pay the difference between the market price of oil and USD 50 per barrel. The payments are to be swapped monthly.

Show the results if the future spot price of oil is USD 57 and USD 42 at the end of the next two months.

Solution:

Month	Fixed Payment	Floating Payment	Net Payment
1	+USD 5	−USD 7	−USD 2
2	+USD 5	USD 0	+USD 5

The excess return swap works as a hedge for the oil company, as it acts like a series of options on oil. When the price rises, the cost of the option reduces the effective selling price per barrel of oil, but when prices fall, the oil company can effectively sell the oil for USD 5 more than the market price. For the oil company, the swap is similar to writing call options, while for the opposite party, such as a refinery, the swap is similar to being long a series of call options. At the end of the second month, there is no floating payment made from the oil company to the counterparty because the embedded option expires worthless.

Total Return Swap

A total return swap is an exchange of the return on a commodity index for a money market return plus a spread. This swap is typically used by institutional investors as a means to gain exposure to the commodity asset class.

Example 6-4

A hedge fund manager seeks exposure to the energy sector by agreeing to pay a 2% money market yield plus 300 basis points and receive the return on the energy index. The notional amount is EUR 10 million, and the payments are made monthly.

Show the results if the monthly return on the index is 10% and 1% during the next two months.

Solution:

Month	Fixed Payment	Floating Payment	Net Payment
1	–EUR 500,000	+EUR 1,000,000	+EUR 500,000
2	–EUR 500,000	+EUR 100,000	–EUR 400,000

The hedge fund wins in the derivative when the index return exceeds 5% and loses otherwise.

Basis Swap

A basis swap is one in which the return on two commodities that are not highly correlated is exchanged. The basis swap typically involves commodities of two different liquidity levels, and the basis can be defined in almost any way as the difference between two commodity prices.

Example 6-5

A farmer agrees to pay the basis of corn and receive the basis of soybeans at monthly intervals. Both commodities have standard amounts of 5,000 bushels in the futures market, and the notional for the swap is 100,000 bushels. Payments are netted monthly.

Show the results of the swap if the corn basis is USD 0.55 per bushel and the soybeans basis is USD 0.75 per bushel at the end of the first month.

Solution:

Month	Corn Payment	Soybeans Payment	Net Payment
1	–USD 55,000	+USD 75,000	+USD 20,000

The farmer wins in the derivative when the corn basis is less than the soybeans basis and loses when the corn basis is higher than the soybeans basis. This swap can be used by a farmer who harvests corn, soybeans, or both. It can also be used by investors who want to gain exposure to differences in pricing in two commodity markets.

Variance Swap

A variance swap is similar to a fixed-for-floating interest rate swap, but the variance of a commodity is used as the reference point instead of an interest rate. Variance swaps are volatility bets in which one party believes the variance in one commodity will exceed the variance of the other one.

Example 6-6

A hedge fund manager agrees to pay the variance of oil prices and receive the variance of natural gas prices, both variances computed using one-month futures prices.

Describe the conditions under which the hedge fund manager suffers a loss while pursuing this strategy.

Solution:

The hedge fund manager is making a relative volatility bet. Since the manager agrees to pay the variance of oil and receive the variance of natural gas, the manager will suffer a loss if the variance of oil exceeds that of natural gas. For example, if the variance of oil is 17% and the variance of natural gas is just 5% over the next month, the hedge fund manager potentially will suffer a large loss, depending on the notional amount.

Volatility Swap

A volatility swap is one in which actual volatility is swapped for expected volatility of one specific commodity.

Example 6-7

An investor expects that over the next year the volatility of cattle prices will be different from the long-term average of 20%. The investor enters a volatility swap in which she agrees to pay if volatility is less than 20% and will receive if volatility exceeds 20%, based on the one-month futures contract standard deviation.

Describe the conditions under which the investor generates a gain while pursuing this strategy.

Solution:

If cattle prices are more volatile than 20%, the investor will generate a gain in the futures market.

LESSON 7: COMMODITY INDEXES

LOS 46j: Describe how the construction of commodity indexes affects index returns. Vol 6, pp 226–230

Commodity Indexes

Commodity indexes are useful to a wide variety of investors, both those who can be directly or indirectly exposed to commodity price risk as well as those who follow inflation trends. To be effective as reference tools, commodity indexes should be investable.

Benefits of Commodity Indexes

Commodities indexes provide:

- A benchmark to evaluate diversified or concentrated commodity investments
- Inputs to make macroeconomic forecasts
- A reference value or return to price derivative securities

Key Characteristics of Commodity Indexes

Indexes are characterized by the following differences, each of which can affect the index and benchmark return:

- Breadth of coverage refers to the number of different commodities and sectors represented. The returns will depend on both performance of the individual commodities and their concentration.
- Each index must have relative weightings assigned to each commodity or component of the index.
- The methodology for rolling the contracts as they mature will have an impact on returns.
- Rebalancing techniques and frequency of rebalancing may provide an opportunity to earn extra returns if there are strong positive or negative correlations between index components and the likelihood of the components to exhibit mean reversion.
- Rules-based indexes and selection-based indexes govern the manner in which the key characteristics are implemented. Rules basing is a quantitative method to determine breadth, relative weightings, roll, and rebalancing. Selection basing, in contrast, is a qualitative method that is subject to committee biases.

Table 7.1 summarizes the key characteristics of an index construction.

Table 7-1: Characteristics of Index Construction

	Number of Commodities	Adoption Date	Weighting Method	Rolling Method	Rebalance Frequency	Availability of Individual Investor Funds
S&P Goldman Sachs Commodity Index	24	1991	Production weighted	Near most liquid monthly contract	Annually	Yes
Bloomberg Commodity Index	22	1998	Production and liquidity weighted	Front month to first or second month	Annually	Yes
Deutsche Bank Liquid Commodity Index	14	2003	Fixed weight	Optimized on roll return	Annually	Yes
Thomson Reuters CoreCommodity CRB Index	19	2005	Fixed weight	Front month to next month	Monthly	No (ETF available)
Rogers International Commodity Index	37	1998	Fixed weight	Front month to next month	Monthly	No

Major Commodity Indexes

S&P Goldman Sachs Commodity Index

The S&P Goldman Sachs Commodity Index (GSCI) is constructed in a highly similar manner to most market capitalization equity and fixed income indexes, which is a production or value-weighting scheme. Those commodities with the highest prices will tend to have the most influence on performance, which tends to make the energy sector the most critical component of this index. The rolling method always chooses to own the nearest-term contract for liquidity purposes and where economic shocks will have the most dramatic impact on returns.

Bloomberg Commodity Index

The Bloomberg Commodity Index (BCI) is a selection-based index in which a committee picks the commodities, and liquidity is used to determine weights. There is a cap of 33% and a floor of 2% placed on the inclusion of each of the 22 commodities in the index.

The construction of the BCI means it has much less exposure to oil than the GSCI but more exposure to natural gas. With the highest roll cost of any commodity and the inclusion of such a high weight of natural gas in the index, there is pressure for the index to deliver price and rebalance returns.

Deutsche Bank Liquid Commodity Index

The Deutsche Bank Liquid Commodity Index (DBLCI) uses a unique optimized rolling method in which backwardation is maximized and contango is minimized to generate maximum roll yield. The DBLCI combines a fixed weighting scheme and active rolling techniques.

Thomson Reuters CoreCommodity CRB Index

The TR/CC CRB Index is a selection-based index in which weights are determined by liquidity of each commodity, the economic impact of commodities, sector importance, and diversification. Each of these factors is determined by the investments committee. The fixed weighting scheme clusters the commodities into various tiers. Rolling is done using either the first or second month contracts.

Rogers International Commodity Index

The Rogers International Commodity Index (RICI) is very similar to the TR/CC CRB Index in its fixed weighting scheme, and selection by an investments committee with clustering among the 37 commodities included in the index. The one unique aspect of the RICI is that it includes some non-U.S. commodities such as Japanese rubber and British cocoa, thus making potential currency returns a part of the index performance.

Summary of Important Index Characteristics

Value weighting tends to place more emphasis on energy companies' returns because they tend to have higher prices. Index weighting schemes can be determined by committees or they can be fixed. Investors must become familiar with each index and its construction, as these choices will influence index returns.

The rolling method selected for each index is critical in that some indexes specifically choose commodities that trade in backwardation, which will give the appearance of higher returns because of the positive roll yield. In fact, some indexes pursue a policy to maximize weights of commodities in backwardation and minimize weights in commodities in contango. Many indexes try to avoid any weights in commodities trading in contango. Finally, some indexes include near-term contracts with only the highest liquidity to avoid any drag on returns.

The rebalancing method will influence returns on an index mostly when frequent rebalancing hurts performance, especially when markets are trading with momentum or significant trends. Rebalancing influences index returns more significantly when prices are mean reverting. Timing is critical, as reversion to the mean creates more opportunities for the index to generate more return when commodities with rising prices are sold and when commodities with falling prices are purchased. If the rebalancing date matches the mean reversion, rebalancing can add significant returns to the index. Frequent rebalancing, however, can lead to opportunity costs as upward-trending commodities are sold before they reach their peaks and downward-trending commodities are bought before they reach their bottoms.

For indexes that rebalance monthly, returns will be higher when mean reversion occurs more frequently. For indexes that rebalance annually, returns will be higher when mean reversion occurs less frequently or not at all.

STUDY SESSION 16: PORTFOLIO MANAGEMENT: PROCESS, ASSET ALLOCATION, AND RISK MANAGEMENT

READING 47: THE PORTFOLIO MANAGEMENT PROCESS AND THE INVESTMENT POLICY STATEMENT

LESSON 1: THE PORTFOLIO MANAGEMENT PROCESS

LOS 47a: Explain the importance of the portfolio perspective. Vol 6, pg 246

The portfolio management readings at Level I and Level II have spent considerable time on the Markowitz framework and the impact of covariance of returns on the risk-return tradeoffs of a portfolio. One of the key takeaways is that when evaluating a security for inclusion in a portfolio, analysts should not consider its risk-return characteristics in isolation, but consider the merits of the security based on how it interacts with the other securities in the portfolio and how it impacts the overall portfolio's risk-return characteristics.

One of the main conclusions from the various asset pricing models that we have studied is that only systematic risk is priced in the market. Firm-specific risks vanish from a portfolio once the portfolio consists of a sufficient number of securities. Therefore, only the systematic risk associated with a security (the risk that the security adds to the portfolio) for example, its sensitivity to GDP growth, unexpected inflation, and the business cycle, is relevant in portfolio construction.

LOS 47b: Describe the steps of the portfolio management process and the components of those steps. Vol 6, pp 247–253

The portfolio management process is an integrated set of steps undertaken in a consistent manner to create and maintain combinations of investment assets suitable to the client's investment objectives. The three basic elements of the process are (1) planning, (2) execution, and (3) feedback.

Planning

The planning phase consists of:

- Identifying and specifying the investor's objectives and constraints;
- Creating the investment policy statement;
- Forming capital market expectations; and

> Each of the components of the planning phase is discussed in more detail later in the reading.

Execution: Portfolio Construction and Revision

In this step, the manager integrates the investment strategy with capital market expectations to select the specific assets for the portfolio.

- Optimization techniques are used to determine the composition of the portfolio.
- Sometimes the actual compositions of the portfolio may differ from the strategic asset allocation (SAA). This may be caused by:
  - A temporary change in the client's circumstances.
  - Changes in short-term capital market expectations.
- Execution of the strategy is as important as planning because it can have a significant impact on portfolio returns. Poorly executed strategies can increase transaction costs, reducing investment returns.
  - Transaction costs can be both explicit (e.g., commissions, fees, and taxes) and implicit (e.g., missed trade opportunity costs and market price impact of large trades).

- The execution step interacts constantly with the feedback step to ensure that the portfolio is adjusted to reflect any changes in the client's circumstances and/or capital market expectations.

Feedback

This step has two components:

Monitoring and rebalancing:
- Processes are put in place to ensure that portfolio managers stay informed on any changes in the client's individual circumstances and changes in economic or market factors that may require portfolio revision.
- Rebalancing may also be required when significant differences in the relative performance of various asset classes cause the portfolio weights to deviate substantially from the target strategic asset allocation.
    - Portfolio managers should consider transaction costs and taxes when considering portfolio rebalancing.

Performance evaluation: Investors should periodically evaluate the performance of portfolio managers to assess (1) the progress of the portfolio in achieving investment objectives and (2) portfolio management skill.

- *Performance measurement* involves the calculation of the portfolio's rate of return and risk.
- *Performance attribution* determines the sources of the portfolio's performance.
- *Performance appraisal* evaluates the manager's performance in light of the performance of the benchmark.

The three sources of absolute return are (1) the strategic asset allocation, (2) security selection, and (3) market timing.

LOS 47e: Define investment objectives and constraints, and explain and distinguish among the types of investment objectives and constraints.
Vol 6, pp 253–260

Investment Objectives and Constraints

When formulating an investment plan, portfolio managers should first identify and specify the investor's:

- Objectives, that is, her desired investment outcomes; and
- Constraints, that is, limitations on her ability to take advantage of certain investments.

The two objectives in this framework are risk and return. They are both interdependent.

Risk Objective

In considering the risk objective, the following issues must be considered:

- *How should risk be measured?* Risk may be measured in absolute terms (standard deviation, variance, value at risk) or relative terms (tracking error).
- *What is the investor's willingness to take risk?* The willingness to take risk depends on the behavioral and personality factors.
- *What is the investor's ability to take risk?* An investor's ability to take risk is influenced by the following factors:
  - *Spending needs*, which determine the level of short-term volatility the investor can tolerate.
  - *Long-term wealth targets*, which determine the level of volatility that the investor can tolerate with out jeopardizing the achievement of those targets.
  - *Liabilities*. For example, an institution's legal obligations to make future payments to beneficiaries, or an individual's future retirement spending needs limit the amount of risk that the investor would be able to take.
  - *The investor's financial strength* or the investor's ability to increase savings if portfolio returns are insufficient to support planned spending.

  Generally speaking, investors with longer time horizons, high expected incomes, and greater net worth have a greater ability to bear risk.

- *How much risk is the investor both willing and able to bear?* An investor's ability and willingness to bear risk determines her risk tolerance, i.e., capacity to accept risk. Managers should formulate risk objectives in line with an investor's risk tolerance.
  - When the willingness to take risk exceeds the ability to do so, ability places a prudent limit on the amount of risk that the investor should take.
  - When the ability to take risk exceeds the willingness to do so, willingness may place a limit on the amount of return that can be targeted.

See Table 1-1.

Table 1-1: Risk Tolerance[1]

	Ability to Take Risk	
Willingness to Take Risk	*Below Average*	*Above Average*
Below Average	Below-average risk tolerance	Resolution needed
Above Average	Resolution needed	Above-average risk tolerance

- *What are the specific risk objectives?* A risk objective may be specified in absolute or relative terms. Risk objectives convert risk tolerance into operational guidelines. For example, a "lower than average risk tolerance" may be converted into a risk objective that "annual volatility of portfolio returns should not exceed x%."
- *How should the investor allocate risk?* After the appropriate measure of risk (e.g., VAR) has been identified along with the desired total amount of risk, overall risk is allocated to specific investments with a view to maximizing risk-adjusted return.

---

1 - Table 1, Volume 6, CFA Program Curriculum 2018

Return Objective

The return objective must be consistent with the risk objective. The formulation of the return objective requires addressing the following issues:

- *How should return be measured?*
  - Typically, total return (the sum of price appreciation and investment income) is used.
  - Returns may be stated in absolute terms (e.g., 5% per year) or relative terms (e.g., 1% greater than the return on the S&P 500).
  - Returns may be expressed in real (adjusted for inflation) or nominal (not adjusted for inflation) terms.
  - Returns may be expressed as pre-tax or post-tax returns.
- *How much return does the investor desire?* **The return desired by the investor may be** realistic or unrealistic. The portfolio manager must evaluate an investor's desired return in light of her ability to assume risk and capital market expectations.
- *How much return does the investor require?* **Required return is usually more stringent** than desired return as it is the level of return that an investor must attain on average to meet her financial obligations. The following issues relating to the required return may arise given specific situations:
  - The required return may conflict with the investor's tolerance for risk.
  - The return requirement may require consideration of needs for current spending versus ending wealth.
  - If the liabilities that are funded by the portfolio are subject to inflation, the required return should reflect expected rates of inflation.
- *What is the specific return objective?* The return objective incorporates the required return, desired return and risk objective into a measurable total return specification.

Table 1-2 summarizes the risk and return objectives of various categories of investors.

Table 1-2 Return Requirements and Risk Tolerances of Various Investors[2]

Type of Investor	Return Requirement	Risk Tolerance
Individual	Depends on stage of life, circumstances, and obligations	Varies
Pension Plans (Defined Benefit)	The return that will adequately fund liabilities on an inflation-adjusted basis	Depends on plan and sponsor characteristics, plan features, funding status, and workforce characteristics
Pension Plans (Defined Contribution)	Depends on stage of life of individual participants	Varies with the risk tolerance of individual participants

---

2 - Table 2, Volume 6, CFA Program Curriculum 2018

Table 1-2: (*continued*)

Type of Investor	Return Requirement	Risk Tolerance
Foundations and Endowments	The return that will cover annual spending, investment expenses, and expected inflation	Determined by amount of assets relative to needs, but generally above-average or average
Life Insurance Companies	Determined by rates used to determine policyholder reserves	Below average due to factors such as regulatory constraints
Non-Life Insurance Companies	Determined by the need to price policies competitively and by financial needs	Below average due to factors such as regulatory constraints
Banks	Determined by cost of funds	Varies

Investment Constraints

As mentioned earlier, investment constraints refer to limitations on the investor's ability to take advantage of certain investments. These include the following:

Liquidity Requirements

Liquidity requirements refer to an investor's need for cash from her investment portfolio to meet (anticipated and unanticipated) spending needs. Liquidity requirements can be met by (1) holding cash or cash equivalents in the investment portfolio or (2) by converting assets into cash equivalents.

Liquidity risk refers to the risk that an asset may have to be sold at a discount to its fair market value if it needs to be converted into cash quickly. It arises because of two reasons: an asset-side reason (i.e., the ability to readily convert it into cash), and a liability-side reason (i.e., the investor's liquidity requirements). Portfolio managers can only control for asset selection (not for investors' liquidity requirements) and this is primarily done by ensuring that the portfolio (1) generates sufficient current income, (2) consists of an appropriate amount of relatively liquid assets, and (3) consists primarily of assets that face minimal price risk (i.e., the risk of fluctuations in market price).

Time Horizon

Time horizon refers to the time period between putting funds into an investment and requiring those funds for use. Investment horizons may be short term (e.g., funding children's education), long term (e.g., saving for retirement), or a combination of two.

- Generally speaking, the longer the time horizon, the easier it would be for the investor to replenish any investment losses through savings, and the greater the ability to take risk.

LOS 47f:
Contrast the types of investment time horizons, determine the time horizon for a particular investor, and evaluate the effects of this time horizon on portfolio choice.
Vol 6, pp 258–259

- Unique circumstances and liquidity requirements can also affect an investor's time horizon.
    - For example, an individual may want her portfolio manager to account for (1) a down payment for a home purchase, (2) financing her children's education, and (3) providing for retirement, which would necessitate a multistage approach to her time horizon constraint.
- Investors generally allocate a greater proportion of their portfolios to risky assets when addressing long-term investment objectives as opposed to short-term objectives.
- The investor's willingness to take risk may require modifications of the asset allocation even if her ability to take risk is greater given her time horizon.
    - For example, an investor with a long time horizon may still prefer a less risky strategic asset allocation if (for whatever reason) she is very concerned about the possibility of substantial interim losses.

Tax Concerns

Taxes play an important role in investment planning because (taxable) investors are really only concerned with after-tax returns on their portfolios.

- Investors' choice of investments and timing of sales are affected by the differences between tax rates applicable on investment income and capital gains.
- Estate taxes on wealth that are triggered by the individual's death can also affect investment decisions.
- Changes in tax policies that affect security prices must be considered by both taxable and tax-exempt investors.

Legal and Regulatory Factors

These are external constraints imposed by governmental, regulatory, or oversight authorities. For example:

- Some countries impose a limit on the proportion of equity securities that can be held in a pension fund's portfolio.
- Directors and members of senior management of a company may be restricted from selling their shares in the company for a period of time if they have access to material nonpublic information about the company.

Unique Circumstances

These are internal constraints that affect portfolio choices. An investor may want to exclude certain investments from her portfolio based on personal or socially conscious reasons. For example, some individuals do not want to invest in tobacco companies because of the harmful effects of smoking.

LOS 47c: Explain the role of the investment policy statement in the portfolio management process and describe the elements of an investment policy statement. Vol 6, pp 247–250

LOS 47d: Explain how capital market expectations and the investment policy statement help influence the strategic asset allocation decision and how an investor's investment time horizon may influence the investor's strategic asset allocation. Vol 6, pp 247–259

The Planning Step

1. Identifying and specifying the investor's objectives and constraints: These have been described in detail earlier in the reading.
2. Creating the investment policy statement (IPS): The IPS serves as a governing document for all investment decision-making. A typical IPS includes the following elements:

    - A description of the client.
    - A statement of purpose.
    - A statement of duties and responsibilities of all the parties involved.
    - A statement of investment goals, objectives, and constraints.
    - A schedule for review of investment performance as well as the IPS itself.
    - Performance measures and benchmarks to be used in performance evaluation.
    - Any considerations to be taken into account in developing the strategic asset allocation.
    - Investment strategies and investment style.
    - Guidelines for rebal.ancing the portfolio based on feedback.

3. Forming capital market expectations: In this step, the manager makes long-run forecasts of the risk-return characteristics of different asset classes. These forecasts form the basis for constructing optimal portfolios.
4. Creating the Strategic Asset Allocation (SAA): In this step, the IPS is combined with capital market expectations to determine the target asset class weights for the investor's portfolio.

Investment Strategies

The strategic asset allocation may be implemented using any of the following approaches:

- Passive investment strategy: The portfolio's asset allocation is not adjusted in response to changing market conditions. Passive investment strategies include:
    - Indexing, in which the portfolio holds a specific portfolio of securities designed to replicate the returns on a specified index.
    - Buy and hold strategies.

- **Active investment strategy:** The portfolio's asset allocation is continually adjusted to reflect any changes in capital market conditions. The aim is to tilt asset weights away from those of the benchmark to generate positive excess risk-adjusted returns (alpha).
- **Semi-active strategy:** A combination of active and passive strategies. The aim here is to seek positive alpha, but to keep a tight control over risk relative to the benchmark.

A portfolio's SAA is important because it is a portfolio's allocation across various asset classes (not its allocation across securities within those asset classes) that is the primary determinant of investment returns.

LOS 47g: Justify ethical conduct as a requirement for managing investment portfolios. Vol 6, pg 261

Portfolio managers generally have more knowledge regarding capital markets and investment principles than their clients. Further, they are in a position of trust, and should therefore hold themselves to the highest standards of competence and standards of conduct.

READING 48: AN INTRODUCTION TO MULTIFACTOR MODELS

LESSON 1: INTRODUCTION AND ARBITRAGE PRICING THEORY

LEVEL I RECAP

Modern Portfolio Theory

Harry Markowitz introduced the world to modern portfolio theory (MPT), which concludes that in constructing a portfolio, each security must be considered in the context of the overall portfolio rather than in isolation. To model asset returns, Markowitz used a multivariate normal distribution, which completely defines the distribution of returns in terms of (1) mean returns, (2) return variances, and (3) return correlations. One of the important takeaways from MPT is that if the correlation between any two assets is less than 1, there exists the possibility of risk reduction through diversification.

William Sharpe introduced us to the capital asset pricing model (CAPM), which illustrated important concepts such as alpha (excess risk-adjusted return), beta (the sensitivity of an asset's return to the return on the overall market), and systematic risk (non-diversifiable risk).

When we move into our discussion on multifactor models, there will be a focus on systematic risk. As you know, not all types of risk are important for investment valuation. In theory, the risk that can be diversified away by holding an asset in a portfolio (non-systematic or diversifiable risk) should not be compensated by a higher expected return. Investors should expect to be compensated for only an asset's non-diversifiable or systematic risk (also referred to as priced risk). In the CAPM, an asset's systematic risk is positively related to its beta. Further, the CAPM asserts that differences in expected returns across assets can be explained by a single factor, the return on the market portfolio. The higher the asset's beta risk (or sensitivity to the market), the higher its expected return.

To summarize, under the CAPM:

A factor can be defined as a variable or a characteristic with which individual asset returns are correlated.

- The return on the market portfolio is the single factor that explains differences in expected returns on different assets.
- Beta measures a particular asset's sensitivity to that single factor.

As you will see, multifactor models assert that there is more than just the one factor that can explain differences in expected returns across assets; that is, these models incorporate multiple sources of systematic risk.

LOS 48a: Describe arbitrage pricing theory (APT), including its underlying assumptions and its relation to multifactor models. Vol 6, pp 275–281

LOS 48b: Define arbitrage opportunity and determine whether an arbitrage opportunity exists. Vol 6, pp 276–280

LOS 48c: Calculate the expected return on an asset given an asset's factor sensitivities and the factor risk premiums. Vol 6, pp 277–278

Arbitrage Pricing Theory

Arbitrage pricing theory (APT) was developed as an alternative to the CAPM. It describes the expected return of an asset (or portfolio) as a linear function of the risk of the asset (or portfolio) with respect to a set of factors that capture systematic risk. Like the CAPM, APT provides an expression for the expected return on as asset assuming that financial markets are in equilibrium. However, APT is different from the CAPM in that it does not indicate the identity or even the number of risk factors. The CAPM is a single-factor model that asserts that differences in expected return are explained by the market portfolio return.

APT simply describes the return on a well-diversified portfolio as a linear function of the risk of the portfolio with respect to a set of factors.

Before moving into the APT equation, we first discuss a **multifactor model** that describes the expected return for asset i:

$$R_i = a_i + b_{i1}I_1 + b_{i2}I_2 + \ldots + b_{iK}I_K + \varepsilon_i,$$ ... (Equation 1)

where:
K = Number of factors that are assumed to generate returns
R_i = Return to asset i
a_i = Intercept term

- Represents the return on asset i if all factors take on a value of 0.

I_k = Return to factor k, k = 1, 2, ..., K
b_{ik} = Sensitivity of the return on asset i to the return to factor k, k = 1, 2, ..., K
ε_i = Error term

- Assumed to have a mean of 0.
- Represents the portion of the return to asset i that is not explained by the model.

Another formulation of this multifactor model subtracts the risk-free rate from both sides of the equation, so that the dependent variable is excess return. The Carhart model (discussed later) is an example of such a formulation.

Now moving back to the APT, the theory makes three important assumptions. These are not as strong as those made by the CAPM.

1. Asset returns are described by a factor model.
   - However, the theory does not specify the number of factors, nor does it offer any guidance for identifying risk factors.
2. There are many assets, so investors can form well-diversified portfolios that have zero asset-specific risk; that is, unsystematic risk is diversified away and is therefore not priced.
3. No arbitrage opportunities exist among well-diversified portfolios.
   - This assumption implies that asset prices adjust quickly to their equilibrium values.
   - An arbitrage opportunity refers to a risk-free investment opportunity that is expected to earn a positive net profit, but requires no net investment of money.

According to APT, if these three assumptions hold, the following equation holds:

$$E(R_p) = R_F + \lambda_1\beta_{p,1} + \ldots + \lambda_K\beta_{p,K}$$

... (Equation 2)

where:
$E(R_p)$ = Expected return to portfolio p
R_F = Risk-free rate
λ_j = Expected reward for bearing the risk of factor j
$\beta_{p,j}$ = Sensitivity of the portfolio to factor j
K = Number of factors

It is very important that you recognize that the **APT equation** (Equation 2) asserts that the expected return on any **well-diversified portfolio** is linearly related to the factor sensitivities of that portfolio. Also notice that the CAPM can be considered a special case of the APT, where there is only one risk factor.

- The factor risk premium (or factor price), λ_j, represents the expected reward for bearing the risk of a portfolio with a sensitivity of 1 to factor j, and a sensitivity of 0 to all other factors. Such a portfolio is called a pure factor portfolio (or more simply, the factor portfolio for factor j.
  - For example, given a portfolio with a sensitivity of 1 with respect to factor 1, and a sensitivity of 0 to all other factors, we can write the APT equation as:

    $$E(R_P) = R_F + \lambda_1 \qquad (1)$$

    Now, if $E(R_P)$ equals 11% and R_F equals 6%, then we can calculate λ_1 as 5%. This implies that an increase of 1 in the sensitivity to the portfolio to factor 1 ($\beta_{p,1}$) will lead to a 5% increase in the portfolio's expected return.
- The sensitivity of the portfolio's return to factor j, $\beta_{p,j}$, represents the increase in portfolio return in response to a one-unit increase in factor j, holding all other factors constant. Each factor in the APT model represents a priced risk.
  - The intercept term in the model is the risk-free rate. It represents the rate of return if the portfolio has 0 sensitivity to all risk factors (or 0 systematic risk).

> The exact interpretation of expected reward depends on the construct of the multifactor model (Equation 1) that forms the basis of the APT model (Equation 2). This point will become clear when we discuss the Carhart four-factor model toward the end of this lesson.

Example 1-1: Determining the Parameters in a One-Factor APT Model

A portfolio manager is presented with two well-diversified portfolios that are each sensitive to the same single factor. The following table lists the factor sensitivities and expected returns for these portfolios over a one-year investment horizon. Also assume that all investors agree that the expected returns presented in the table are accurate.

Portfolio	Expected Return	Factor Sensitivity
A	16%	1.5
B	10%	0.5

Based on the information given, calculate the parameters of the APT equation (i.e., the risk-free rate and the factor risk premium).

Solution:

According to Equation 2, for any well-diversified portfolio, the APT equation with a single factor will be in the following form:

$$E(R_p) = R_F + \lambda_1 \beta_{p,1}$$

Based on the information provided, we can state the following equations:

$$E(R_A) = R_F + 1.5 \lambda_1$$
$$0.16 = R_F + 1.5 \lambda_1 \text{ ... (Equation 3)}$$
$$E(R_B) = R_F + 0.5 \lambda_1$$
$$0.10 = R_F + 0.5 \lambda_1 \text{ ... (Equation 4)}$$

Rearranging Equation 3, we have:

$$R_F = 0.16 - 1.5 \lambda_1$$

Substituting this expression for R_F in Equation 4, we have:

$$0.10 = (0.16 - 1.5 \lambda_1) + 0.5 \lambda_1$$
$$\lambda_1 = 0.06$$
$$R_F = 0.16 - 1.5 \lambda_1$$
$$R_F = 0.16 - (1.5 \times 0.06)$$
$$R_F = 0.07$$

Therefore, the APT equation is:

$$E(R_p) = 0.07 + 0.06 \beta_{p,1}$$

Example 1-2: Calculating Expected Return Using the Arbitrage Pricing Model

Continuing from Example 1-1, suppose that there is another portfolio, Portfolio C, that has a factor sensitivity of 2 to the same factor. Calculate the expected return on Portfolio C based on the model derived in Example 1-1.

Solution:

In Example 1-1 we obtained the following APT equation:

$$E(R_p) = 0.07 + 0.06 \beta_{p,1}$$
$$E(R_c) = 0.07 + (0.06 \times 2.0) = 0.19 \text{ or } 19\%$$

Example 1-3: Checking for and Exploiting Arbitrage Opportunities

Suppose the portfolio manager forms two portfolios, Portfolios D and E, which are sensitive to the same single factor.

- Portfolio D has been formed by investing 50% in Portfolio A and 50% in Portfolio C
- The expected return and the factor sensitivity for Portfolio E are 18.5% and 1.75, respectively.

Evaluate whether any arbitrage opportunity exists, and comment on how an investor may exploit it.

Solution:

Given that Portfolio D has been formed by investing 50% in Portfolio A and 50% in Portfolio C, its expected return and factor sensitivity can be calculated by computing weighted averages:

Expected return = $(0.16 \times 0.5) + (0.19 \times 0.5) = 17.5\%$

Beta = $(1.5 \times 0.5) + (2.0 \times 0.5) = 1.75$

Notice that Portfolios D and E have the same sensitivity (1.75) to the risk factor. However, Portfolio E offers a higher return (18.5%) than Portfolio D (17.5%). Therefore, Portfolio E is undervalued relative to its factor risk. We can exploit this arbitrage opportunity by going long on Portfolio E and selling short Portfolio D. If we sell $1,000 worth of Portfolio D and invest the $1,000 in Portfolio E, the net cash flows and factor sensitivity of our arbitrage position are provided in this table:

Portfolio	Initial CF	Final CF	Factor Sensitivity
D	1,000	−1,175	−1.75
E	−1,000	1,185	1.75
Sum	**0**	**10**	**0**

The factor sensitivity of our overall portfolio is 0. Further, since both portfolios are welldiversified, there is minimal asset-specific risk. APT assumes that investors would engage in arbitrage until financial market equilibrium is established. The price of Portfolio E would increase and the price of Portfolio D would fall until the expected returns for both are the same.

The Carhart Model

The Carhart four-factor model (also known as the four-factor model and the Carhart model) is a commonly used multifactor model. It asserts that the excess return on a portfolio is a function of:

1. Its sensitivity to the market index (RMRF).
2. A market capitalization factor (SMB).
3. A book-value-to-price factor (HML).
4. A momentum factor (WML).

The equation for the Carhart model is given by:

$$R_p - R_F = a_p + b_{p1}RMRF + b_{p2}SMB + b_{p3}HML + b_{p4}WML + \varepsilon_P \qquad \text{... (Equation 5)}$$

where:
R_p = Return on the portfolio
R_F = Risk-free rate
b_p = Sensitivity of the return on the portfolio to the given factor
RMRF = Return on a value-weighted equity index in excess of the T-bill rate

- This factor represents exposure to the overall market.

SMB = Small minus big, the average return on three small-cap portfolios minus the average return on three large-cap portfolios

- This factor represents a market capitalization factor.

HML = High minus low, the average return on two high book-to-market portfolios minus the average return on two low book-to-market portfolios

- This factor represents exposure to a value orientation (value stocks have low P/B ratios, or high book-to-market ratios).

WML = Winners minus losers, the return on a portfolio consisting of the past year's winners minus the return on a portfolio consisting of the past year's losers

- This factor represents a momentum factor.

Let's go back to our use of the term "expected reward" in defining the factor risk premium. We stated that the interpretation of the term "expected reward" depends on the construct of the model. In the context of the Carhart model, SMB refers to the expected reward from holding small-cap stocks rather than large-cap stocks. Similarly, HML refers to the expected reward from holding value stocks over growth stocks.

Now let's build on Equation 5. In financial market equilibrium, since the expected value of alpha is zero, the Carhart model can be used to compute the equilibrium expected return:

$$E(R_p) = R_F + \beta_{p,1}RMRF + \beta_{p,2}SMB + \beta_{p,3}HML + \beta_{p,4}WML \qquad \text{... (Equation 6)}$$

If you look at Equation 6 closely, you will notice that the Carhart model is simply an extension of the CAPM; it incorporates three additional drivers of expected return: size, value, and momentum.

- In the CAPM world, the only factor that drives differences in expected returns across assets is exposure to the market. Any observed mispricing caused by size, value, or momentum is considered an anomaly.
  - An anomaly is defined as a capital market observation that is not explained by a theory of asset pricing.
- In the Carhart model, these three factors are considered systematic risk factors; exposure to these factors gives rise to an expectation of additional return.

LESSON 2: TYPES OF MULTIFACTOR MODELS AND SELECTED APPLICATIONS

LOS 48d: Describe and compare macroeconomic factor models, fundamental factor models, and statistical factor models. **Vol 6, pp 281–282**

Multifactor Model: Types

Multifactor models are used extensively in both passive and active portfolio management. They can be classified as follows:

- Macroeconomic factor models use surprises in macroeconomic variables that significantly explain returns as factors.

- **Fundamental factor models** use company- or stock-specific fundamentals (e.g., P/B ratio, P/E ratio, market capitalization, etc.) that explain cross-sectional differences in stock prices as factors.
- **Statistical factor models** apply statistical methods on historical returns of a group of securities to extract factors that explain observed returns.
  - In statistical factor models, the factors are actually portfolios of the securities in the subject group, and are therefore defined by portfolio weights.
  - These models may further be categorized as:
    - Factor analysis models, in which the factors are portfolios that explain historical *return covariances*.
    - Principal components models, in which the factors are portfolios that explain historical *return variances*.
  - While they offer an advantage in that they make minimal assumptions, the drawback lies in the fact that they are difficult to interpret. Further, they require a substantial background in quantitative methods.

Analysts generally prefer to use fundamental and macroeconomic models as they are easier to interpret. Therefore, these two will be the focus of our attention in this section.

The Structure of Macroeconomic Factor Models

Macroeconomic factor models assume that return on each asset is correlated with **surprises** in certain factors related to the broader economy.

- A surprise refers to the difference between the actual value and the expected value of a variable. For example, if the expected inflation rate is 4.5% but actual inflation equals 5%, the surprise in the inflation rate equals +0.5% (Actual inflation = Expected inflation + Surprise inflation).
- A factor's surprise refers to the component of the factor's return that was unexpected, and factor surprises serve as explanatory or independent variables in the model.
- Notice how the representation of independent variables here (i.e., as factor surprises) contrasts with the representation of independent variables in Equation 2 (where they were represented as returns).

If K macro factors explain asset returns, then the return on asset i in a macroeconomic factor model can be expressed as:

$$R_i = a_i + b_{i1}F_1 + b_{i2}F_2 + \ldots + b_{iK}F_K + \varepsilon_i$$ ... (Equation 7)

where:
R_i = Return to asset i
a_i = Expected return to asset i
F_K = Surprise in the factor k, k = 1, 2, ..., K
b_{iK} = Sensitivity of the return on asset i to a surprise in factor k, k = 1, 2, ..., K
ε_i = An error term with a zero mean that represents the portion of the return to asset i that is not explained by the factor model

Let's work with real-world macroeconomic variables now. Assuming that a stock's returns can be explained by (1) surprises in inflation rates and (2) surprises in GDP growth rates, the equation for a macroeconomic factor model would be expressed as:

$$R_i = a_i + b_{i1}F_{INFL} + b_{i2}F_{GDP} + \varepsilon_i$$

where:
R_i = Return to stock i
a_i = Expected return to stock i
F_{INFL} = Surprise in inflation rates
F_{GDP} = Surprise in GDP growth
b_{i1} = Sensitivity of the return on stock i to surprises in inflation
b_{i2} = Sensitivity of the return on stock i to surprises in GDP growth
ε_i = An error term with a zero mean that represents the portion of the return to stock i that is not explained by the factor model

An important assumption we are making in this model is that the two factors in the model, the surprise in inflation rates and the surprise in GDP growth, are uncorrelated. Further, our model assumes that inflation rates and GDP growth rates are both priced risks. However, we do not use predicted values of these variables as independent variables in this model, because their predicted (expected) values are already reflected in the stock's current price and therefore in its current expected return.

The intercept term (a_i) reflects the effects of the predicted values of inflation and GDP growth on the expected return on stock i. On the other hand, any surprise in either of the priced risk factors contains new information that is not reflected in the current price or expected return on the stock. Therefore, the macroeconomic factor model breaks down the return on stock i into (1) the unexpected return as a result of surprises, (2) the expected return based on predicted values of priced risk factors, and (3) an error term.

In order to interpret the intercept term, recall that the expected value of the error term (ε_i) equals 0. Therefore, if surprises in both the inflation rate and the GDP growth rate are 0 (or, stated differently, actual inflation equals expected inflation, and actual GDP growth equals expected GDP growth), the expected return on stock i will equal a_i. Therefore, a_i represents the expected return on stock i based on current expectations of the inflation rate and the GDP growth rate.

The slope coefficients in the model (b_{i1} and b_{i2}) are known as factor sensitivities, factor betas, or factor loadings. A factor sensitivity measures the change in the dependent variable to a one-unit change in the factor, holding all other factors constant. Our model predicts that, holding all other factors constant, a one-unit surprise in the inflation rate will increase the return on stock i by b_{i1} units. Similarly, a one-unit surprise in the GDP growth rate will increase the return on stock i by b_{i2} units, holding all other factors constant.

Finally, let us consider the error term (ε_i). We already know that:

- a_i represents the expected return on stock i based on current expectations of the inflation rate and the GDP growth rate.
- $b_{i1}F_{INFL} + b_{i2}F_{GDP}$ represents the return resulting from surprises in the inflation rate and GDP growth rate.

Taken together, a_i and ($b_{i1}F_{INFL} + b_{i2}F_{GDP}$) represent the total (expected plus unexpected) return on stock i from the systematic factors identified in the model (inflation rate and GDP growth rate). Therefore, the error term reflects the portion of the return on stock i that is unexplained by the systematic factors included in the model. If the model incorporates all systematic factors (i.e., all sources of common risk), then ε_i must represent stock- or company-specific risk.

Typically, the risk premium for the GDP growth factor is positive, while the risk premium for the inflation rate factor is negative. Therefore, an asset with a positive sensitivity to the inflation factor (i.e., its returns tend to have a positive response to unexpectedly high inflation) would have a lower required return than one with a negative sensitivity to inflation, due to its unique ability to act as an inflation hedge. Table 2-1 illustrates how different asset classes perform in different inflation rate and GDP growth environments.

Table 2-1: Growth and Inflation Factor Matrix

	Inflation	
	Low Inflation/Low Growth Cash Government bonds	High Inflation/Low Growth Inflation-linked bonds Commodities Infrastructure
Growth	Low Inflation/High Growth Equity Corporate debt	High Inflation/High Growth Real assets (real estate, timberland, farmland, energy)

In order to develop macroeconomic factor models, regression analysis is used to estimate individual assets' sensitivities to the factors. After obtaining these parameters for individual assets in the portfolio, we calculate the portfolio's parameters as the weighted average of the parameters of its individual assets. Each individual asset's weight is based on the proportion of the portfolio's total market value that it represents.

Example 2-1: Calculating Stock Returns Using a Macroeconomic Factor Model

Sophia derived the following two-factor model to explain the returns on the stock of Pyramid Construction (PC):

$$R_{PC} = a_{PC} + 1.5F_{GDP} - 2F_{INFL} + \varepsilon_{PC}$$

The following information is also available:

- Expected return on the company's stock = 12%
- Over the past year, the actual value of GDP exceeded its predicted value by 2.5 percentage points, while actual inflation was lower than its predicted value by 1 percentage point.
- Company-specific return (i.e., unrelated to GDP and the inflation rate) = 1.5%

Calculate the return on the company's stock for the year based on the macroeconomic factor model.

Solution:

$$R_{PC} = 0.12 + (1.5 \times 0.025) - [2 \times (-0.01)] + 0.015 = 19.25\%$$

The return on PC was greater than expected because the actual return was positively affected by the higher-than-expected GDP and the lower-than-expected inflation rate. Note that the negative surprise in inflation (actual inflation is less than expected inflation) is good news for the stock as it has a negative sensitivity to surprises in inflation (coefficient on F_{INFL} is negative).

Example 2-2: Estimating Returns for a Two-Stock Portfolio Given Factor Sensitivities

Alex Stuart is analyzing the returns on a portfolio of two stocks, Sun Corporation (SC) and Moon Corporation (MC). The following macroeconomic model results are provided:

$$R_{SC} = 0.10 - 2F_1 + 4F_2 + \varepsilon_{SC}$$
$$R_{MC} = 0.15 + 4F_1 + 2F_2 + \varepsilon_{MC}$$

Given that 40% of the portfolio is invested in SC and 60% is invested in MC, calculate:

1. The expected return on the portfolio.
2. The actual return on the portfolio, given that F_1 and F_2 equal 0% and 1% respectively, and that the error terms for both stocks equal 0.3%.

Solutions:

1. Since the intercept term in macroeconomic factor models represents the expected return on the stock, we can state that the expected return on SC equals 10%, and that the expected return on MC equals 15%. The expected return on the portfolio is calculated as the weighted average of the returns on the two stocks:

$$\text{Expected return} = (0.4 \times 0.1) + (0.6 \times 0.15) = 13\%$$

2. The *portfolio* sensitivity to each factor equals the weighted average of the sensitivities of the two stocks to each factor. Therefore:
   - The portfolio's sensitivity to F_1 equals $[(0.4 \times (-2)] + (0.6 \times 4) = 1.6$
   - The portfolio's sensitivity to F_2 equals $(0.4 \times 4) + (0.6 \times 2) = 2.8$

   Therefore, the portfolio's actual return can be calculated as:

$$R_P = 0.13 + 1.6F_1 + 2.8F_2 + 0.4\varepsilon_{SC} + 0.6\varepsilon_{MC}$$
$$= 0.13 + 1.6(0) + 2.8(0.01) + 0.4(0.003) + 0.6(0.003) = 16.1\%$$

The Structure of Fundamental Factor Models

The equation that represents the fundamental factor model is the same as the equation we presented earlier (Equation 7) for the macroeconomic factor model:

$$R_i = a_i + b_{i1}F_1 + b_{i2}F_2 + \ldots + b_{iK}F_K + \varepsilon_i$$

However, there are important differences between fundamental factor models and macroeconomic factor models. In order to highlight those differences, we shall work with the following fundamental factor model, where the dividend yield and the price-to-earnings (P/E ratio) are the two factors:

$$R_i = a_i + b_{i1}F_{DY} + b_{i2}F_{PE} + \varepsilon_i$$

where:
R_i = Return to stock i
a_i = Intercept
F_{DY} = Return associated with the dividend yield factor
F_{PE} = Return associated with the P/E factor
b_{i1} = Sensitivity of the return on stock i to the dividend yield factor
b_{i2} = Sensitivity of the return on stock i to the P/E factor
ε_i = An error term

In fundamental factor models, the factors (F_{DY} and F_{PE}) are stated as **returns** rather than return surprises in relation to predicted values (as is the case with macroeconomic factor models). Therefore, the factors do not usually have an expected value of zero.

The factor sensitivities (b_{i1} and b_{i2}) are also interpreted differently. In a fundamental factor model, the factor sensitivities can be attributes of the security (dividend yield and P/E ratio in our example) or of the issuing company (e.g., industry membership). Further, the factor sensitivities in these models are typically standardized. Standardized sensitivities are computed as follows:

$$b_{ik} = \frac{\text{Value of attribute } k \text{ for asset } i - \text{Average value of attribute } k}{\sigma \,(\text{Values of attribute } k)}$$

For example, if the average dividend yield across all stocks being considered is 2.5%, and the standard deviation of dividend yields across all stocks is 1%, a stock with a dividend yield of 4% has a standardized sensitivity to dividend yield of $(4 - 2.5)/1 = 1.5$. A standardized value of 1.5 simply indicates that the subject stock's dividend yield is 1.5 standard deviations above average. This process of standardizing is similar to how we computed z-values for the normal distribution at Level I.

Sometimes, however, fundamental models also incorporate factors, such as industry membership, that are represented as binary dummy variables. In interpreting the sensitivities to such factors, a sensitivity of 0 indicates that the company does not belong to the particular industry, whereas a sensitivity of 1 indicates membership in that industry.

In fundamental factor models, the intercept is not interpreted as expected return (as was the case in the macroeconomic factor model). The intercept has no economic interpretation when the factor sensitivities are standardized (which is typically the case). If the factor sensitivities are not standardized, the intercept term could be interpreted as the risk-free rate, because it would represent the return on an asset with no factor risk (zero factor betas) and no asset-specific risk (error term = 0).

Finally, note that in macroeconomic factor models we develop the factor (surprise) series first and then use regression analysis to estimate the factor sensitivities. In fundamental factor models, in contrast, we generally specify the factor sensitivities (attributes) first and then estimate the factor returns through regression analysis. For example, we would use the dividend yields of stocks (factor sensitivity, b_{i1}) as inputs in the regression to determine the average return associated with the dividend yield factor (F_{DY}).

Fundamental factor models are used for several purposes, including **portfolio performance attribution** and risk analysis. Portfolio performance attribution includes return attribution and risk attribution.

- Return attribution seeks to identify the sources of excess return of the portfolio relative to its benchmark.
- Risk attribution identifies sources of portfolio volatility (when the portfolio aims to generate absolute returns) and sources of tracking risk (when the portfolio's performance is evaluated relative to a benchmark).

Generally speaking, the factors that are used in most fundamental factor models for equities can be placed into three broad groups:

- Company fundamental factors are related to the company's internal performance (e.g., factors related to earnings growth, earnings variability, and financial leverage).
- Company share-related factors include valuation measures and other factors that are related to share price or the trading characteristics of the shares (e.g., price multiples, and variables relating to share price momentum and stock price volatility).
- Macroeconomic factors include systematic risk measures (e.g., CAPM beta), sector or industry membership factors, and yield curve–level sensitivity.

Comparing Types of Factor Models

A study that aimed to contrast macroeconomic factor models with fundamental factor models in terms of their ability to explain the returns of 779 U.S. large-cap stocks found the following:

- Five macroeconomic factors (inflation, term structure, industrial production, default premium, and unemployment) combined explained almost 11% of the variation in stock returns.
- Thirteen fundamental factors (industries, volatility, momentum, size, trading activity, growth, earnings yield, book-to-price ratio, earnings variability, financial leverage, foreign investment, labor intensity, and dividend yield) explained almost 43% of the variation in stock returns.
- These findings should not be used to conclude that fundamental factor models are superior to macroeconomic factor models. The factors in macroeconomic factor models are individually backed by statistical evidence that they represent systematic risk. This is not true for each factor in the fundamental factor model.
- The macroeconomic factor set includes a smaller number of variables and is relatively straightforward. Further, it allows a portfolio manager to incorporate economic views into portfolio construction by adjusting portfolio exposures to macro factors.
- The fundamental factor set is much larger, and often includes dummy variables, which make it much more complex. The upside is that it offers a more detailed picture of risk in terms that are easily related to company and security characteristics.
- The study also found that the macroeconomic factor model had no marginal explanatory power when added to the fundamental factor model, implying that fundamental risk attributes capture all the risk characteristics represented by the macroeconomic factor betas. However, this was only because the fundamental factor set used in the study supplied a very detailed description of the characteristics of a stock and its issuer.

LOS 48e: Explain sources of active risk and interpret tracking risk and the information ratio. Vol 6, pp 292–296

LOS 48f: Describe uses of multifactor models and interpret the output of analyses based on multifactor models. Vol 6, pp 289–298

MULTIFACTOR MODELS: SELECTED APPLICATIONS

Factor Models in Return Attribution

Managers are commonly evaluated based on the performance of their portfolios relative to a specified benchmark. Multifactor models can be used to understand the sources of a manager's returns relative to the benchmark. The return on a portfolio (R_p) can be viewed as the sum of the benchmark's return (R_B) and active return. Active return therefore equals portfolio return minus benchmark return.

$$\text{Active return} = R_p - R_B$$

Active return can be broken down into:

- **The return from the portfolio manager's factor tilts:** This refers to overweights or underweights relative to the benchmark factor sensitivities. The return from factor tilts is calculated as the product of the portfolio manager's active factor sensitivities (factor tilts) and the factor returns.

- The return from individual asset selection or security selection: This reflects the manager's skill in individual asset selection (i.e., ability to overweight securities that outperform the benchmark or underweight securities that underperform the benchmark).

Active return = Return from factor tilts + Return from asset selection

$$f_0(T) = S_0(1 + r)^T + FV(CB,0,T)$$

Example 2-3 illustrates how active returns are computed and how the performance of an active portfolio manager is computed using a fundamental factor model.

Example 2-3: Four-Factor Model Active Return Decomposition

Arsene Wenger, an investment manager, uses the following fundamental factor model to evaluate equity portfolios:

$$R_p - R_F = a_p + b_{p1}F_{RMRF} + b_{p2}F_{SMB} + b_{p3}F_{HML} + b_{p4}F_{WML} + e_P$$

where:
  R_p = Return on the portfolio
  R_F = Risk-free rate
  b_k = Unstandardized regression coefficient. This represents the unstandardized sensitivity of the return on the portfolio to Factor k.
F_{RMRF} = The return on a value-weighted equity index in excess of the T-bill rate. This factor represents exposure to the overall market.
 F_{SMB} = The return on small-cap portfolios in excess of the return on large-cap portfolios. This factor represents exposure to the size (market capitalization) factor.
 F_{HML} = The return on high book-to-market portfolios minus the return on low book-to-market portfolios. This factor represents exposure to a value orientation (value stocks have low P/B ratios, or high book-to-market ratios).
 F_{WML} = The return on past year's winners minus the return on past year's losers. This represents a momentum factor.

Table 2-2 provides a decomposition of the active return earned by a portfolio managed by Santi Cazorla.

Table 2-2: Active Return Decomposition

	Factor Sensitivity				Contribution to Active Return	
Factor	Portfolio (1)	Benchmark (2)	Difference (3) = (1) − (2)	Factor Return (4)	Absolute (3) × (4)	Proportion of Total Active
F_{RMRF}	0.75	0.80	−0.05	4.45%	−0.223	−19.44%
F_{SMB}	0.05	0.08	−0.03	−3.50%	0.105	9.15%
F_{HML}	1.25	1.00	0.25	4.50%	1.125	98.08%
F_{WML}	0.10	0.08	0.02	8.75%	0.175	15.26%
Return from factor tilts (= −0.223 + 0.105 + 1.125 + 0.175)					1.182	103.05%
Return from asset selection					−0.035	−3.05%
Total active return [= 1.182 + (−0.035)]					1.147	100%

> When we described fundamental factor models earlier, we said that factor sensitivities were typically standardized in these models. However, in this example, notice that the factor sensitivities are not standardized.

Further, we are given the following information:

- The benchmark for Cazorla's portfolio is the Russell 1000, which includes large-cap U.S. stocks.
- Cazorla tells Wenger that he is a "stock picker" and points to the positive active return earned by his portfolio (1.147%) to support his assertion.
- From his experience, Wenger knows that returns to growth-oriented portfolios have a positive sensitivity to the momentum factor (F_{WML}), while value-oriented portfolios typically have low or negative sensitivity to the momentum factor.

Using the information given:

1. Determine Cazorla's investment style mandate.
2. Evaluate the sources of Cazorla's portfolio's active return for the year.
3. What concerns might Wenger have regarding Cazorla's portfolio's performance upon examining his active return decomposition?

Solutions:

1. Cazorla's anticipated investment style can be inferred by comparing his portfolio's actual factor exposures to the factor exposures of his benchmark. An analysis of the numbers in Columns 1 and 2 of Table 2-2 tells us the following:
   - The benchmark portfolio had the highest sensitivity to the HML factor. Value stocks have relatively high book-to-market ratios, so we can infer that Cazorla has a value orientation. The fact that his portfolio's sensitivity to the HML factor is even higher than the benchmark's (1.25 vs. 1.00) indicates that Cazorla's portfolio has a greater exposure to value stocks than the benchmark has.
   - Cazorla's portfolio and the benchmark portfolio both have relatively low sensitivities to the WML (momentum) and SMB (size) factors.
     - The low sensitivities of Cazorla's portfolio and the benchmark (0.10 and 0.08 respectively) to the momentum factor are in line with the value orientation. Note that the question tells us that value-oriented portfolios typically have low or negative sensitivity to the momentum factor.
     - The low sensitivities (0.05 and 0.08) to the size factor indicate no net exposure to small-cap stocks for Cazorla's portfolio or for the benchmark.
   The benchmark chosen for Cazorla's portfolio (the Russell 1000) suggests that the portfolio is geared toward large-cap stocks. Overall, we can conclude that Cazorla has a large-cap, value orientation.
2. Cazorla's active return primarily comes from his positive active exposure to the HML factor.
   - This bet contributed $(1.25 - 1.00)(4.50\%) = 1.125\%$, or approximately 98.08% of the total realized active return (1.147%). Cazorla tilted his portfolio more heavily toward a value orientation (portfolio sensitivity = 1.25 vs. benchmark sensitivity = 1.00) and, since the return on the value factor was significantly positive (4.50%), Cazorla's portfolio benefited from the tilt.
   - Cazorla's active exposures to the RMRF, SMB, and WML factors were relatively small (there are insignificant differences between the portfolio and the benchmark's sensitivities to these factors). Therefore, the effects of these bets on total active return were dwarfed by the impact of his large successful bet on value stocks.

- His active exposure to the overall market (RMRF) was not profitable as the return on the factor was positive (4.45%), but his portfolio was less sensitive to this factor than the benchmark was (portfolio factor sensitivity = 0.75 vs. benchmark factor sensitivity = 0.80).
- His active exposure to the size factor (SMB) was profitable as the return on the factor was negative (−3.50%), and his portfolio was less sensitive to this factor than the benchmark was (portfolio factor sensitivity = 0.05 vs. benchmark factor sensitivity = 0.08).
- His active exposure to the momentum factor (WML) was profitable as the return on the factor was positive (8.75%), and his portfolio was more sensitive to this factor than the benchmark was (portfolio factor sensitivity = 0.10 vs. benchmark factor sensitivity = 0.08).

3. Cazorla claims to be a "stock picker" but his return from asset selection is actually negative (−0.035%) over the period. As already discussed, the main reason that Cazorla was able to outperform the benchmark was his sizable bet on value stocks over a period during which value stocks significantly outperformed growth stocks. Wenger should try to establish whether Cazorla can consistently make successful bets on value as an investment style. The bottom line is that the active return on Cazorla's portfolio (while impressive due to the fact that it is positive) cannot be attributed to his ability to pick stocks (which is where Cazorla claims his expertise lies).

Factor Models in Risk Attribution

Active risk (also known as tracking error, TE, or tracking risk) is the standard deviation of active returns.

$$TE = s(R_p - R_B)$$

In the previous section, we learned how fundamental factor models were used to identify the sources of a portfolio manager's **active return**. In this section, our objective is to measure the portfolio's active exposure along each dimension of risk, or, stated differently, to understand the sources of tracking error. Decomposition of active risk allows us to answer the following questions regarding a portfolio's performance:

- What active risk exposures contributed most significantly to the portfolio's tracking risk?
- Can the portfolio manager justify the nature of her active exposures?
- Are the portfolio's active risk exposures consistent with her stated investment philosophy?
- Which active bets earned an adequate return for the level of active risk taken?

As was the case in the previous section, we will use a fundamental factor model (see Example 2-4) to illustrate the decomposition of active risk.

It is more convenient to analyze risk in terms of variances rather than standard deviations (as variances of uncorrelated variables are additive). Therefore, we work with active risk squared, which is the variance of active **return**. A portfolio's active risk squared can be separated into two components:

1. Active factor risk is the component of active risk squared that can be attributed to differences in factor exposures (to the same set of factors) between the portfolio and the benchmark.

2. **Active specific risk** or **security selection risk** is the component of active risk squared that can be attributed to differences in the weights of individual securities between the portfolio and the benchmark after accounting for the differences in factor sensitivities between the portfolio and the benchmark.

$$\text{Active risk squared} = s^2\,(R_P - R_B)$$

Note that active factor risk and active specific risk both refer to variances rather than standard deviations. When applied to an investment in a single asset class, active risk squared has two components:

$$\text{Active risk squared} = \text{Active factor risk} + \text{Active specific risk}$$

For example, consider an active portfolio manager who decides to overweight or underweight particular industries in her equity portfolio (single asset class), which causes her portfolio's industry factor sensitivities to be different from those of the benchmark.

- The difference between the returns on the benchmark and the portfolio that results from these differences in factor weights is the return from factor tilts.
- Active factor risk refers to the deviation of the portfolio's returns from the benchmark's returns caused by differences in factor sensitivities.

The manager may also decide to overweight or underweight particular stocks within a specific industry in her portfolio.

- The difference between the return on the benchmark and the return on the portfolio that results from these differences in individual asset or security weights is the return from security selection.
- Active specific risk or security selection risk refers to the deviation of the portfolio's returns from the benchmark's returns caused by differences in security weights. It arises from individual securities' residual risk.

Active specific risk can be computed as:

$$\text{Active specific risk} = \sum_{i=1}^{n} w_i^a \sigma_{\varepsilon_i}^2$$

where:
W_i^a = The ith asset's active weight in the portfolio (i.e., the difference between the asset's weight in the portfolio and its weight in the benchmark)
$\sigma_{\varepsilon_i}^2$ = The residual risk of the ith asset (i.e., the variance of the ith asset's returns that is not explained by the factors)

Active factor risk can then be computed as the difference between active risk squared and active specific risk.

$$\text{Active factor risk} = \text{Active risk squared} - \text{Active specific risk}$$

Example 2-4: Comparing Active Risk

An investment manager is using a fundamental factor model to evaluate the performance of four portfolios that have the same benchmark. The model incorporates two dimensions of risk: (1) risk indexes and (2) industrial categories.

- "Risk indexes" measures various fundamental aspects of companies and their stocks (e.g., size, leverage, dividend yield, etc.).
- "Industrial categories" is a binary variable. Companies have non-zero exposures to industries in which they operate.

Table 2-3 decomposes the active risk squared of the four portfolios. Active risk squared is broken down into (1) active factor risk and (2) active specific risk. Active factor risk is further broken down by individual factors (i.e., industry membership and risk indexes).

Table 2-3: Active Risk Squared Decomposition

	Active Factor Risk			Active Specific Risk	Active Risk Squared
Portfolio	Industry (1)	Risk Indexes (2)	Total Factor (3) = (1) + (2)	(4)	(5) = (3) + (4)
A	7.2	12.6	19.8	16.2	36
B	0.8	8.0	8.8	7.2	16
C	0.56	10.64	11.2	4.8	16
D	0.02	0.48	0.5	0.5	1

Note:

All figures are $\%^2$.

Column (1) and Column (2) list the sources of active factor risk in the portfolios.

Column (4) lists active specific risk in the portfolios.

Based on the information provided in Table 2-3, answer the following:

1. Contrast the active risk decomposition of Portfolios A and B.
2. Contrast the active risk decomposition of Portfolios B and C.
3. Comment on the investment approach adopted by Portfolio D.

Solutions:

Table 2-4 reorganizes the information provided in Table 2-3 to show the contribution of each source of risk to the portfolio's total active risk squared. Presenting the information in this manner makes it easier to analyze the sources of the portfolios' active risk squared.

When we described fundamental factor models earlier, we also said that sometimes factor sensitivities are presented as binary variables, which is the case here with industrial categories.

Table 2-4: Active Risk Decomposition (Restated)

Portfolio	Active Factor Risk (% of Total Active)			Active Specific Risk (% of Total Active)	Active Risk (%)
	Industry	**Risk Indexes**	**Total Factor Risk**		
A	20	35	55	45	6
B	5	50	55	45	4
C	4	67	70	30	4
D	2	48	50	50	1

Note:

All figures are in %.

All exposures have been rounded off to the nearest integer.

Note that in addition to focusing exclusively on active risk, multifactor models can also be used to decompose and attribute sources of total risk.

Explanatory calculations for Table 2-4 are provided here (for Portfolio A):

- Contribution of "Industry categories" factor to active risk squared = $7.2/36 = 20\%$
- Contribution of "risk indexes" factor to active risk squared = $12.6/36 = 35\%$
- Contribution of active factor risk to active risk squared = $20\% + 35\% = 55\%$ or $(7.2 + 12.6)/36 = 55\%$
- Contribution of active specific risk to active risk squared = $16.2/36 = 45\%$
- Active risk = Active risk squared$^{0.5}$ = $36^{0.5} = 6$

1. Portfolio A has a higher tracking risk (active risk) than Portfolio B (6% vs. 4%)
   - Both the portfolios entail the same proportions of active factor risk and active specific risk (55/45 splits for both).
   - Portfolio A carries significant exposure to the industry factor (20% of active risk squared). Portfolio B is almost industry neutral (exposure to the industry factor only contributes 5% of active risk squared).
   - Portfolio B makes a larger active bet on risk indexes relative to Portfolio A.
2. Portfolios B and C carry the same amount of active risk (4%).
   - Both are also relatively industry neutral (exposure to the industry factor contributes only around 5% of active risk squared).
   - More of Portfolio C's active risk comes from risk indexes (and consequently from active factor risk).
   - More of Portfolio B's active risk comes from active specific risk (45% for B vs. 30% for C), which suggests that Portfolio B is somewhat less diversified that Portfolio C.
3. Portfolio D's relatively insignificant active risk (1%) suggests that it is passively managed. It closely matches the benchmark in terms of its exposure to both dimensions of risk identified by the model. This is evidenced by its low absolute amount of active factor risk (0.50, which is equal to 0.7071% when expressed as a standard deviation) relative to Portfolios A, B, and C in Table 2-3.

Notice that the portfolios in Example 2-4 tended to have more active factor risk than active specific risk. This is typically the case, as active specific risk can be mitigated by holding an adequate number of individual securities in the portfolio, or a well-diversified portfolio (as we learned earlier in the reading). Therefore, the challenge for managers lies in managing active factor risk in their portfolios.

As a broad indication of the range for tracking error, in U.S. equity markets:

- A passive investment strategy should aim for a tracking error of 0.10% or less per annum.
- A low-risk active or enhanced index investment strategy, which makes tightly controlled use of managers' expectations, should have a tracking error goal of 2% per annum.
- A diversified active large-cap equity strategy should have a tracking error in the range of 2%–6% per annum.
- An aggressive active equity manager might have a tracking error in the range of 6%–10% or more.

Bear in mind that while our examples have focused on analysis of equity portfolios, multifactor models can be used for performance attribution of portfolios consisting of other asset classes as well.

The Information Ratio

We cannot use active return alone to evaluate the performance of active portfolio manager. Active return must be evaluated in light of the active risk taken by the manager to evaluate her performance.

Consider the performance of two portfolio managers.

- Manager A has earned an active return of 1.0% for each of the past four years.
- Manager B has earned active returns of 4%, 1%, −1%, and 0% over the past four years.

Even though the average active return for both the managers is the same (1%), it is obvious that Manager A has performed better (more consistently).

The information ratio (IR) is used to evaluate mean active return per unit of active risk.

$$IR = \frac{\bar{R}_p - \bar{R}_B}{s(R_p - R_B)}$$

The information ratio is conceptually similar to the Sharpe ratio. They both calculate excess return per unit of excess risk. See Example 2-5.

- The numerators compare average portfolio return to a benchmark. The Sharpe ratio uses the risk-free rate as the benchmark return, while the IR uses the return on an appropriate benchmark (relevant to the portfolio manager's investment style).
- The denominators use standard deviation to reflect dispersion. The Sharpe ratio uses the standard deviation of the portfolio's returns, while the IR uses the standard deviation of active returns (active risk).

The higher the information ratio, the better the risk-adjusted performance of the portfolio.

Example 2-5: Calculating the Information Ratio

An analyst gathered the following information regarding the performance of a portfolio and its benchmark:

Average return on the portfolio = 8.5%
Average return on the benchmark = 7%
Portfolio's tracking error = 5%

Calculate the information ratio.

Solution:

$$IR = \frac{\bar{R}_p - \bar{R}_B}{s(R_p - R_B)}$$

$$= \frac{(0.085 - 0.07)}{0.05} = 0.3$$

Factor Models in Portfolio Construction

In the previous section, we illustrated the application of multifactor models in analyzing a portfolio's active returns and active risk. In this section, we describe how multifactor models are used in portfolio construction.

When it comes to portfolio construction, multifactor models can be used to make focused bets or to control portfolio risk relative to the risk inherent in the benchmark. Further, they can be used in both active and passive management.

- **Passive management:** If a portfolio manager wants a fund to track the performance of a particular index that consists of many securities, she may need to choose a representative sample of securities from the index for her fund. Multifactor models can be used to align the fund's factor exposures with those of the index.
- **Active management:** Multifactor models are used to predict alpha (excess risk-adjusted returns) and relative return under various active investment strategies. They are also used to establish desired risk profiles when constructing portfolios.
- **Rules-based active management (alternative indexes):** These strategies routinely tilt toward factors such as size, value, quality, or momentum when constructing portfolios. Multifactor models are used in these strategies to tilt the portfolio's factor sensitivities and style biases relative to capitalization-weighted indexes.

We now move into a discussion of factor portfolios, which are commonly used to establish a desired risk profile for a portfolio.

A factor portfolio is constructed to have a sensitivity of 1 to a specific factor and a sensitivity of 0 to all other factors in the model. Therefore, it has exposure to only one risk factor and exactly represents the risk of that factor. Factor portfolios are of interest to managers who want to (1) hedge against a particular risk or (2) speculate on a particular outcome.

For example, consider a portfolio manager who believes that GDP growth will be stronger than is generally expected. She wants to bet on GDP growth but at the same time hedge against all other factor risks. The appropriate position for her would be to take a long position on a portfolio that has a sensitivity of 1 to the GDP risk factor (a factor portfolio exposed to the GDP risk factor) and a sensitivity of 0 to all other factors.

Now consider a portfolio manager who wants to hedge her portfolio against GDP factor risk. Her current portfolio has a sensitivity of 0.5 to GDP factor risk. The portfolio also has non-zero sensitivities to other risk factors, but the manager wants to retain her existing exposure to those risks. The appropriate position for the manager in this case would be to take a 50% short position in a GDP risk factor portfolio. Her long exposure to GDP risk in her existing portfolio (with a sensitivity of +0.5) would be completely offset (hedged) by the −0.5 factor sensitivity on her short position in the GDP factor portfolio.

LOS 48g: Describe the potential benefits for investors in considering multiple risk dimensions when modeling asset returns. Vol 6, pg 299

How Factor Considerations Can Be Useful in Strategic Portfolio Decisions

Multifactor models can help investors make investing decisions that are better aligned with their requirements. Given a sound model that incorporates the systematic risk factors that affect an asset's expected returns, investors can take on exposure to risks that they understand and are willing to bear, and avoid risks that they are unwilling to take on.

For example, consider university endowments. These institutions typically have very long investment horizons, offering them a comparative advantage when it comes to their ability to bear the business cycle risk inherent in equities and the liquidity risk associated with private equity investments. As a result, they may tilt their strategic asset allocations toward these asset classes to take advantage of the risk premiums on offer (for bearing the mentioned business cycle and liquidity risks). At the same time, these university endowments are typically very wary of inflation because the costs of the activities they support tend to increase at a rate higher than the average inflation rate. Therefore, they seek protection from inflation risk in their portfolios.

This example shows us how multifactor models offer us a framework that is so much richer than the CAPM, which simply asserts that all investors should invest in some mix of the market portfolio and the risk-free asset.

Practically speaking, a CAPM-oriented investor might hold a money-market fund and a portfolio of capitalization-weighted broad market indexes across many asset classes, varying the weights in these two in accordance with risk tolerance. However, multifactor models force investors to think about the priced risks that they face, analyze the extent of their exposure, and offer ways to mitigate exposure to undesirable risks. The end result is better-diversified portfolios that are possibly also more efficient. For example, the characteristics of a portfolio can be better explained by its sensitivities to momentum, size, value, and market factors (as is the case in the Carhart model) than by the market factor alone (as is the case with the CAPM).

READING 49: MEASURING AND MANAGING MARKET RISK

LESSON 1: VALUE AT RISK

LOS 49a: Explain the use of value at risk (VaR) in measuring portfolio risk.
Vol 6, pp 315–317

A firm's risk management process requires it to measure risk, set acceptable risk levels, and continually monitor the risks it accepts. Some risks are easier to measure and monitor than others.

Market risk, for example, arises from potential changes in interest rates, stock prices, commodity prices, and exchange rates. This differs from credit risk, operational risk, and other types of risk to which the firm may be exposed.

Risk managers often use *value at risk (VaR)* to describe a minimum loss to which a portfolio or portfolios of assets might be subject over a particular time period with a certain degree of probability.

- Minimum amount—The loss may be greater than the minimum amount or percentage, but VaR identifies a loss of *at least* some minimum amount or percentage.
- Time frame—The period over which the firm is subject to the minimum loss may be a day, two weeks, a month, or other.
- Degree of probability—The probability that the loss will exceed the minimum amount established as the threshold. Probabilities of 1% and 5% are common but may be stated as levels of confidence such as 99% and 95%, respectively.

Because of its use in identifying potential loss, VaR will often be stated in positive terms rather than negative terms (Figure 1-1).

Figure 1-1: The 1% VaR of the Equity Large-Cap Value Portfolio Is £7.5 Million over a Two-Week Period

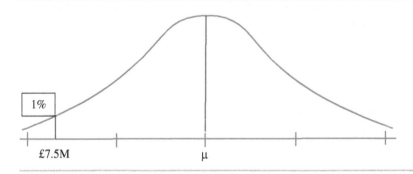

Although this VaR statement indicates the probability of minimum loss, a VaR statement could also indicate level of confidence: that is, a 99% probability it would not have a loss of that amount or greater over the period.

This explanation should make apparent that a higher level of confidence results in a greater value at risk, although there will be less likelihood of that greater loss.

Estimating VaR

LOS 49b: Compare the parametric (variance-covariance), historical simulation, and Monte Carlo simulation methods for estimating VaR. Vol 6, pp 317–320

LOS 49c: Estimate and interpret VaR under the parametric, historical simulation, and Monte Carlo simulation methods. Vol 6, pp 320–329

Although each VaR estimation method decomposes risk into a set of risk factor exposures, the methods use different approaches to specifying inputs and estimating VaR. The data set in Table 1-1 will be used to illustrate each method.

Table 1-1: Input Assumptions

| Security | Allocation | 5-year Annualized | |
		Return	Standard Deviation
Big Equity Fund	60%	9.32%	13.97%
Big Bond Fund	40%	2.66%	4.30%
$Corr_{A,B}$	−0.75		
Portfolio value	$300 million		

Parametric Method

The parametric method generates a VaR estimate based on return and standard deviation, typically from a normal distribution. VaR estimates based on other distributions are possible, but require skewness and kurtosis parameters in addition to return and standard deviation.

Calculations for VaR using the parametric method consider the number of standard deviations appropriate for the level of risk assumed, usually 2.33, 1.65, or 1 standard deviation corresponding to 1%, 5%, or 16% in the left tail, respectively. This becomes a fairly simple process using the normalization formula:

$$z = \frac{R - \mu}{\sigma}$$

Using this formula requires estimating μ as expected return for the portfolio:

$$E(R_P) = \sum_{i=1}^{n} w_i R_i$$

where i identifies each security or asset, w_i is the weight of each asset in the portfolio, and R_i is the return of each asset in the portfolio.

Calculations for portfolio standard deviation must consider not only the standard deviation of each asset, but also the correlation between assets:

$$\sigma_P = \sqrt{w_i^2 \sigma_i^2 + w_j^2 \sigma_j^2 + 2w_i \sigma_i w_j \sigma_j \rho_{i,j}}$$

where σ_i is the standard deviation of each security or asset and ρ is the correlation of the asset pair i and j. Note that $cov_{i,j}$ may be substituted (if known) in the portfolio standard deviation formula for the terms $\sigma_i \, \sigma_i \, \rho_{i,j}$.

However, the annual return and standard deviation data must be adjusted based on the time frame specified for the VaR. Assuming we use 250 trading days and are interested in the one-day VaR, the portfolio expected return must be divided by 250 and the portfolio standard deviation by the square root of 250.

Annual expected return for the portfolio is:

$$
E(R_P) = \sum_{i=1}^{n} w_i R_i
$$
$$
= 0.60(9.32\%) + 0.40(2.66\%) = 6.66\%
$$

Daily return equals 6.66% / 250 = 0.0266%

Annual standard deviation of portfolio returns is:

$$
\sigma_P = \sqrt{w_i^2 \sigma_i^2 + w_j^2 \sigma_j^2 + 2 w_i \sigma_i w_j \sigma_j \rho_{i,j}}
$$
$$
= \sqrt{0.36(0.01952) + 0.16(0.00185) + 2(0.60)(0.1397)(0.40)(0.0430)(-0.75)}
$$
$$
= 0.0718 = 7.18\%
$$

Daily standard deviation of portfolio returns equals $0.0718 / (250)^{1/2} = 0.00454$ or 0.454%.

Note that we're looking for a 5% VaR, which would indicate a return 1.65 standard deviations below the mean daily return of 0.0266%. If each standard deviation is 0.454%, then we can calculate the return that is 1.65 standard deviations below the mean:

$$
z = \frac{R - \mu}{\sigma}
$$
$$
-1.65 = \frac{R - 0.0266\%}{0.454\%}
$$
$$
R = -1.65(0.454\%) + 0.0266\% = -0.7225\%
$$

VaR will, however, typically be stated in positive terms. Therefore, you could expect to lose $2,167,500 ($300M × 0.007225) or more 5% of the time.

The parametric method using the normal distribution is easy to use and employs historical values that can be adjusted for reasonableness in any environment. It does not, however, reflect the nonparametric losses that result from unexercised options in a portfolio that expire worthless. Additionally, the distribution changes as time value diminishes and the option value approaches the underlying security value at maturity. Finally, sensitivity to correlation changes between portfolio assets adds instability to the estimate.

Historical Simulation Method

Rather than assuming a normal distribution and calculating VaR using statistical parameters such as mean, standard deviation, and correlations for the assets, the historical simulation method uses current portfolio weights for each asset multiplied by its percentage return for each period (e.g., daily). All available returns representing expected reality would be used. (See Table 1-2.)

Table 1-2: Historical Simulation Method—Portfolio Repricing

Period	Asset i (60%)	Asset j (40%)	Portfolio Return
A	$A_i\%$	$A_j\%$	$R_A = w_i(A_i\%) + w_j(A_j\%)$
B	$B_i\%$	$B_j\%$	$R_B = w_i(B_i\%) + w_j(B_j\%)$
…	…	…	…
Z	$Z_i\%$	$Z_j\%$	$R_Z = w_i(Z_i\%) + w_j(Z_j\%)$

Returns for the repriced portfolio are ranked lowest to highest, and VaR is then determined for the required confidence interval.

Given that data have been sorted low to high, the 1% VaR would be the first return observation at the low end of a 100-period data set, the 5% VaR would be the fifth return observation, and so on.

While both the parametric and historical simulation methods use an assumption of equal weightings for periodic results, the historical simulation method can be adjusted by overweighting more current or more realistic returns while underweighting older or less realistic outcomes. Additionally, historical simulation can accommodate options in a portfolio because it uses outcomes that actually occurred.

On the other hand, the historical simulation method suffers from the disadvantage of representing only historical reality rather than extreme outcomes that can result. For that reason, historical simulation is recommended only when the future appears likely to reflect past results.

Monte Carlo Simulation

Monte Carlo simulation employs user-developed assumptions to generate a distribution of random outcomes. This method overcomes the problem of potential outcomes outside past results as in a historical simulation, while avoiding complexity inherent in correlations among a wide variety of assets as in the parametric method.

A distribution of returns for each risk factor (each asset, in this case) will be generated. Distributions can be assumed normal or non-normal. The two distributions are then combined according to our exposure to each asset (60% equity and 40% debt) and considering the correlation of asset returns, and ranked low to high as in historical simulation.

VaR will then be determined much as in the historical simulation method.

The challenge lies in the tradeoff between greater reliability of many simulation runs versus the time and cost of many runs. This becomes important because a Monte Carlo simulation samples from each return distribution whereas the parametric method draws from the entire range of outcomes possible within a distribution. A greater number of samples, then, will tend to move the Monte Carlo outcome closer to parameters for the population of portfolio return outcomes. The distribution resulting from a Monte Carlo simulation will also tend to resemble the distribution from which it is drawn; that is, a simulation drawn from risk factors with normal distribution will tend to produce normally distributed returns.

Advantages and Limitations of VaR

LOS 49d: Describe advantages and limitations of VaR. Vol 6, pp 329–332

Risk managers can verify by backtesting whether actual results exceed VaR the percentage of time indicated by the level of confidence.

VaR not only is simple and easy to communicate in terms of percentage or currency effect on the portfolio, but it also provides a convenient method for risk managers to compare asset classes, portfolios, or trading units across the organization. This allows risk managers to allocate total assets according to the risk-return needs of the organization.

Just as it can help allocate capital across the organization, it can be used to evaluate performance for individuals at the portfolio or business unit level and is a measure of risk widely accepted by regulators throughout the world.

In addition to the incorrect belief that VaR is a worst-case scenario, limitations of the VaR process include:

- *Oversimplification*—Although VaR conveniently reports risk as a minimum loss, it tends to oversimplify the risk itself as well as the contributing factors to the overall risk.
  - *Underestimating outlier events*—Use of the normal distribution and other symmetric distributions tends to underestimate the percentage of time that "left tail events" occur. This is especially important in parametric and Monte Carlo methods; the historical method uses whatever distribution the data indicates.
  - *Illiquidity risk*—Related to left tail events, this refers specifically to asset illiquidity during stressful times in financial markets.
  - *Correlation risk*—Also related to left tail events, this refers specifically to assets becoming more highly correlated as people "rush to the doors" in a financial market.
- *Disregarding potential reward*—VaR focuses only on left tail events, which makes analyzing asset risk-return opportunities difficult.
- *Subjectivity*—VaR requires various decisions requiring judgment. Specifically, VaR computations require decisions on time horizon, estimation method, and level of confidence.
- *Trending*—A portfolio can remain under VaR and still incur substantial losses each period on an ongoing basis.

Extensions of VaR

LOS 49e: Describe extensions of VaR. **Vol 6, pp 332–334**

Although any risk model will be unlikely to independently answer all of a risk manager's questions, variations on VaR can help uncover additional aspects of risk.

Conditional VaR

Also known as *expected shortfall* or *expected tail loss*, conditional VaR describes the *average* loss expected outside confidence limits. Therefore, it is not technically a VaR measure.

Conditional VaR will most likely be developed using historical or Monte Carlo approaches because the average of the values left of the level of confidence is observable. The expected value in the relevant area of the tail can, however, be developed mathematically using approaches outside the scope of this lesson.

Incremental VaR (IVaR)

IVaR examines how the minimum loss will change if a position within the portfolio changes. It could, for example, be used to identify the VaR change expected from adjusting the previous 60–40 stock–bond allocation to 75–25.

Marginal VaR (MVaR) is a related concept that uses calculus to identify the change to minimum loss from some marginal change in portfolio positions. MVaR is often interpreted as the change in minimum loss resulting from a $1 or 1% change in a portfolio position; while not technically correct, it provides a reasonable explanation.

Relative VaR

Also known as *ex ante tracking error*, this extension describes the minimum loss at a given level of confidence of the manager's bets relative to a benchmark. In effect, the benchmark is entered as a short position in calculating portfolio VaR. If the portfolio exactly matches the benchmark, relative VaR will be 0.

LESSON 2: OTHER RISK MEASURES

LOS 49f: Describe sensitivity risk measures and scenario risk measures and compare these measures to VaR. **Vol 6, pp 344–345**

LOS 49h: Describe the use of sensitivity risk measures and scenario risk measures. **Vol 6, pp 334–343**

Risk managers often address shortcomings of VaR with other measures. Sensitivity analysis, for example, allows a risk manager to see how underlying risk factors affect gains and losses. Various types of scenario analysis allow a risk manager to determine how a portfolio performs under historical or hypothetical market conditions, especially during times of stress.

Sensitivity Analysis

Risk management requires understanding how an asset's exposure to risk factors affects financial performance. Sensitivity analysis addresses how an asset responds to changes in a single risk factor.

LOS 49g: Demonstrate how equity, fixed income, and options exposure measures may be used in measuring and managing market risk and volatility risk.
Vol 6, pp 335–339

Equity Exposure

Beta, the covariance of the asset return with the market return divided by variance of the market return, is the primary risk factor affecting securities. This sensitivity does not recognize factors specific to the company, industry, and so forth, except to the extent they impact the overall market for equity securities. Clearly, these idiosyncratic factors have a negligible impact on overall market movements.

Beta's impact on return becomes clear from the capital asset pricing model (CAPM):

$$E(r_a) = r_f + \beta \left[E(r_M) - r_f \right]$$

In this formulation, the sensitivity of the asset to the market is applied to the market return less the risk-free rate (i.e., equity risk premium) to establish compensation for the individual asset's risk. The equity risk premium $[E(r_M) - r_f]$ describes the additional return investors require for holding equity securities rather than risk-free instruments.

Fixed Income Exposure

The primary risk factor affecting fixed income securities is changes in yield curve upon which the bond is valued. This will typically be measured by *duration* (i.e., percentage change in price for a given change in yield). Duration is a first-order (i.e., straight-line) relationship, however, and will work well only with relatively small yield changes. *Convexity* captures the second-order relationship between bond price and yield.

The following formula captures both the first- and second-order yield effects on bond price:

$$\frac{\Delta B}{B} = -D \frac{\Delta y}{1+y} + \frac{1}{2} C \frac{(\Delta y)^2}{(1+y)^2}$$

Convexity becomes important as yield changes become larger and holding periods become longer.

Options Exposure

Exposures on derivatives such as forwards, futures, and swaps that have a price change directly related to changes in the price of an underlying security can be evaluated based on sensitivity of the underlying. Risk managers must, however, use special measures to evaluate the non-linear exposures of options.

For purposes of further discussion in this section, c represents call price and S represents stock price. Variables preceded by Δ will indicate the change in that variable.

Delta

Option *delta* is similar to duration in that it measures price sensitivity to changes in some other factor (i.e., changes in the underlying price in the case of options):

$$Delta = \frac{\Delta c}{\Delta S}$$

Call option deltas range between 0 and 1 due to the direct non-linear relationship between call option price and the underlying price. As expiration approaches, delta approaches 1 for deeply in-the-money calls and 0 for deeply out-of-the-money calls.

Put option deltas range between 0 and –1 due to the inverse non-linear relationship between put option price and the underlying price. As expiration approaches, delta approaches –1 for deeply in-the-money puts and 0 for deeply out-of-the-money puts.

Gamma

Option price gamma is similar to bond price convexity in that it measures the second-order sensitivity (i.e., changes in delta given changes in the price of the underlying):

$$\Gamma = gamma = \frac{\Delta delta}{\Delta S}$$

Gamma reflects uncertainty about an option expiring out-of-the-money. Gamma increases as the option approaches in-the-money because a small price change in the underlying can determine whether the option becomes exercisable—resulting in a gain—or will expire worthless, causing loss of the option premium.

The formula for estimating the new call price based on changes in the underlying stock S using Δ_c for delta of the call option and Γ_c for gamma of the call option closely resembles first- and second-order price effects of changes in interest rates on bond prices:

$$c + \Delta c \approx c + \Delta_c \Delta S + \frac{1}{2} \Gamma_c (\Delta S)^2$$

Vega

Price changes in the underlying help determine an in-the-money exercise or a worthless expiration. The more volatile the price changes, the greater likelihood of being in-the-money. Therefore, changes in price volatility of the underlying affect option prices as captured in vega:

$$Vega \approx \frac{\Delta c}{\Delta \sigma_S}$$

The new value of a call price given changes in price and volatility of the underlying is:

$$c + \Delta c \approx c + \Delta_c \Delta S + \frac{1}{2} \Gamma_c (\Delta S)^2 + vega \Delta \sigma_S$$

For a portfolio that includes options, the composite position for each of the Greeks is the currency-weighted values for delta, gamma, and vega of the options positions. Sensitivity to market risk factors for a diversified portfolio can then be calculated if the risk manager knows the beta of the equity portfolio, the duration and convexity of the bond portfolio, and the Greeks for any options.

Scenario Analysis

Scenario analysis develops risk measures for extreme outcomes similar to VaR, but is not bound by the parameters of a probability distribution developed for results from recent history. Historical simulation repeats a particular period of financial markets history to see how well a current portfolio performs, while hypothetical simulation uses extreme variations and co-variations to develop a nonprobabilistic extreme outcome.

Stress tests are related to hypothetical scenario analysis by stressing the portfolio with extremely low-probability/high-loss outcomes. Scenario analysis may, however, be useful for determining potential gain as well as loss.

Risk managers should be careful not to attempt to remove all risk; that would likely lead to a risk-free return. They should, however, focus on low-probability events that will result in unacceptable losses.

Historical Scenarios

Historical scenarios are created by putting the current portfolio into a valuation model representing some historical period such as the financial crisis of 2008–2009 or the market crash of 1987. While equities can often be valued using their price history or modeling changes via factor analysis, bonds and derivatives may have different characteristics than during the historical time. Any collateral requirements or cash needs should also be considered by the scenario, including a lack of liquidity that may have resulted during the crisis period.

For example, bonds will have a different duration based on the maturity date now versus during the historical period. Alternatively, a bond may not have been issued yet during the historical period. A derivatives position may not have been created during that historical period, but the changes relative to the underlying can still be modeled.

Risk managers can note each asset's price before the scenario and then reprice the portfolio after applying changes in interest rates, volatility, and other risk factors that occurred during the historical period. The changes are often assumed to occur simultaneously and immediately, and without rebalancing by the portfolio manager, but may also be modeled over several days or the entire historical period while allowing for manager decisions normally made during such a crisis.

Although portfolio total return will generally always be important, risk managers for different types of portfolios will often look at different measures. Specifically, long-only managers will tend to look at the portfolio return relative to their benchmark return (which must also be simulated for the historical period), whereas asset-liability managers (e.g., pensions, insurers) will also want to view the effect on liabilities.

Rather than fully considering price changes during the scenario period, some managers apply risk changes during the scenario period to the securities based on their sensitivity to such factors. This should not be done for options or securities with embedded options, because gamma and convexity will not be accurate enough to use for the scenario.

Risk managers must determine appropriate reactions to factor sensitivities for assets not present during the historical period, such as credit default swaps during the market crash of 1987. Similarly, equities not issued yet must be mapped according to their factor sensitivities or to a relevant index.

Although historical simulation can be helpful, the probability of a repeat performance will be low. Managers who have protected their portfolios from the set of events during the historical crisis may have introduced other problems.

Hypothetical Scenarios

Hypothetical scenarios can often point out weaknesses in portfolios that were not evident during a historical period. *Reverse stress testing* can be used against a current portfolio's sensitivities to test behaviors during any assumed crisis, even one that appears outside the bounds of probability or has not occurred in the past.

A stress test may not be required for all of the portfolio's sensitivities, but just those to which it is most vulnerable. Reverse stress testing can also expose portfolio vulnerabilities when problems in unrelated markets occur, causing managers in those markets to sell off parts of their portfolios to which there is exposure. Hypothetical scenario analysis can also assess the impact of markets crowding into the same exposures.

Risk managers may also develop market scenarios for geopolitical events, natural disasters, or any number of other events that could create unacceptable losses.

Comparisons to VaR

Although both VaR and sensitivity measures can help estimate potential losses, sensitivity and scenario analysis disclose nothing about the probability of such. They do, however, allow risk managers insight into the factors driving losses during such events. Clearly, it makes sense to use VaR and other risk factors to estimate the probability of large losses as well as determine how to guard against them.

LOS 49i: Describe advantages and limitations of sensitivity risk measures and scenario risk measures. Vol 6, pp 345–347

An experienced risk manager may be able to assess potential loss simply by the size of a position, but will have less ability to understand *how* the portfolio will be stressed by changes in specific factors. In other words, the potential loss is not the only consideration. VaR and other risk measures overcome position-size analysis limitations.

Sensitivity measures can determine the portfolio effects of specific changes in risk exposures, but are less helpful in understanding changes in risk exposures on specific securities. For example, a portfolio with both triple-A and high-yield bonds will have assets that respond differently to a 1% change in rates or changes in credit spreads. Correlation risk may also vary for non-parallel interest rate changes; that is, one-year bonds may react very differently from longer-term bonds. Getting too specific, however, runs the risk of missing the bigger picture regarding portfolio vulnerability.

Scenario analysis has the distinct disadvantage of having to be believable in order to result in change. A risk manager would have been reluctant to suggest large losses resulting from high-rated mortgage securities as occurred from 2008 to 2010, and asset managers may have shelved a report with recommendations resulting from such a scenario.

Historical scenario analysis assumes that risk factor effects on an asset during a historical period will be similar for the current period. One example is duration changing based on the new time to maturity for a bond. Some changes in factor sensitivities may be more difficult to account for.

LESSON 3: RISK MEASUREMENT APPLICATIONS

In general, market participants use risk measures based on:

- Degree of leverage, which affects minimum capitalization,
- Mix of risk factors related to specific asset types within a portfolio, and
- Accounting and regulatory requirements.

Highly leveraged asset managers tend to favor high confidence levels and focus on short intervals, while long-only asset managers focus more on avoiding underperformance over longer measurement periods. Long-only managers have little interest in the difference between 5 and 6 standard deviation events because it will have little relevance to their portfolios. The magnitude of such differences is greater for extremely leveraged portfolios.

Portfolios with bonds will often be concerned with duration, credit spread analysis, and so on. Their analysis will focus on inflation expectations and central bank policy change, or fiscal policy. Equity funds may be more concerned with beta or fundamental factors (firm size, momentum, industry developments, etc.).

Capital adequacy measures and VaR apply more to portfolios using fair value accounting (e.g., held-for-sale bank portfolios, U.S. mutual funds, and European funds organized as Undertakings for Collective Investment in Transferable Securities). *Asset-liability gap modeling*, on the other hand, will be common for entities subject to book value accounting.

LOS 49j: Describe risk measures used by banks, asset managers, pension funds, and insurers. Vol 6, pp 348–356

Banks

It is common for banks to assess risk by geographic areas or business units, and aggregate these outcomes to a top-level view of the entity.

Banks will typically use fair value accounting on risk measures applicable to being "held for sale" or in a trading portfolio. Banks will use book value for "held to maturity" and longer-term assets in an investment portfolio.

- *Liquidity gap*—The difference between assets and liabilities and the ability to raise cash to fund the gap; repayment dates for debt.
- *VaR*—For the held-for-sale or trading portion of the portfolio.
- *Leverage ratio*—May be based on internal measures or regulatory requirements, often weighted based on riskiness to allow more equity backing for riskier investments.
- *Sensitivities*—Key rate or partial duration, credit spread duration, or general duration will be applied to the held-for-sale portfolio. Equity, commodity, and foreign exchange exposures will be measured. Delta, vega, and gamma will be measured for options exposures, possibly by expiration time frames to differentiate longer expirations.
- *Scenario analysis*—Used to assess effects of extreme, targeted shocks against all firm capital, including effects of high unemployment on credit card delinquencies and other operational factors.
- *Economic capital*—Market, credit, and operational risks may be blended and applied to all the firm's capital over a longer period (e.g., one year) to estimate losses at high confidence levels.

Banks will tend to view risks in currency terms based on the balance sheet currency.

Asset Managers

While regulation focuses more on fair treatment of investors, the firm itself often wishes to ensure its survival by balancing performance against risk. Thus, risk management focuses on the probability of underperforming a benchmark as well as on volatility and the probability of large losses.

Asset managers may need to aggregate individual portfolio holdings across the entity to ensure it meets requirements both at the portfolio level and at the firm level, and a fund of funds will likely wish to view its exposure at a master fund level. A hedge fund manager may wish to aggregate its firm's side-by-side investments in funds managed for clients.

In addition, backward-looking measures (e.g., historical beta, standard deviation, *ex post* tracking error, etc.) may show performance, but must be augmented with current portfolio measures (e.g., VaR, duration, forward-looking beta, *ex ante* tracking error, and scenario analysis/stress testing).

Traditional Asset Managers

These managers will often seek to outperform in relative terms (i.e., relative to a benchmark). Absolute return strategies will tend to use cash return as a benchmark. Asset allocation funds can use a combination of market indexes or a custom benchmark.

Long-only asset managers will tend to assess risk as some percentage of assets, thus dividing VaR or currency duration by the asset base.

- *Tracking error*—Asset managers use *ex post* tracking error to assess manager performance (i.e., how the manager did relative to some benchmark). Risk managers are more likely to use *ex ante* tracking error to assess whether unexpected results are likely to unfavorably impact future *ex post* tracking. This essentially involves exposing the current portfolio to historical scenarios to determine the benchmark-relative result. *Active share* is the portion of the portfolio different from the benchmark, which may be assessed separately.
- *Liquidity*—Daily average trading volume and days to liquidate.
- *Redemption risk*—Related to liquidity risk, the portion of the fund subject to redemption during peak times.
- *VaR*—Not as common for traditional managers who judge performance relative to a benchmark, but common for absolute return managers (who usually do not use a benchmark).
- *Sensitivities*—Beta for equities, various duration measures for bonds, and delta measures for options.
- *Scenario analysis*—Primarily to ensure full disclosure or compliance with disclosed risks.
- *Position limits*—A specific amount, easily understood by investors, often based on asset class, currency, country, or sector.

Hedge Fund Managers

Hedge funds often use leverage and therefore must consider market risk in the context of other factors such as likelihood of redemptions, withdrawal of liquidity lines, and margin calls.

- *Liquidity*—Hedge funds often experience a non-normal distribution of returns; standard deviation doesn't provide a useful measure of potential loss or when withdrawals are likely to make the problem worse. Therefore, hedge funds rely on quarterly or peak-to-trough *maximum drawdown* as a measure of liquidity risk. This applies specifically to:

- ○ Correlation relationships—equity market neutral
- ○ Embedded options—buy bonds or sell options
- ○ Credit risk—long/short credit, credit arbitrage, and distressed investments
- ○ Events—merger arbitrage
- ○ Illiquidity bets—large positions in small-capitalization investments or in illiquid investments
- ○ Opaque markets—infrequently valued or poorly valued assets

- *VaR*—Hedge funds seldom use benchmark-relative measures (e.g., tracking risk) but frequently use VaR with high confidence levels (i.e., greater than 90%) and short periods (i.e., weekly, daily).
- *Leverage*—Many measures are common; understand the numerator and denominator of the ratio.
- *Sensitivities*—A full range of exposures relevant to the subject fund.
- *Scenario analysis*—Common, and appropriate for the risks taken by the fund.
- *Position limits*—Long exposure and short exposure are common. Gross exposure, the absolute value of long and short positions, is also an important measure of correlation risk.

Pension Funds

Pension funds in this context refer to defined benefit plans that have an obligation based on some function of a retiree's final income. Such funds must be liquid enough to fund such future payments. Plan sponsors will typically not be required to make contributions when the ratio of assets to the present value of future liabilities exceeds 100% or some other suitable percentage, but must make contributions when that ratio falls below the minimum.

Market risk measures for pension plans, then, will be important to both plan sponsors and beneficiaries.

- *Interest rate/yield curve*—Expected future cash flows are grouped by maturity and currency in the case of international pension funds. Any liability along the yield curve will be shown as a short position.
- *Surplus at risk*—Assets are expressed in a VaR model as long positions whereas liabilities are expressed as short fixed-income positions. Pension fund managers then use a confidence level to assess probable underfunding (i.e., long positions are insufficient to fund the liabilities). Zero surplus at risk will result by precisely funding liabilities with long positions in fixed income securities with comparable maturities. Surplus at risk will typically arise due to higher volatility than for low correlation of assets with liabilities. When surplus at risk exceeds an acceptable level, fund managers will reset the assets to better match the liabilities (i.e., liability-driven investing). A *glide path* (i.e., multiyear plan) may be used to bring assets and liabilities back in synch when they become significantly over- or underfunded.
- *Liability hedging/return-generating exposures*—Although liabilities may not always be linkable directly to an offsetting asset, it may be possible for a fund manager to link to an asset that will *at least* generate the minimum required or may even generate a surplus. The return-generating assets may also help avert the need for additional fund sponsor contributions if actuarial expectations (e.g., wage growth, life expectancy, etc.) exceed expectations.

Insurers

Due to a variety of regulations specific to lines of insurance, insurers often aggregate risk at the business unit level to understand risk at the firm level. In addition to regulatory differences, life insurance and annuities have a different risk profile than property/casualty (P&C) insurance and health insurance. Therefore, correlations with asset classes tend to be very different for different lines of insurance.

Insurers as a whole do not attempt asset-liability matching, but instead rely on premium revenues to claims. Regulations often place greater discount requirements on riskier assets when determining financial strength for P&C insurers. Life insurers will generally be tied more to financial markets with financial strength more dependent on discount rate assumptions.

Property/casualty insurers typically focus on the following exposures:

- *Sensitivities*—Managers set exposure limits and design an asset allocation to remain within the limits.
- *Scenario analysis*—Risk managers may combine market risks and insurance risks into the same scenario to see the effects of outsize investment losses and operational losses.
- *Economic capital/VaR*—Additional capital will typically be needed only when payouts exceed premium revenue. Risk modeling must consider risk for the payouts as well as market risk on investments.

Life insurers consider the following exposures:

- *Sensitivities*—Exposures of the investment portfolio are measured and monitored relative to the annuity liabilities.
- *Scenario analysis*—Market risks should consider both actuarial changes (e.g., longevity of the insured) and operational risks (i.e., differences between expected and actual) to see the full picture.
- *Asset-liability matching*—While the investment portfolio will not be directly matched to liabilities, it is more aligned than with property/casualty insurers.

LESSON 4: USING CONSTRAINTS TO MANAGE MARKET RISK

LOS 49k: Explain constraints used in managing market risks, including risk budgeting, position limits, scenario limits, and stop-loss limits. Vol 6, pp 357–360

Risk managers are often responsible for determining the correct balance between profitability on the investment portfolio and the degree of loss it cannot exceed. Setting high confidence limits results in larger potential losses but higher profitability. Setting a lower confidence limit results in smaller potential losses but lower profitability.

Management of risk exposure should also consider the level of organization. For example, managing risk at a very low, granular level seems like it provides the greatest safety, but does not take advantage of the diversification benefits of other portfolios in the organization, assuming all portfolios are not perfectly correlated.

One possible method of managing by individual portfolio allows overallocation to the extent that portfolio correlation provides diversification. Investments can then be reduced to specific allocations as portfolios across the organization become more correlated. Alternatively, firms may be able to reinvest a VaR budget generated by correlations across trading desks and in the context of each portfolio's VaR when aggregated to the firm level.

Risk Budgeting

Risk budgeting occurs when the firm chooses a desired maximum risk and then budgets this out to business units or individual portfolios. The risk will generally be based on *ex ante* tracking error or VaR.

Banks might establish risk budgets by parceling out the firm's total appetite for risk type (e.g., market, operational, credit) within business units, geographical areas, or activity. These budgets will be established based on the profitability of the risk, expectations of shareholders, and so forth.

Pension fund sponsors are more likely to look at surplus at risk (i.e., the difference between assets and liabilities). They may then assign the risk of asset underperformance by allocating *ex ante* tracking error risk for each asset in the portfolio. The portfolio manager retains responsibility for aligning reward from the investment with tracking error risk from bets outside the benchmark.

Position Limits

VaR has certain logical appeal, but performs poorly in circumstances such as a portfolio with highly concentrated investments. This is especially true when liquidity becomes an issue. Position limits, by contrast, provide excellent controls against overconcentration. Position limits can be formulated to avoid event risk and overconcentration, but should not be so constraining they prevent outperforming a benchmark.

Position limits might include limits on:

- Issuer
- Currency or country
- High-risk strategies such as high-yield debt or emerging market equity
- Long/short positions
- Derivative activities
- Concentration (e.g., percentage of daily average trading volume)

Scenario Limits

Scenario limits address potential correlation changes and results from a non-normal distribution as with VaR. Scenario limits can be used to trigger asset manager actions to help protect the portfolio.

Risk managers typically set the limits for each scenario, but allow greater tolerance for extreme scenarios to avoid limiting all funding. For example, if an extreme scenario were to suggest an incredibly high interest rate increase, a low tolerance (high confidence level) would prevent investing in the scenario due to potentially unsustainable losses.

Stop-Loss Limits

Stop-loss limits require reduction in position or portfolio size, or even complete liquidation, when positions exceed their limit over a specified period. Stop-loss limits may be employed to eliminate the trending problem with VaR (i.e., positions have losses just under VaR each period over some time).

This can be accomplished by requiring that positions be reduced or liquidated if losses exceed some threshold over a period of time. Alternatively, the manager may be forced to assume a hedge that protects portfolio value but decreases potential upside (e.g., protective puts). The latter approach is called portfolio insurance or drawdown control.

Capital Allocation

LOS 49l: Explain how risk measures may be used in capital allocation decisions. Vol 6, pp 360–361

Capital allocation aligns risk and reward by putting limits on capital assigned to each of the firm's activities. This prevents an unproven strategy from potentially siphoning away all risk capital from other potentially lucrative strategies.

In a process similar to risk budgeting for an asset management firm, a company must decide the level of *economic capital*, defined as the capital required to maintain solvency if it incurs severe losses up to some level of confidence (i.e., the VaR for some period at some level of confidence).

Although risk budgeting generally focuses on losses at the one standard deviation level, capital allocation is more likely to focus on losses at the 1% risk level (i.e., 99% confidence) to assess how much equity could be required for a particular strategy. Investors not only expect higher returns for a higher level of risk, but they also expect the company to invest in areas in which the company has enough expertise to successfully execute a strategy.

The capital allocation process—where projects exceeding a hurdle rate of return are accepted and others rejected—has been explored in great detail in corporate finance. Economic capital will not be the binding constraint, then, when actual cash on hand or regulatory capital requirements are higher than economic capital. It will be the binding constraint when assets available to handle business risk are less than required.

Study Session 17: Portfolio Management: Economic Analysis, Active Management, and Trading

READING 50: ECONOMICS AND INVESTMENT MARKETS

LESSON 1: FRAMEWORK FOR THE ECONOMIC ANALYSIS OF FINANCIAL MARKETS AND THE DISCOUNT RATE ON REAL RISK-FREE BONDS

LOS 50a: Explain the notion that to affect market values, economic factors must affect one or more of the following: (1) default-free interest rates across maturities, (2) the timing and/or magnitude of expected cash flows, and (3) risk premiums. Vol 6, pp 376–378

The Present Value Model

The impact of economic factors on asset values can be studied in the context of the present value model and how they affect discount rates and future cash flows. This is because the value of an asset must reflect the benefits of holding it and that money received in the future is worth less than money received today. This is why an investor needs an incentive to defer using cash into the future, with greater incentives needed for more uncertain future outcomes. These considerations provide the rationale for using discounted future cash flows to determine the present value of an asset, as shown in Equation 1, which values financial assets at a given time t.

$$P_t^i = \sum_{s=1}^{N} \frac{E_t[\widetilde{CF}_{t+s}^i]}{(1+l_{t,s}+\theta_{t,s}+\rho_{t,s}^i)^s}$$

... (Equation 1)

where:
P_t^i = Value of the asset i at time t (today)
N = Number of cash flows in the asset's lifespan
$\widetilde{CF}_{t+s}^i$ = Uncertain, nominal cash flow paid s periods in the future
$E_t[\widetilde{CF}]$ = Expectation that the random variable CF is conditional on the information available today (t)
$l_{t,s}$ = Yield to maturity on a real default-free investment today (t), which pays one unit of currency s periods in the future
$\theta_{t,s}$ = Expected inflation rate between t and t + s
$\rho_{t,s}^i$ = Risk premium required today (t) for taking on cash flow risk of asset i, s periods in the future

This basic equation can be used to value any financial instrument, with the present values of all cash flows being summed from 1 to N. Moreover, the economy's effect on asset prices is reflected through expected cash flows (numerator) and the discount rate applied to them (denominator), which can include a risk premium for economic uncertainty. In fact, most financial assets are defined by their potential cash flows and the certainty thereof.

This uncertainty is reflected in the discount rate in Equation 1, which has three distinct components:

1. $l_{t,s}$ is the required return on a real default-free bond at time t for cash flows paid s periods in the future. For example, a U.S. Treasury Inflation-Protected Security (TIPS) yield could be used.

2. The discount rate ($\theta_{t,s}$) is the marginal return that investors require above the real default-free rate for investing in a nominal default-free investment. This is the compensation required for taking inflation risk, because investors are concerned about the future real purchasing power of their investments.

3. $\rho_{t,s}^i$ is the marginal return that investors require for investing in financial assets that have uncertain future cash flows. This premium will:

   ○ Vary among asset classes based on their respective characteristics and how they respond to changes in the real economy, including default-free government bonds.

   ○ Vary over time as perceptions about economic growth, inflation, and cash flow risk change, and can reflect other factors such as illiquidity risk.

In summary, the expected cash flows for any financial asset, i, can be discounted using the following expression for the discount rate:

$$1 + l_{t,s} + \theta_{t,s} + \rho_{t,s}^i \text{ for } s = 1, \dots N \qquad \dots \text{(Equation 2)}$$

LOS 50b: Explain the role of expectations and changes in expectations in market valuation. Vol 6, pg 379

Equation 1 reveals some important conclusions:

- Asset values depend on the expectation of future cash flows.
- These expectations are based on information at time t relevant to forecasting future cash flows.

Because asset values depend on future cash flow expectations, any information that changes these expectations will affect prices. However, this does not mean all news will affect asset valuations, as sometimes "news" is already anticipated and priced into markets. Generally speaking, prices rise on good news and fall on bad news, but this is not always the case. This is because investors react to new information based on their perceptions of it being positive or negative relative to their original expectations. How investors react to earnings data for corporations is a great example of this, as stock prices often decline on positive earnings news simply because a firm failed to meet investor expectations. Other factors can also affect expectations, including investor sentiment and economic events that directly impact future cash flows and the risk premium required to calculate a discount rate.

The Discount Rate on Real Default-Free Bonds

LOS 50c: Explain the relationship between the long-term growth rate of the economy, the volatility of the growth rate, and the average level of real short-term interest rates. Vol 6, pp 379–391

The Inter-Temporal Rate of Substitution

The relationship between the economy and investment markets is based on the concept that purchasing an asset involves the opportunity cost of lower current consumption and that these investor decisions collectively impact capital markets valuations. To demonstrate the importance of these decisions, consider the following example of how individuals can determine the real default-free interest rate ($l_{t,s}$) in an economy.

- An individual can choose between using some portion of his or her wealth today (t) and investing it in real default-free bonds.
- The question then is what rate of return an investor would require given there is no default or inflation risk.
- Given there is no risk of losing money over the investment period, one might say an investor would require no return for holding a real default-free bond.
- However, investing today involves the opportunity cost of not consuming today, which will cause an investor to require some return for holding an asset.
- This required return is the opportunity cost of consuming today.
- If potential returns increase, then an investor would purchase more assets and substitute current for future consumption.
- Thus an investor must consider the relative prices of the two alternatives:
  1. Pay price $P_{t,s}$ today (t), for a default-free bond paying 1 monetary unit of income s periods in the future, or
  2. Buy goods worth $P_{t,s}$ dollars today.

The willingness of individuals to substitute current for future consumption will depend on the price of the bond. This trade-off is measured by the marginal utility of consumption s periods in the future relative to the marginal utility of consumption today (t). The ratio of the marginal utility for future consumption (numerator) to the marginal utility of current consumption (denominator) is known as the inter-temporal rate of substitution, denoted as $\widetilde{m}_{t,s}$.

Some important points about how individuals assess marginal utility as a function of the economic environment are the following:

- During good economic times, individuals may have relatively high levels of current consumption such that the utility derived from an additional unit of consumption will be relatively low, and vice versa during bad economic times.
- Additionally, the marginal utility of consumption diminishes with higher wealth because individuals have already satisfied their fundamental needs. This is why investors receive a larger utility from assets that do well in bad economic times than ones that do well during good economic times.

The rate of substitution between current and future consumption is a random variable because individuals do not know how much income they will have in the future, which is also the case for investments, given that their prices are determined by investor utility. Given this uncertainty, investors must decide today based on future expectations that are conditional on the information available when the decision is made.

Therefore, if an investor wants to consider a zero-coupon bond at time t that is certain to pay off one unit of real consumption in s periods, then:

$$P_{t,s} = E_t[1\widetilde{m}_{t,s}] = E_t[\widetilde{m}_{t,s}]$$

where $\widetilde{m}_{t,s}$ is the investor's marginal willingness to trade consumption at time t for (real) wealth at time t + s.

Example 1-1 illustrates the inter-temporal rate of substitution.

Example 1-1: The Inter-Temporal Rate of Substitution

Suppose an investor's willingness to trade current for future consumption can be represented as:

$$\widetilde{m}_{t,1} = e^{a+b\tilde{z}}$$

In this instance, $\tilde{z}$ represents a random shock to the economy that affects investor cash flows. It is $\tilde{z}$ that makes $\widetilde{m}_{t,1}$ a random variable. Suppose that $\tilde{z}$ takes on one of two values:

1. A negative value indicates a bad state.
2. A positive value indicates a good state.
   - The probabilities of bad and good states are 0.3 and 0.7, respectively.
   - 0.98 and 0.95 are the asset's prices in bad and good states, respectively.
   - Note that investors are less willing to invest in good economic times, meaning a positive economic shock is associated with a higher level of current consumption.

What price would the investor be willing to pay for a 1-year default-free bond in exchange for $1 at maturity?

Solution:

Using market-consistent values for the exponent in the expression for $\widetilde{m}_{t,1}$, we can calculate the price of a 1-year default-free bond that pays $1 at maturity as the expected value of investor willingness to trade current for future consumption:

$$E_t[\widetilde{m}_{t,1}] = 0.3e^{a+b\times(z \text{ for a bad state})} + 0.7e^{a+b\times(z \text{ for a bad state})}$$

$$= 0.3 \times 0.98 + 0.7 \times 0.95 = 0.959$$

The results show that the investor is willing to buy the default-free bond today for $0.959 in exchange for $1 at maturity.

Because investors cannot affect the price of the bond, they must decide whether to buy or sell based on the price, $P_{t,1}$ (0.959). If this price were less than investors' expectations of the inter-temporal rate of substitution, say 0.97, they would buy more of the bond. However, as more bonds are purchased, current consumption falls, which then leads to a higher marginal utility for current consumption. This in turn makes expectations for the inter-temporal rate of substitution ($E_t[\widetilde{m}_{t,s}]$) fall as bond prices rise. This process continues until the rate of substitution equals the bond price, as shown in Example 1-1, and vice versa if the inter-temporal rate of substitution is below the bond price. This means the equilibrium price for a real default-free bond equals the investors' collective expectation for the inter-temporal rate of substitution.

Default-Free Interest Rates and Economic Growth

Theoretically, there should be a connection between real short-term interest rates and current and future economic growth for an economy. More specifically, interest rates should be positively correlated to economic growth and the volatility thereof. This means that strong economic growth and high levels of volatility should lead to higher real interest rates, while lower levels of growth and volatility should lead to lower rates. This is because in fast-growing economies people tend to save and invest less and borrow more to fund current consumption, which tends to increase interest rates. Moreover, when economic volatility rises, investors require higher interest rates as compensation for heightened economic risks and the associated uncertainty about future interest rates.

This same logic holds true among nations that have different interest rates as a function of their long-term economic growth expectations. More specifically, interest rates in fast-growing, developing economies should be higher than in more slowly growing, developed economies, regardless of short-term expectations. This is best illustrated by the prevalence of higher interest rates in emerging markets countries relative to the G7 nations. This is due to emerging economies having systematically higher growth rates relative to developed economies, thereby causing higher interest rates until they too are developed.

To examine the relationship between real interest rates and gross domestic product (GDP) growth, inflation-linked bonds can be used as a proxy for real interest rates. This is because these bonds pay a yield that is linked to an inflationary index, thereby producing a real return. Many countries offer these types of bonds; in the United States, they are called Treasury Inflation-Protected Securities (TIPS).

To illustrate the relationship between economic growth and real interest rates in the United States, the chart in Figure 1-1 shows the 5-year TIPS yield relative to the associated rolling 5-year U.S. GDP growth rates. Unfortunately, there are no 1-year TIPS available to compare the short-term real interest rates, but the general relationship holds over bonds of various maturities. As you can see from the chart, there is clearly a direct relationship between economic growth and real interest rates.

Figure 1-1: 5-Year TIPS Yield vs. U.S. GDP Growth

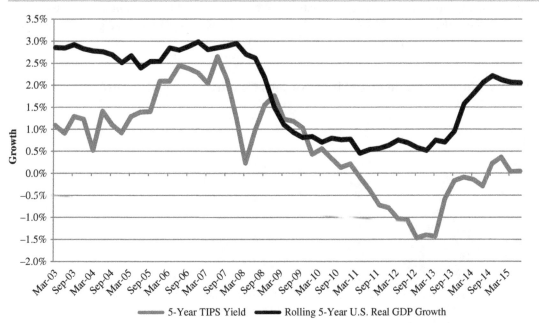

LESSON 2: THE YIELD CURVE AND THE BUSINESS CYCLE

LOC 50d: Explain how the phase of the business cycle affects policy and short-term interest rates, the slope of the term structure of interest rates, and the relative performance of bonds of differing maturities. Vol 6, pp 371–385, 391–400

A direct relationship between short-term interest rates and economic growth exists because of investor willingness to substitute current for future consumption, which is positively correlated to changes in real GDP growth. This means that nominal interest rates will equal the real interest rate required to balance investor saving and investment needs, plus inflationary expectations. Moreover, because GDP growth rates are volatile and unpredictable, there should also be a direct relationship between the volatility of real GDP growth and short-term interest rates. For broad evidence of the relationship between interest rates and GDP growth, we can look at the most prominent developed economies, the G7 nations:

- Canada
- France
- Germany
- Italy
- Japan
- United Kingdom
- United States

As seen in Figures 2-1A and 2-1B, there is clearly a direct relationship between the strength of economic growth over time and interest rates. This relationship is demonstrated between the faster-growing and slower-growing G7 nations. We can also see how economic volatility is directly related to interest rates in the case of Italy, which has very low economic growth but high volatility, and relatively high interest rates (bond yields) as a result.

Figure 2-1A: Government Bond Yields for Various Countries, December 2014

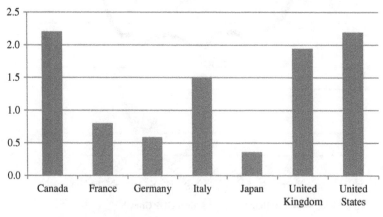

Source: Barclays

Figure 2-1B: GDP Growth and Volatility for Various Countries, 2005–2014

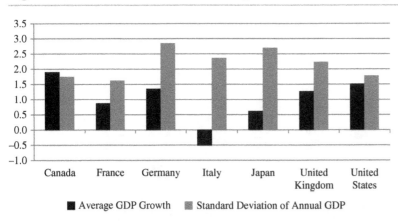

Sources: International Monetary Fund, Barclays, Petroff Institutional

We can further examine this relationship by comparing U.S. Treasury bill rates alongside inflation and economic growth over time, as shown in Figures 2-2A and 2-2B. The expected direct relationship between interest rates and GDP and inflation is obvious over time. There is an exception in recent periods, however, as the U.S. Federal Reserve is keeping short-term policy rates at historic lows even though the U.S. economy is growing.

Figure 2-2A: U.S. GDP Growth vs. Short-Term Interest Rates

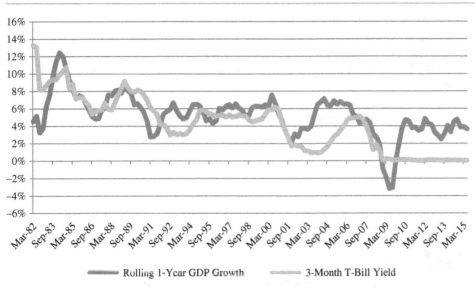

Source: Federal Reserve, Bureau of Economic Analysis, Petroff Institutional

Figure 2-2B: U.S. Inflation vs. Short-Term Interest Rates

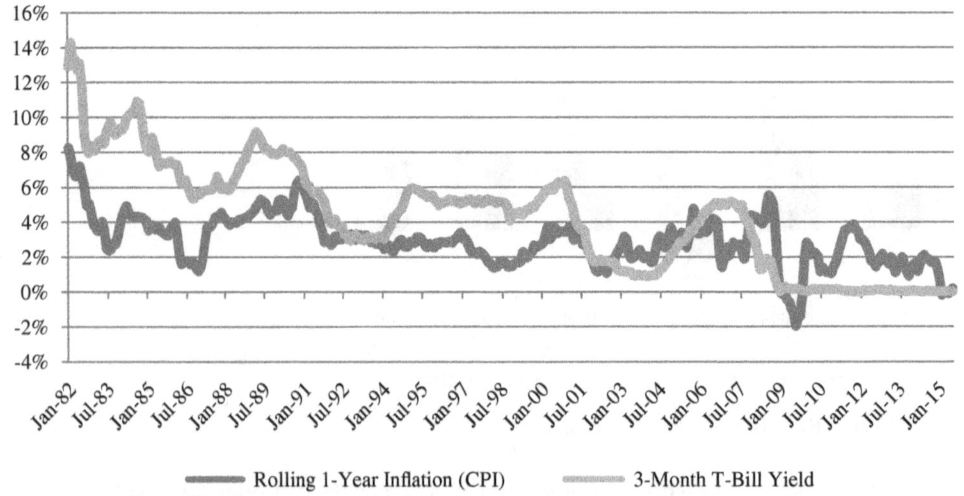

Legend: Rolling 1-Year Inflation (CPI) — 3-Month T-Bill Yield

Sources: Federal Reserve, Bureau of Labor Statistics, Petroff Institutional

Central Banks and Short-Term Policy Rates

Central banks and monetary authorities are responsible for setting interest rates in response to the economy's position in the business cycle:

- Rates are cut when GDP or inflation is judged to be too low.
- Rates are raised when GDP or inflation is too high.

Figures 2-3A and 2.3B show these relationships in the United States with the Federal Reserve short-term policy rates alongside GDP and inflation.

Figure 2-3A: U.S. GDP Growth vs. Federal Reserve Policy Rate

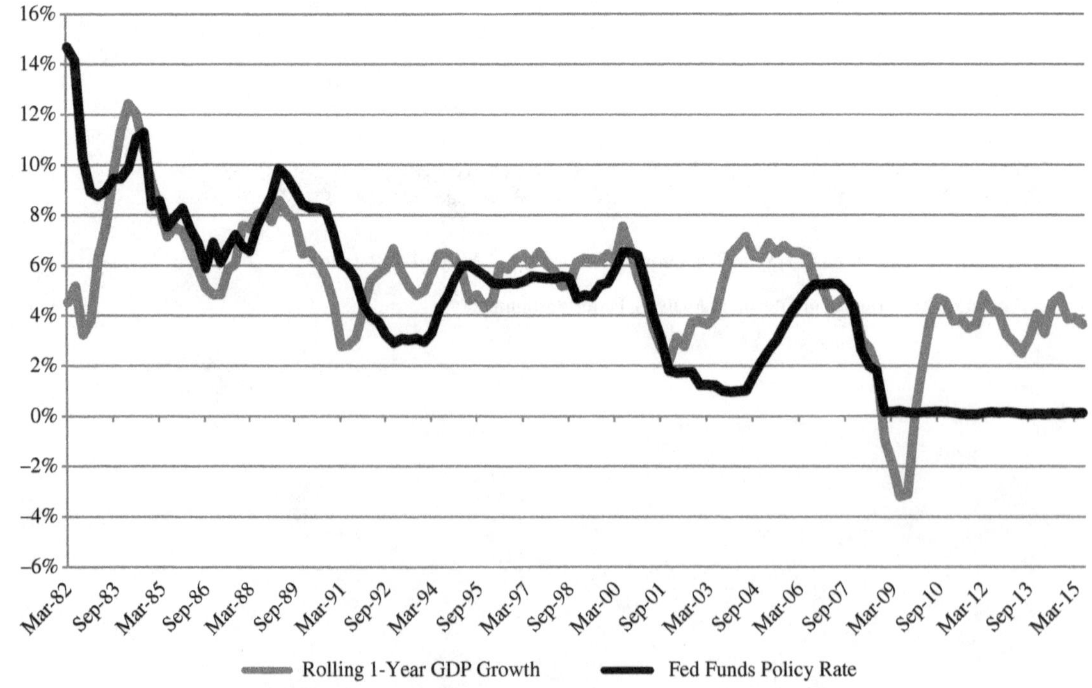

Legend: Rolling 1-Year GDP Growth — Fed Funds Policy Rate

Sources: Federal Reserve, Bureau of Economic Analysis, Petroff Institutional

Figure 2-3B: U.S. Inflation vs. Federal Reserve Policy Rate

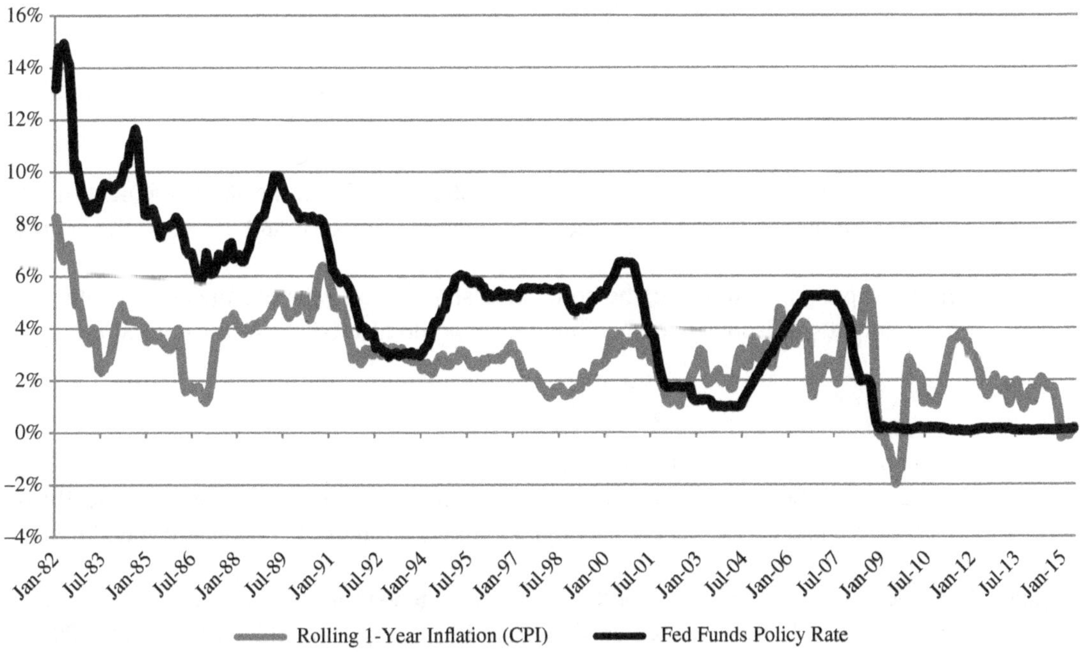

Sources: Federal Reserve, Bureau of Labor Statistics, Petroff Institutional

Taylor Rule

A U.S. economist, Professor John Taylor, devised a rule that could help central banks gauge whether their policy rate is at an "appropriate" level. This rule takes the following form:

$$pr_t = l_t + \iota_t + 0.5(\iota_t - \iota_t^*) + 0.5(Y_t - Y_t^*)$$
$$= l_t + 1.5\iota_t - 0.5\iota_t^* + 0.5(Y_t - Y_t^*)$$

... (Equation 3)

where:
pr_t = Policy rate at time t
l_t = Level of real short-term interest rates that balance long-term savings and borrowing in the economy
ι_t = Rate of inflation
ι_t^* = Target rate of inflation
Y_t = Logarithmic level of actual real GDP
Y_t^* = Logarithmic level of potential real GDP

The difference between Y_t and Y_t^* is known as the "output gap." When the output gap is positive, this implies that an economy is producing beyond its sustainable capacity. Conversely, when the output gap is negative, it implies that the economy is producing below its sustainable capacity. This is why positive output gaps are usually associated with high inflation and negative gaps are accompanied by high unemployment.

Neutral Policy Rate

When inflation is close to the targeted rate and the output gap is zero, the appropriate policy rate will be equal to the level of the short-term real interest rates (l_t) that balances savings and borrowing in the economy, plus the targeted rate of inflation. This policy rate is the neutral policy rate, or the rate that neither bolsters nor slows real economic growth.

- When inflation is above the targeted level, the policy rate should be above the neutral rate, and when inflation is below the targeted level, the policy rate should be below the neutral rate.
- When the output gap is positive, the policy rate should also be above the neutral rate, and when the output gap is negative, the policy rate should also be below the neutral rate.

Level and Slope of the Yield Curve

The level of a yield curve indicates whether rates are high or low, and the slope indicates the steepness of the curve, or how quickly or slowly rates change with maturity. More specifically, the slope of the yield is defined by the difference in yield between long-dated and short-dated bonds.

The business cycle has a direct effect on both the level of interest rates and the slope of the yield curve. This can be seen in Figure 2-4, which shows the U.S. Treasury yield curve before (2006) and during the 2008 recession. This chart demonstrates how the level of interest rates is higher and the slope of the yield curve is flatter during economic expansions, and the level of interest rates is lower and the slope of the yield curve is steeper during economic recessions. This is because central banks keep short-term interest rates higher during expansions and lower during recessions, though they do not directly control long-term interest rates. This is how flat and high yield curves occur during expansions and the opposite occurs during recessions.

Figure 2-4: U.S. Treasury Yield Curves

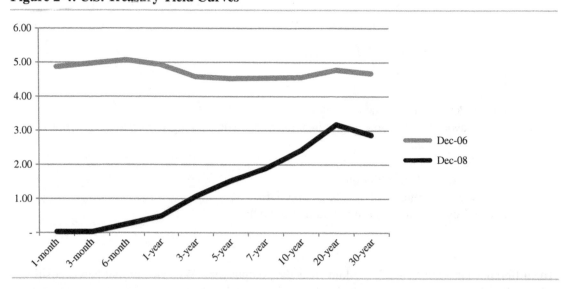

Generally speaking, the following rules apply to the slope of the yield curve and subsequent economic activity:

- A flat yield curve usually indicates a forthcoming recession.
- An inverted yield curve is a strong sign of a forthcoming recession.
- A steep yield curve usually precedes economic recoveries.

Relative Performance of Bonds of Differing Maturities

Investors generally have a preference for assets that do well during recessions, and they will pay a premium for them relative to other assets. This preference should be reflected in government bond yield curves and appears to be the case historically. For example, following World War II, the average spreads (or slopes) of the U.S. and UK government bond curves were 0.50% and 0.40%, respectively. This slope suggests that investors have been willing to pay a premium for shorter-dated bonds, implying that long-dated bonds may not be a good hedge against recessions. Alternatively, an upward-sloping yield curve may be illustrative of short-dated bonds being more negatively correlated with recessions than long-dated bonds, and are preferable to investors as a result.

Table 2 1 demonstrates this relationship with government bonds ranging in maturities from a selection of countries.

- Panel A shows the average yield difference between long and short bond maturities.
- Panel B shows that returns rise with maturity.
- Panel C shows the correlation between the return on bonds and the economic growth of the relevant economy.

Given that investors are willing to place a premium on short-term bonds as a hedge against recessions, why have long-term bonds performed better than short-term bonds?

Table 2-1: Government Bond Spreads, Total Returns, and GDP Growth Correlations for Four Markets

A. Spreads

Years		5 vs. 2	10 vs. 5	30 vs. 10
Australia	—	0.34%	0.21%	—
Canada	—	0.43%	0.38%	0.37%
United Kingdom	—	0.21%	0.15%	−0.24%
United States	—	0.54%	0.39%	0.32%

B. Total returns

	2	5	10	30
Australia	8.12%	9.52%	10.61%	—
Canada	6.78%	7.94%	9.22%	10.73%
United Kingdom	8.54%	8.83%	10.96%	11.28%
United States	6.96%	8.27%	9.01%	9.97%

C. Correlation with GDP growth

	2	5	10	30
Australia	−42.80%	−43.29%	−35.64%	—
Canada	−30.95%	−37.10%	−28.44%	−12.50%
United Kingdom	−23.82%	−19.79%	−18.24%	−5.11%
United States	−14.85%	−25.52%	−22.24%	−19.73%

Note: The sample period for the United Kingdom and the United States is January 1980 to December 2011. For Australia, it is January 1987 to December 2011, and for Canada, it is January 1985 to December 2011.

Sources: Thomson Reuters, Economics and Investment Markets

The answer to this question is in the correlations between bond returns and economic growth. First we see that all the government bond correlations to economic growth are negative, meaning they do well in bad times and investors are willing to pay a premium for them. Additionally, the correlations between short-dated government bond returns and economic growth are generally more negative than the correlations for long-dated government bonds. This means that short-term bonds have done better in recessions than long-term bonds. Therefore, because short-term bonds outperform during recessions, investors require a risk premium to invest in long-term bonds, which causes the yield curve to be upward sloping.

LOS 50e: Describe the factors that affect yield spreads between non-inflation-adjusted and inflation-indexed bonds. Vol 6, pp 406–411

The difference between the yields of zero-coupon, default-free nominal and real bonds of the same maturity is known as the break-even inflation (BEI) rate. An example of a BEI rate can be seen in Figure 2-5, which shows the difference in yield between 10-year nominal and inflation-protected U.S. Treasury bonds. We can see that the BEI rate is a realistic measure of the capital markets' inflation expectations given the significant drop seen in the middle of the 2008 recession when economic expectations were at their lowest in decades.

Figure 2-5: U.S. 10-Year Treasury Break-Even Inflation Rate, 2005–2014

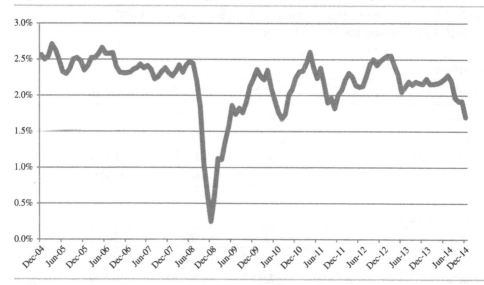

The BEI rate only partially represents inflation expectations and includes a risk premium to compensate investors for uncertainty about future inflation. Real bond yields are primarily driven by society's need to balance borrowing and saving alongside the pace of economic growth as demonstrated through the inter-temporal rate of substitution. However, nominal bond yields are also affected by perceptions of future inflation due to changing economic and monetary policy conditions, and have an embedded risk premium as a result. In short, there are two major factors driving differences in yields between nominal and inflation-protected bonds:

1. Prevailing economic conditions and the associated inflation expectations.
2. An investor risk premium for bearing uncertainty about future inflation.

LESSON 3: CREDIT PREMIUMS AND THE BUSINESS CYCLE

LOS 50f: Explain how the phase of the business cycle affects credit spreads and the performance of credit-sensitive fixed-income instruments. Vol 6, pp 421–427

Credit Risk Premium

While holders of default-free bonds do not require compensation for default or credit risk, corporate or government bonds with a realistic possibility of default will require a credit risk premium.

To account for the separate role credit risk plays in pricing a bond, the basic financial asset pricing model can be adapted to include a credit risk premium, $(\gamma^i_{t,s})$, which is different from the inflation-based risk premium for default-free bonds $(\pi_{t,s})$, as shown in the following equation:

$$P^i_t = \sum_{s=1}^{N} \frac{E_t[\widetilde{CF}^i_{t+s}]}{(1 + l_{t,s} + \theta_{t,s} + \pi_{t,s} + \gamma^i_{t,s})^s}$$

Example 3-1 illustrates calculation of the credit risk premium.

Example 3-1: Credit Risk Premium

Suppose an analyst estimates that the real risk-free rate is 1.5%, inflation will be 2.5% the next year, and the premium required by investors for inflation uncertainty is 0.50%. If the price of a 1-year corporate bond with a face value of $100 is $94, what would be the implied credit risk premium for inflation uncertainty?

Solution:

The (approximate) implied premium can be calculated as follows:

$$\gamma^i_{t,s} = 100/94 - (1 + 1.50\% + 2.50\% + 0.50\%) = 1.38\%$$

Credit Risk Premium and the Business Cycle

The difference between the yield of a corporate bond and the yield of a default-free government bond is called the credit spread and represents the compensation that investors require for bearing risk relative to a default-free bond. However, it is important to note that the yield for credit-risky bonds also entails the same premium for interest rate risk as default-free bonds. This means that default-free and credit-risky bonds will move in a similar manner up and down with the business cycle, creating parallel rate curve shifts over time. The only exceptions to seeing parallel rate shifts are during shifts in the business cycle when credit and default-free yields diverge, which is a risk covered by $\gamma^i_{t,s}$ in the previous equation.

This is why there is an inverse relationship between the business cycle and credit spreads, and a direct relationship between the business cycle and performance on credit-sensitive bonds relative to default-free bonds. This means that as the economy expands, credit spreads narrow and returns on credit-sensitive bonds are higher than those of similar default-free bonds. Conversely, as the economy weakens, credit spreads widen and bondholders suffer relative losses. This relationship makes sense because investors will demand a premium for taking credit risk during times of economic weakness when the chances of bond defaults and corporate bankruptcies are highest.

This relationship can be seen in Figure 3-1, which shows rolling 1-year annualized U.S. GDP growth versus the credit spreads on the Moody's AAA and BAA bonds relative to the U.S. 10-year Treasury bond. As you can see, there is clearly an inverse relationship between U.S. GDP growth and credit spreads over time. This was especially apparent during the 2008 recession, when spreads reached historic levels in a short period of time.

Figure 3-1: Moody's Credit Spreads vs. U.S. 10-Year Treasury Yields/U.S. GDP Growth

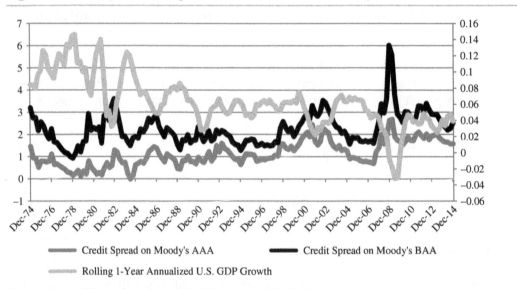

Credit Spread on Moody's AAA   Credit Spread on Moody's BAA

Rolling 1-Year Annualized U.S. GDP Growth

Sources: Bureau of Economic Analysis, Federal Reserve, Petroff Institutional

Corporate Bond Default Rates and the Business Cycle

If investors are risk neutral, they will demand a higher yield on their credit-risky bonds to compensate them for the possible losses. These losses depend on the probability of default and the expected recovery rate as shown in the following equation:

$$\text{Expected loss} = \text{Probability of default} \times (1 - \text{Recovery rate})$$

Theoretically, when investors are risk neutral, the expected return on a default-free bond should be equal to the loss-adjusted expected return on a comparable credit-risky bond. However, in practice investors are risk-averse and credit-risky bonds have higher yields than default-free bonds, even if holding a diversified bond portfolio can mitigate most of the credit risk. This is because investors can still be exposed to considerable risk of loss, given that defaults are not steady and tend to move in tandem with the business cycle.

This historical relationship of clustered defaults can easily be seen in Figures 3-2A, 3-2B, and 3-2C, which show, respectively, the number of defaults, the rate of defaults as a percentage of outstanding issuance, and the loss rates per annum for corporate bonds.

Figure 3-2A: Number of Corporate Bond Defaults

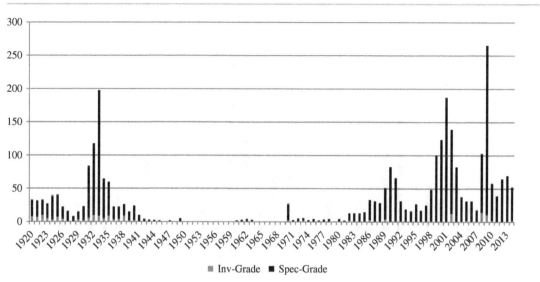

Inv-Grade Spec-Grade

Source: Moody's

Figure 3-2B: Default Rates as Percentage of Outstanding Issuance

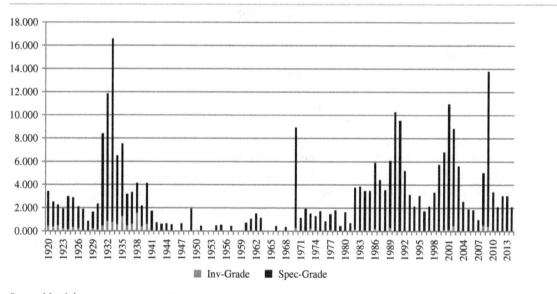

Inv-Grade Spec-Grade

Source: Moody's

Figure 3-2C: Annual Credit Loss Rates

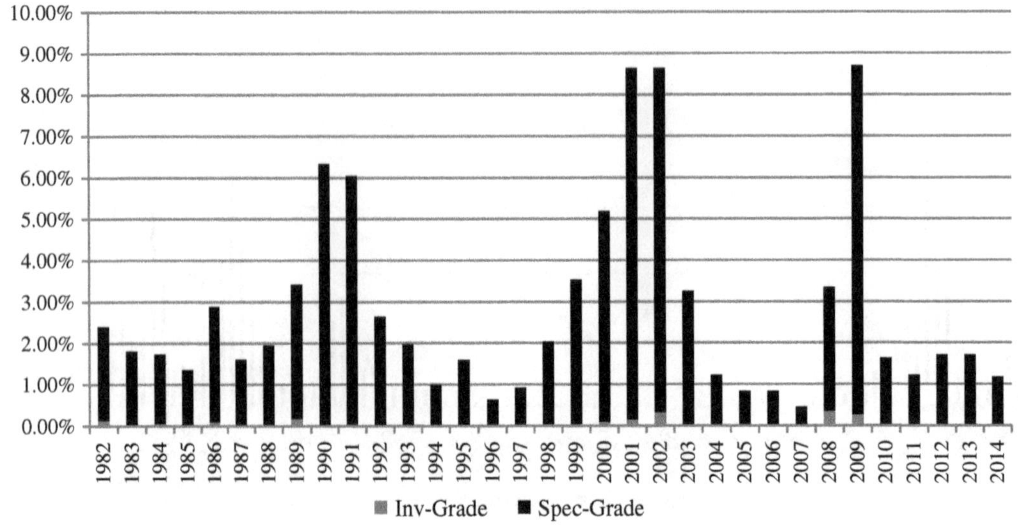

Source: Moody's

LOS 50g: Explain how the characteristics of the markets for a company's products affect the company's credit quality. Vol 6, pp 427–429

A corporation's credit quality and its associated bond spreads are driven by the business cycle. However, the impact of the economy on a company's credit quality will depend on whether the company is cyclical or non-cyclical and its industrial sector. This is because the business cycle does not affect every company the same way.

Some products and services are relatively insensitive to economic conditions, and firms that provide these are called non-cyclicals. Conversely, some firms are highly sensitive to economic conditions and are called cyclicals. Dishwashing detergent is a good example of a non-cyclical product because people need to wash dishes just as often during a recession as they would during an economic expansion. Airline tickets are an example of a cyclical service because people tend to travel and spend more during times of economic growth than they would during a recession. One way to illustrate this relationship is to compare the credit spreads of cyclical and non-cyclical bonds to Treasuries.

As seen in Figure 3-3, non-cyclical credit spreads (option-adjusted spreads [OAS]) expand less during recessions and are generally lower than those of cyclical stocks, which is a result of their lower earnings volatility over time. Conversely, investors need a higher credit premium for firms in cyclical industries due to the higher volatility of earnings and potential to repay debt.

Figure 3-3: Industrial Credit Spreads vs. GDP Growth

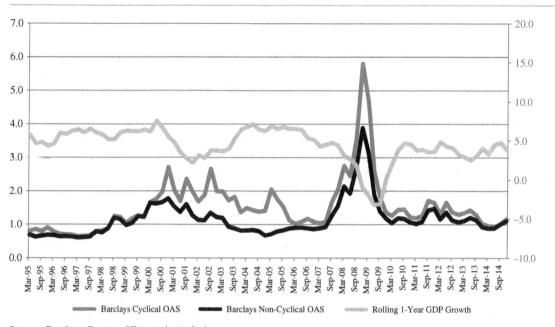

Sources: Barclays, Bureau of Economic Analysis

Another important determinant of credit spreads for companies is their industrial sector, as various sectors have different sensitivities to the business cycle and credit ratings as a result. These sensitivities can be related to the types of goods and services sold (i.e., cyclical or non-cyclical) or to the general level of indebtedness for companies in the sector. Clearly, the more cyclical the corporation's earnings and the higher the industry debt level, the lower the credit quality of the firm and the higher the credit spread for its debt and vice versa. This relationship between credit quality and associated credit spreads can be seen in Figure 3-4, which clearly shows that the lower the credit quality, the greater the sensitivity to economic conditions.

Figure 3-4: Industrial Credit Spreads vs. GDP Growth

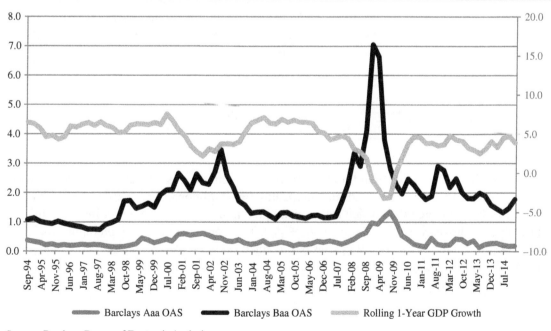

Sources: Barclays, Bureau of Economic Analysis

LOS 50h: Explain how the phase of the business cycle affects short-term and long-term earnings growth expectations. Vol 6, pp 435–440

The phase of the business cycle can have a tremendous effect on short- and long-term earnings growth expectations. On a short-term basis, these effects are most prominent around economic recessions when declining consumer spending leads to significantly lower earnings growth. Therefore, during the initial phases of a recession, short-term earnings growth expectations tend to drop quickly and by large amounts, and do not begin recovering until market participants can see a forthcoming nadir in economic activity. A great example of this was the 2008 recession, when trailing 12-month reported earnings for the S&P 500 fell from $84 to $7 per share between March 2007 and March 2009. It was not until later in 2009 that earnings growth and expectations started to recover in any significant way.

After this initial drop in economic activity expectations, investors tend to become more positive about future earnings. This is because firms usually cut costs significantly at the beginning of a recession, and when consumer demand starts growing again, there can be sharp increases in corporate profits at the end or even during a recession. These profits should improve earnings expectations even further as they lead the economy out of recession through increased hiring and investment in capital equipment. Furthermore, it is during these times that central banks apply monetary stimulus, which is yet another positive for earnings growth on a longer-term basis. This is why some analysts consider corporate profits and earning expectations to be an important leading indicator of the business cycle.

LESSON 4: EQUITIES AND THE EQUITY RISK PREMIUM

LOS 50i: Explain the relationship between the consumption-hedging properties of equity and the equity risk premium. Vol 6, pp 433–435

Equity Risk Premium

There are financial instruments for which the size and the timing of cash flows are uncertain. The best example of this is equities because dividend payments can rise and fall over time, fail to be paid, or even cease if the corporation becomes bankrupt. To express this in an equation, we can rewrite the basic financial asset pricing equation as follows:

$$P_t^i = \sum_{s=1}^{\infty} \frac{E_t[\widetilde{CF}_{t+s}^i]}{(1 + l_{t,s} + \theta_{t,s} + \pi_{t,s} + \gamma_{t,s}^i + \kappa_{t,s}^i)^s} \quad \ldots \text{(Equation 4)}$$

This equation is similar to that used for credit-risky bonds, but there is no maturity on cash flows because investors are buying dividends into perpetuity (∞). Additionally, we need to add a new term for the discount rate ($\kappa_{t,s}^i$), which is the equity premium investors require for investing in equities over credit-risky bonds ($l_{t,s} + \theta_{t,s} + \pi_{t,s} + \gamma_{t,s}^i$). This combination of risk premiums for equities ($\kappa_{t,s}^i$) and credit-risky bonds ($\gamma_{t,s}^i$) is best defined as the equity risk premium (i.e., the combined bond and equity holder risks).

The equity risk premium is expressed in Equation 5 through the combination of $\gamma^i_{t,s} + \kappa^i_{t,s}$ into $\lambda^i_{t,s}$, or the total compensation investors require over and above holding a default-free bond.

$$P^i_t = \sum_{s=1}^{\infty} \frac{E_t[\widetilde{CF}^i_{t+s}]}{(1 + l_{t,s} + \theta_{t,s} + \pi_{t,s} + \lambda^i_{t,s})^s} \quad \ldots \text{(Equation 5)}$$

Consumption-Hedging Properties of Equities

Corporate earnings have a strong direct relationship to the underlying economy. This means that as GDP growth rates decline, corporate earnings fall, and equities tend to lose money. This relationship can be seen in Figure 4-1, which shows returns for the S&P 500 relative to GDP growth over time.

Figure 4-1: S&P 500 Returns vs. Rolling 1-Year GDP Growth

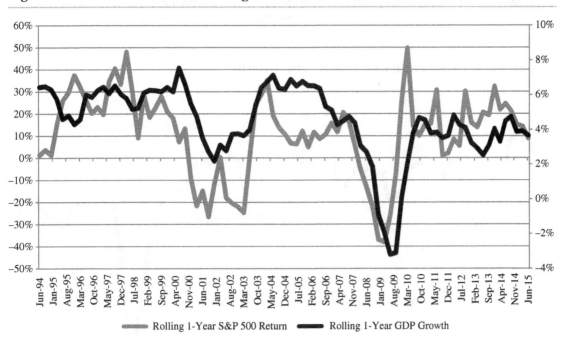

Sources: Standard & Poor's, Bureau of Economic Analysis, Petroff Institutional

The weak performance of equities during bad economic times is why they have poor consumption-hedging properties and investors require a risk premium (or higher expected returns) for holding these assets relative to those with good consumption-hedging properties such as bonds.

LOS 50j: Describe cyclical effects on valuation multiples. Vol 6, pp 441–443

Equity analysts will usually focus on potential earnings and monitor valuation multiples to compare equities within and among sectors. Common valuation ratios used in this process are the price-to-earnings (P/E) ratio and price-to-book (P/B) ratio. The P/E ratio is the ratio of current share price to earnings per share, and the P/B ratio is the ratio of the stock price to the company's net assets per share.

Investors use both these ratios to compare valuations for individual equities, sectors, and markets. For instance, if a stock is trading with a low P/E relative to the rest of the market, it may be because investors believe future earnings growth prospects are relatively low. Conversely, a stock trading with a high P/E relative to the rest of the market may indicate that investors expect earnings to grow relatively quickly. However, it is important to note that relative valuations depend significantly on the market, sector, industry, or type of company in question. Moreover, the cyclical nature of the economy has serious effects on valuation multiples for equities.

For example, increased earnings growth expectations and falling GDP volatility and inflationary expectations can lead to higher P/E ratios or a decline in the equity risk premium. Generally speaking, there is a direct relationship between business cycles and valuation ratios, as demonstrated in Figure 4-2, which shows Shiller P/E ratios for the S&P 500 relative to rolling U.S. GDP growth as a proxy for the business cycle. As can be seen clearly, periods of cyclical growth are associated with higher valuation multiples, and contractions are associated with lower multiples.

Figure 4-2: S&P 500 P/E Ratios vs. U.S. GDP Growth

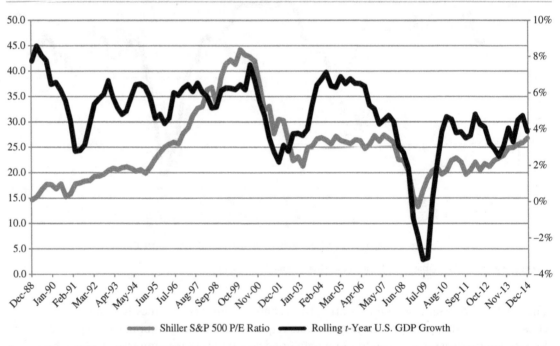

Sources: Robert Shiller online data http://www.econ.yale.edu/~shiller/data.htm, Bureau of Economic Analysis, Petroff Institutional

---

LOS 50k: Describe the implications of the business cycle for a given style strategy (value, growth, small capitalization, large capitalization). Vol 6, pp 444–446

Various equity investment styles have emerged over the years that attempt to outperform markets as a whole over a business cycle. Common investor styles that have developed include value and growth investing, and holding small- versus large-capitalization stocks.

Value versus Growth

Growth stocks tend to trade with high P/E ratios and very low dividend yields. These companies often sell products in immature markets where future sales prospects are much higher than in matured markets. Conversely, value stocks tend to operate in mature markets where earnings are more stable, but there is a lower potential for substantial earnings growth. This is why value stocks typically trade with low P/E ratios and high dividend yields. Historical returns suggest that value stocks tend to outperform growth stocks during the aftermath of a recession, and growth stocks tend to outperform when the economy is expanding. This relative relationship of value to growth can be seen in Figure 4-3, which shows the relative performance of the Russell 1000 value and growth indices relative to GDP growth over time.

Figure 4-3: Russell 1000 Growth and Value Returns vs. GDP Growth

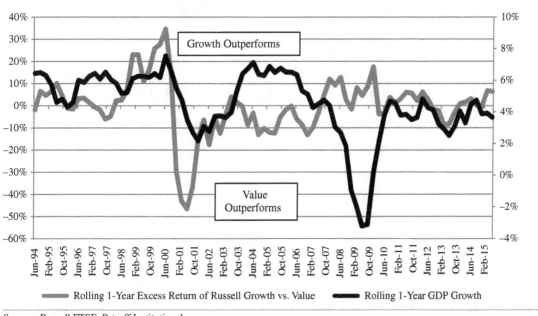

Rolling 1-Year Excess Return of Russell Growth vs. Value   Rolling 1-Year GDP Growth

Sources: Russell FTSE, Petroff Institutional

Small versus Large Cap

Generally speaking, the size of a company can have an effect on its performance during good and bad economic times. Small-cap companies usually have less diversified revenue sources and can suffer serious earnings declines during recessions, making it more difficult to get financing and to continue operating and grow profits. In contrast, large firms with more diversified lines of revenue and greater access to financing are better able to handle recessions. The potential effects of a downturn in the business cycle are why investors demand a return premium for holding small-cap versus large-cap stocks. Small-cap stocks do tend to outperform large-cap stocks coming out of a recession. However, they do so with a greater degree of volatility in earnings, which again warrants investors to require a risk premium for small-cap stocks. This relationship between small- and large-capitalization stocks can be seen in Figure NaN, which shows the relative performance of the Russell 1000 (large-cap) and 2000 (small-cap) indices relative to GDP growth over time.

Figure 4-4: Russell 1000 and 2000 Returns vs. GDP Growth

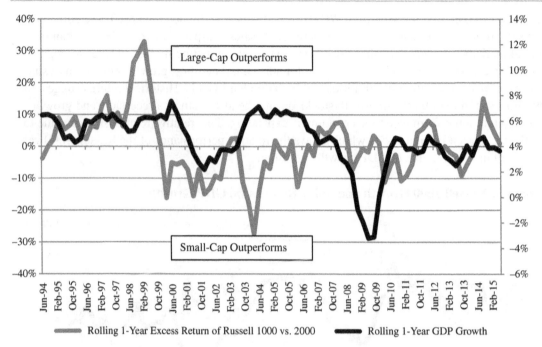

Rolling 1-Year Excess Return of Russell 1000 vs. 2000 ——— Rolling 1-Year GDP Growth

Sources: Russell, Petroff Institutional

LOS 50l: Describe how economic analysis is used in sector rotation strategies.
Vol 6, pp 446–447

The performance of most investment managers is measured against broad market indices that require them to take over- and underweight positions relative to benchmark allocations to add value. Generally, these manager bets take the form of higher and lower allocations to various sectors and styles within their benchmarks. Given that these bets involve beta exposures (systematic risks), there is not much a manager can do to add value other than making correct assumptions about the economy and then rotating exposures among sectors appropriately in advance. The key here is for managers to make correct economic assumptions lest they detract value from their portfolios. In practice, sector rotation strategies tend to be difficult to implement successfully, given the need to accurately predict economic cycles.

This sort of investment analysis centers on the prospective economic cycle relative to current conditions and which sectors are best poised to do well based on historical cyclical patterns of behavior. Examples of sector rotation strategies based on economic analysis include:

- Rotating into growth stocks relative to value stocks at the end of a recession, or from growth into value before a recession begins.
- Moving into small-cap stocks at the onset of an economic expansion to outperform large-cap stocks, or shifting into large caps prior to a recession.
- Shifting to cyclical stocks from non-cyclicals prior to an economic expansion and vice versa for recessions.

LESSON 5: COMMERCIAL REAL ESTATE

LOS 50m: Describe the economic factors affecting investment in commercial real estate. Vol 6, pp 448–453

The Pricing Formula for Commercial Real Estate

Commercial real estate is a unique asset class because it can be viewed as part equity and part bond, and is usually illiquid. With some minor changes to the generic financial asset pricing formula, the unique pricing features of commercial real estate can be expressed as follows:

$$P_t^i = \sum_{s=1}^{\infty} \frac{E_t[\widetilde{CF}_{t+s}^i]}{(1 + l_{t,s} + \theta_{t,s} + \pi_{t,s} + \gamma_{t,s}^i + \kappa_{t,s}^i + \phi_{t,s}^i)^s} \quad \dots \text{(Equation 6)}$$

This formula acknowledges that expected cash flows ($E_t[\widetilde{CF}_{t+s}^i]$) are uncertain because tenants may default on rent. The quality of any rental income may be known and is dependent on the quality of the tenants, just as is the case with a bond and the issuing corporation. However, forecasting the future value of a property is a difficult task, making it hard to construct a discount rate for commercial real estate.

To understand the construction of the discount rate in Equation 6, consider the following three tenants and rental/leasing agreements:

1. A default-free government tenant that agrees to pay rental income that is indexed to inflation, $(1 + l_{t,s})$
2. A default-free government tenant that agrees to pay a fixed nominal rental income, $(1 + l_{t,s} + \theta_{t,s} + \pi_{t,s})$
3. A corporate tenant that agrees to pay a fixed nominal rental income, $(1 + l_{t,s} + \theta_{t,s} + \pi_{t,s} + \gamma_{t,s}^i)$

Given the three tenants, the discount rate that would be applied to the cash flows of these entities would be analogous to the purchase of a:

1. Real default-free government bond
2. Nominal default-free government bond
3. Credit-risky nominal bond

Additionally, a risk premium would need to be added to the discount rate to account for the uncertainty of ending property values when the lease expires, which is analogous to the equity risk premium ($\kappa_{t,s}^i$).

We also need to take into account the illiquidity of commercial real estate, which is better in good economic environments and worse during recessions. This direct relationship between property values and the economy makes commercial real estate a poor consumption-hedging asset. Therefore, investors will require an additional premium for illiquidity, which is expressed in Equation 6 as $\phi_{t,s}^i$.

Bond-Like Cash Flows: Tenant Rents

For commercial real estate investors, the cash flow received is rents paid by tenants. However, the cost of ownership will affect net rental income due to things such as building maintenance and upkeep. Also, the level of rents may go up and down over time depending on the economy and the state of the property. So a single property may not represent a steady income stream, but a well-diversified portfolio of commercial property could be expected to generate a steady stream of rental income analogous to the coupon income derived from a bond. Similar to a bond portfolio, the credit quality (or tenant quality) of a commercial property portfolio will be a function of the underlying cash flows.

Commercial real estate investors receive regular cash flow from rents, but these types of investments are not entirely bond-like. For example, when a bond matures, the investor receives the face value of the bond and its final interest payment. This is in contrast to an expiring lease where the investor (landlord) takes back possession of the property and then either re-leases or sells the property. Whether an investor sells is usually a function of the property value at the time, which can be affected by both national and local real estate trends. Examples of such factors include:

- If the property's local area has become more popular, the property might be sold or redeveloped.
- If the lease expires when the economy is doing well and there is strong demand for commercial real estate, then sale or redevelopment is likely.
- If the lease expires when the property's location is less desirable or the economy is weak, then sale or redevelopment may not be options. During these times, rents may fall and the property may even be sold at a loss.

These are reasons investors can think about a commercial real estate portfolio as having both bond-like and equity-like characteristics.

Rental Income, Property Values, and the Economy

There are two primary sources of returns for commercial real estate, and they are affected differently by economic growth.

- This first aspect of real estate returns is income, which is the cash flow net of operating expenses received from rents.
  - It is important to note that the credit quality of a commercial property will be determined by the credit quality of the underlying tenants and their ability to pay rents.
- The second component of returns is changes in property values that are determined by location, the credit quality of tenants, and underlying economic growth.

Generally speaking, income from commercial real estate remains relatively stable and only fluctuates modestly with the economic cycle. This is one of the more attractive aspects of commercial real estate to investors—the returns generated have reliability similar to that of high-quality investment-grade bonds. This is evident from Figure 5-1, which shows U.S. commercial income returns relative to rolling 1-year U.S. GDP growth. While there is variability in returns from income, it seems more stable in comparison to fluctuations in GDP. This stability in returns from income portends that investors would require a low premium for investing in commercial real estate, at least based on this portion of real estate returns.

Figure 5-1: Real Income Returns vs. U.S. GDP Growth

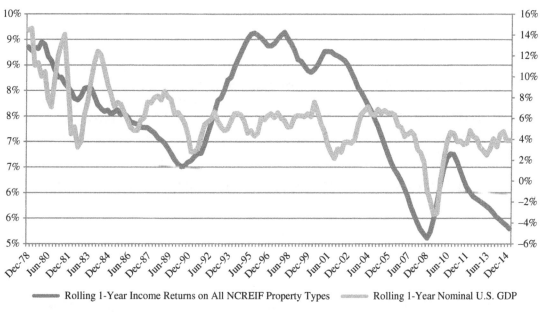

Rolling 1-Year Income Returns on All NCREIF Property Types ▬ Rolling 1-Year Nominal U.S. GDP

Sources: NCREIF, Petroff Institutional

However, returns from property values are affected significantly by the state of the economy and have a direct relationship with GDP. This relationship is shown in Figure 5-2, which compares returns from property values on commercial real estate to U.S. GDP growth. In contrast to returns from income, property values are somewhat volatile and would make investors require a higher risk premium for investing in these assets relative to bonds in spite of their steady income stream.

Figure 5-2: Returns from Property Values vs. U.S. GDP

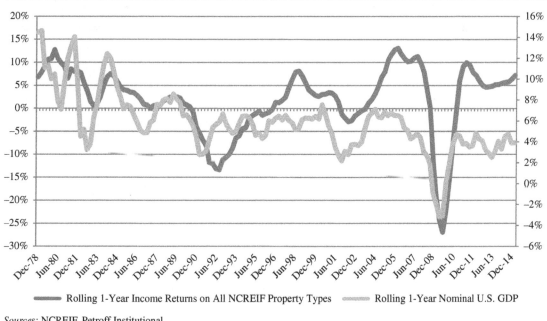

Rolling 1-Year Income Returns on All NCREIF Property Types ▬ Rolling 1-Year Nominal U.S. GDP

Sources: NCREIF, Petroff Institutional

Commercial Real Estate Risk Premiums and the Economy

As discussed previously, there are conflicting forces that affect how large or small a risk premium investors require for real estate, relative to similar opportunities such as high-quality bonds with a steady income stream. We can derive this risk premium by looking at high-quality bond yields relative to the capitalization rate on properties, which is the ratio between net operating income and market value (or the property's yield). This risk premium is not just affected by real estate fundamentals as discussed earlier, but also moves inversely as a function of prevailing economic conditions. This is because as economic conditions worsen, the chance of property value losses goes up, and so does the capitalization rate spread relative to bonds. Figure 5-3 shows this inverse relationship over time.

Figure 5-3: Capitalization Rate and High-Quality Bond Yield Spread vs. U.S. GDP

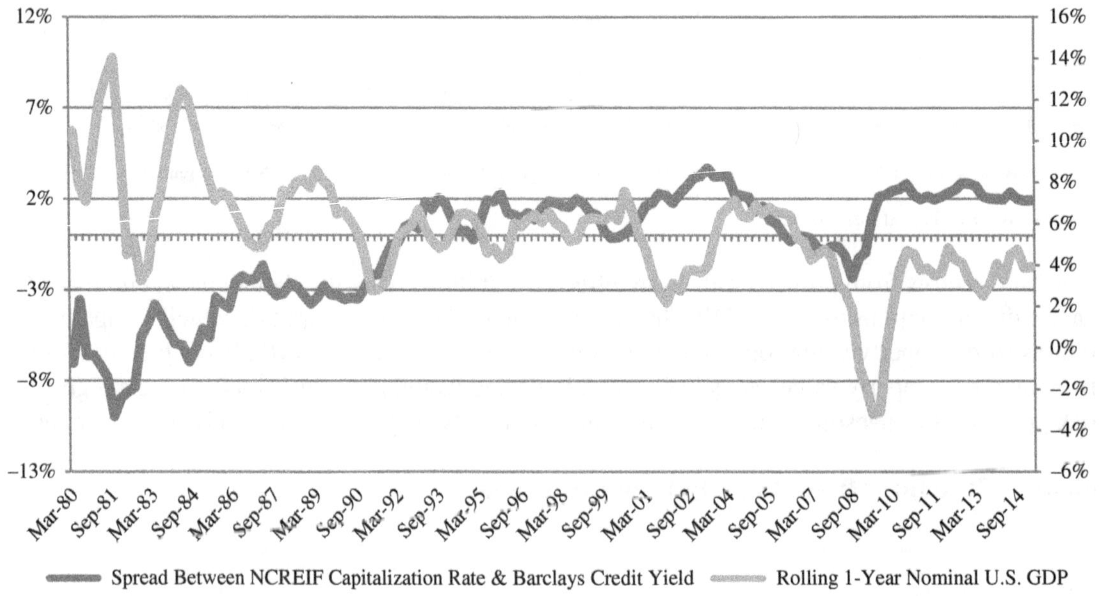

Spread Between NCREIF Capitalization Rate & Barclays Credit Yield — Rolling 1-Year Nominal U.S. GDP

Sources: NCREIF, Petroff Institutional

READING 51: ANALYSIS OF ACTIVE PORTFOLIO MANAGEMENT

LESSON 1: ACTIVE MANAGEMENT AND VALUE ADDED, AND COMPARING RISK AND RETURN

LOS 51a: Describe how value added by active management is measured.
Vol 6, pp 468–473

Introduction

Active portfolio management theory deals with how an investor should construct a portfolio given an assumed competitive advantage or skill in predicting returns. It relies on the assumption that financial markets are not perfectly efficient.

When it comes to evaluating the performance of an actively managed portfolio, its risk and returns must be compared to the risk and return of an appropriate benchmark portfolio. Therefore, we will focus on value added above and beyond the alternative of a low-cost index fund.

ACTIVE MANAGEMENT AND VALUE ADDED

The purpose of active management is to match or surpass the performance of the benchmark portfolio by generating positive value added. Before getting into the measurement and analysis of value added, let's briefly talk about what constitutes an appropriate benchmark for an actively managed portfolio.

Choice of Benchmark

A benchmark should have the following qualities:

- It should be representative of the assets that the investor will want to invest in.
- Investors should be able to replicate positions in the benchmark at a low cost.
- Benchmark weights should be verifiable *ex ante*, and return data should be timely *ex post*.

Both capitalization-weighted and float-adjusted market capitalization–weighted indices have been used as the benchmark portfolio.

- Capitalization-weighted indices have featured prominently as benchmark portfolios in the development of capital market theory in that they are self-rebalancing and can be simultaneously held by many investors.
- Float-adjusted market capitalization–weighted indices offer an improvement in that they account for only securities/assets that are available to the general public for investing.

An important thing to bear in mind is that when capitalization-weighted indices are used as benchmarks, value added from active management becomes a zero-sum game. This is because the market portfolio represents the average performance across all investors that own securities, and as a group active investors cannot outperform the market. Outperformance by one group of investors must be offset by underperformance by the other. However, when float-adjusted market capitalization–weighted indices are used as benchmarks, active management is not necessarily a zero-sum game with respect to the (relatively narrow) benchmark, because investors may invest in securities outside the benchmark.

The return on the benchmark portfolio, R_B, is calculated as the weighted average of the return to the individual securities in the benchmark:

$$R_B = \sum_{i=1}^{N} W_{B,i} R_i \qquad \text{... (Equation 1)}$$

where:
R_i = Return on security i
$w_{B,i}$ = Benchmark weight of security i
N = Number of securities

The return on an actively managed portfolio, R_P, is calculated as the weighted average of the return to the individual securities in the portfolio:

$$R_P = \sum_{i=1}^{N} W_{P,i} R_i \qquad \text{... (Equation 2)}$$

Measuring Value Added

The **value added** (or **active return**) of an actively managed portfolio is calculated as the difference between the return on the portfolio and the return on the benchmark:

$$R_A = R_P - R_B$$

A managed portfolio's **alpha** (which refers to its risk-adjusted value added) incorporates some estimate of portfolio risk relative to its benchmark (typically measured by **beta**). Therefore, alpha is calculated as:

$$\alpha_P = R_P - \beta_P R_B$$

Do not let the practical use of the word *alpha* confuse you here. Alpha, in practice, is often used to refer to active return, with an implicit assumption that the beta of the managed portfolio equals 1.0.

The term **active weight** is used to refer to the difference between the weight of the particular security in a managed portfolio and the weight of that security in the benchmark. The delta (Δ) in the following formula indicates a difference from benchmark weights.

Active weight = Portfolio weight – Benchmark weight
$$\Delta w_i = w_{P,i} - w_{B,i}$$

It can be shown (and we'll spare you the derivation here) that Equations 1 and 2 can be used along with the definition of active weights to come to the conclusion that value added is the sum product of (1) active weights and (2) asset returns:

$$R_A = \sum_{i=1}^{N} \Delta w_i R_i$$

Given that the sum of active weights is zero, we can also write the expression for value added as the sum product of (1) active weights and (2) active security returns:

$$R_A = \sum_{i=1}^{N} \Delta W_i R_{Ai}$$

... (Equation 3)

where R_{Ai} = Active security return = $R_i - R_B$.

Example 1-1 illustrates the application of Equation 3 to compute value added.

Example 1-1: Value Added

Use the information in the table to answer the questions that follow:

Country	Benchmark Weight	Portfolio Weight	2014 Return
A	23%	17%	11.3%
B	21%	14%	12.8%
C	11%	9%	10.8%
D	9%	24%	9.9%
E	36%	36%	12.5%

1. Which countries have the largest overweight and the largest underweight in the managed portfolio relative to the benchmark? Compute the active weights for those two countries.
2. Using active weights and total returns, compute the value added of the managed portfolio for 2014.
3. Using active weights and active security returns, compute the value added of the managed portfolio for 2014.

Solutions:

1. Country D has the largest overweight (24% – 9% = 15%), while Country B has the largest underweight (14% – 21% = –7%).
2. Using active weights and total returns, value added can be computed as:

$$R_A = -0.06(11.3) + -0.07(12.8) + -0.02(10.8) + 0.15(9.9) + 0(12.5) = -0.305\%$$

3. In order to use active weights and active security returns (Equation 3) to compute value added, we first need to compute the return on the benchmark portfolio:

$$R_B = 0.23(11.3) + 0.21(12.8) + 0.11(10.8) + 0.09(9.9) + 0.36(12.5) = 11.866\%$$

Value added can then be computed as the sum product of active weights and active security returns:

$$R_A = -0.06(11.3 - 11.866) + -0.07(12.8 - 11.866) + -0.02(10.8 - 11.866) +$$
$$0.15(9.9 - 11.866) = -0.305\%$$

Decomposition of Value Added

Performance attribution systems can be used to break down value added into multiple sources. For our purposes here, we will focus on the decomposition of value added into:

- Value added from asset allocation. This refers to the value added by changing the weights of various asset classes in the managed portfolio relative to the benchmark. For example, a managed portfolio may hold 35% in equities when the benchmark calls for 30% of the funds to be held in equities.
- Value added from security selection. This refers to the value added by changing the composition of various individual securities within an asset class relative to the benchmark. For example, within the fixed-income asset class, the managed portfolio may have 3% invested in bonds issued by ABC Company when the benchmark weight for those bonds is 2.8%.

Example 2-1 illustrates the attribution of portfolio performance.

Example 1-2: Decomposition of Value Added

Consider the information provided in the table:

Fund	Fund Return (%)	Benchmark Return (%)	Value Added (%)
BMS Equities	34.3	31.3	3.0
BMS Fixed Income	–2.8	–3.0	0.2

The investment policy statement calls for a strategic asset allocation of 60% equities and 40% bonds.

Over the relevant period, the active manager actually invested 70% of the portfolio in equities and 30% in bonds.

1. Compute the contribution to value added from the manager's skill in security selection.
2. Compute the contribution to value added from the manager's active allocation decisions.
3. Compute the total value added by the manager.

Solutions:

1. First, we compute the value added from each asset class held in the portfolio:

   BMS Equities added value of $R_A = R_P - R_B = 34.3\% - 31.3\% = 3.0\%$

   BMS Fixed Income added value of $R_A = R_P - R_B = -2.8\% - (-3.0\%) = 0.2\%$

   We can now compute the combined value added from security selection. Note that actual **portfolio weights** are used in this calculation.

   $0.70(3.0\%) + 0.30(0.2\%) = 2.16\%$

2. The active allocation was 70% – 60% = +10% for equities and 30% – 40% = –10% for fixed income. Therefore the total value added from active allocation is computed as:

   $0.10(31.3\%) - 0.10(-3.0\%) = 3.43\%$

   Note that we used **benchmark returns** in the calculation.

---

3. The total value added (VA) by the portfolio manager is computed as:

Total VA = Value added from security selection + Value added from active allocation

$$= 2.16\% + 3.43\% = 5.59\%$$

We now introduce to you to the general formula for computing the value added from a portfolio with two asset classes, stocks and bonds:

R_A = Value added from security selection + Value added from active allocation

$$= (w_{P,Stocks} R_{A,Stocks} + w_{P,Bonds} R_{A,Bonds}) + (\Delta w_{Stocks} R_{B,Stocks} + \Delta w_{Bonds} R_{B,Bonds})$$

$w_{P,Stocks}$ = Portfolio weight on stocks
$R_{A,Stocks}$ = Active return on stocks
Δw_{Stocks} = Active weight on stocks
$R_{B,Stocks}$ = Benchmark return on stocks

Note that we answered Question 1 using the first parenthetical term in Equation 5 and Question 2 using the second parenthetical term.

Also note that the computed total value added can be confirmed by computing the difference between the return on the policy portfolio and the return on the investor's portfolio:

Return on policy portfolio = 0.60(31.3%) + 0.40(−3.0%) = 17.58%
Return on investor's portfolio = 0.70(34.3%) + 0.30(−2.8%) = 23.17%
Value added = 23.17% − 17.58% = 5.59%

Portfolio attribution systems can be expanded to account for several asset classes. When the number of asset classes is greater than two, the following formula is used to compute the value added from security selection in active allocation decisions.

R_A = Value added from security selection + Value added from active allocation

$$R_A = \sum_{j=1}^{M} w_{P,j} R_{Aj} + \sum_{j=1}^{M} \Delta w_j R_{B,j}$$

where M = Number of asset classes.

The takeaway from this section is that deviations from benchmark portfolio weights drive the value added from active portfolio management. If portfolio weights are identical to benchmark weights, value added would equal zero.

LOS 51b: Calculate and interpret the information ratio (*ex post* and *ex ante*) and contrast it to the Sharpe ratio. Vol 6, pp 473–483

COMPARING RISK AND RETURN

The risk–return trade-off of a portfolio can be represented in absolute or relative terms.

- The Sharpe ratio provides an absolute expected (*ex ante*) or realized (*ex post*) reward-to-risk measure.
- The information ratio provides a relative (to a benchmark) expected (*ex ante*) or realized (*ex post*) reward-to-risk measure.

Sharpe Ratio

The Sharpe ratio measures a portfolio's excess return per unit of risk, where risk is measured by the standard deviation of the portfolio return (also known as total risk or volatility).

$$SR_P = \frac{R_P - R_F}{STD(R_P)}$$

- When used as an *ex ante* measure, the Sharpe ratio uses expected return and risk. Since these forecasts are subjective, the *ex ante* Sharpe ratio will vary across investors.
- When used as an *ex post* measure, the Sharpe ratio uses historical returns and risk. Typically both return and risk are annualized. If we were presented with monthly returns and standard deviations, annual return would be computed by multiplying the monthly return by 12, while the annual standard deviation would be computed by multiplying the monthly standard deviation by the square root of 12.

Also note the following:

- When comparing two funds based on historical Sharpe ratios, we must ensure that they are computed from the same measurement period.
- The Sharpe ratio is unaffected by the addition of cash or leverage to a portfolio.
- The two-fund separation theorem asserts that all investors would hold some combination of the risk-free asset and the risky asset portfolio with the highest Sharpe ratio. If the investor wants to increase the portfolio's expected return, she could add leverage to the portfolio, and if she wants to reduce the expected risk she would hold more cash and less of the risky asset portfolio. (See Example 1-3.)

Example 1-3: Adjusting Risk and Return Using the Sharpe Ratio

An investor is choosing between two portfolios: Portfolio A and Portfolio B. The current risk-free rate is 3%. Further information is provided in the table:

	Portfolio A	Portfolio B
Expected return	11.0%	14.2%
Expected volatility	14.3%	21.9%
Sharpe ratio	0.559	0.511

1. What percentage of the portfolio should the investor hold in cash to reduce the risk of a portfolio entirely invested in Portfolio B to the level of risk of Portfolio A?
2. Compute the Sharpe ratio of the combined Portfolio B plus cash portfolio from Question 1.
3. Compare the expected return of the combined Portfolio B plus cash portfolio to that of Portfolio A.

Solutions:

1. Here, we want to reduce a portfolio volatility of 21.9% to 14.3% by adding cash. Portfolio standard deviation is calculated as:

$$\sigma_P{}^2 = \sigma_B{}^2 w_B{}^2 + \sigma_C{}^2 w_C{}^2 + 2Cov_{B,C} w_B w_C$$

We know that the volatility of cash is zero, and the covariance of returns between cash and Portfolio B is also zero. Therefore:

$$\sigma_P = \sigma_B w_B$$
$$14.3\% = 21.9\% w_B$$
$$w_B = 14.3 / 21.9 = 65.3\%$$

2. The Sharpe ratio of the combined portfolio is unaffected by cash. It remains at 0.511.
3. The expected return of the combined portfolio is calculated as:

$$E(R_P) = w_B E(R_B) + w_C E(R_C)$$
$$E(R_P) = 0.653(14.2\%) + 0.347(3.0\%) = 10.31\%$$

Let's compute the Sharpe ratio of the combined portfolio to confirm our assertion in the solution to Question 2:

$$SR_P = (10.31 - 3.0) / 14.3 = 0.511$$

Information Ratio

The information ratio (IR) measures the active return from a portfolio relative to a benchmark per unit of active risk (which is the volatility of the active return, and also is known as benchmark tracking risk). The information ratio is used to evaluate the consistency of active return, as most investors would prefer a more consistently generated value added (low active risk) rather than a sporadic/highly volatile active return pattern.

The information ratio is calculated as follows:

$$IR = \frac{\text{Active return}}{\text{Active risk}} = \frac{R_A}{\sigma(R_A)} = \frac{R_P - R_B}{\sigma(R_P - R_B)} \qquad \text{… (Equation 4)}$$

*   Active return is the difference between the managed portfolio return (R_P) and the benchmark portfolio return (R_B).
*   Active risk, or the volatility of active return, is measured by the standard deviation of active return (σ_A).
*   In computing the information ratio, both active return and active risk are typically annualized.

> We earlier mentioned the distinction between active portfolio return and alpha (α_p). Similarly, active risk has a more exact beta-adjusted counterpart, which is known as residual risk. For our purposes, however, we will work with the assumption that the beta of the managed portfolio relative to the benchmark is exactly 1.0, although in practice that assumption can be relaxed.

We spent some time on differentiating the Sharpe ratio from the information ratio in an earlier reading. Just to reinforce your understanding:

A closet index fund, which is a fund that advertises itself as being actively managed but is actually close to being an index fund, will have:

- A Sharpe ratio that is close to the benchmark because its return (and therefore return in excess of the risk-free rate) and volatility will be similar to those of the benchmark.
- An information ratio close to zero or even slightly negative, as there will be little (positive) active risk and the return can be negative if it cannot cover management fees.

A market-neutral long-short equity fund, which has offsetting long and short positions and a beta of zero with respect to the market, will have identical Sharpe and information ratios if the risk-free rate is used as the benchmark. In that case, both calculations would be identical, as would total risk and active risk.

Also note the following:

- *Ex post* information ratios will be negative if active return is negative.
- Since active management is a zero-sum game, the realized information ratio across all funds with the same benchmark should be close to zero.
- If an investor does not expect a positive *ex ante* information ratio, she should just invest in the benchmark.
- Rankings based on active risk (standard deviation of active return) can be different from rankings based on total risk (standard deviation of returns).
- Unlike the Sharpe ratio, the information ratio is affected by the addition of cash or leverage to a portfolio. If cash is added to a portfolio, the information ratio of the combined portfolio will fall.
- The information ratio is not affected by the magnitude of active weights. For example, if the active weights in a managed portfolio are all increased by 30%, the active return and active risk would both increase by 30%, resulting in no change in the information ratio.
  - Note that an outside investor cannot change the active risk of a managed portfolio by changing its individual asset active weights. However, she can effectively change the active risk exposure by taking appropriate positions on the benchmark.
  - For example, if the active risk of a fund is 10%, the investor can combine the fund with the benchmark and hold both in equal amounts to reduce the active risk of the combined portfolio to 5%, with a proportionate reduction in active return. Similarly, she can effectively increase active risk by short selling the benchmark portfolio.

Constructing the Optimal Portfolio

When we studied basic portfolio theory (at Level I) we learned that, when a risk-free asset is available, the optimal portfolio on the efficient frontier of risky asset portfolios is the one that lies at the point where a line originating at the risk-free rate is tangent to the efficient frontier (i.e., the risky asset portfolio with the highest Sharpe ratio) regardless of the investor's level of risk aversion.

A similarly important property when it comes to active portfolio management is that, given the opportunity to adjust active risk and active return by investing in both the actively managed portfolio and the benchmark portfolio, the squared Sharpe ratio of the actively managed portfolio is equal to the sum of the squared Sharpe ratio of the benchmark and the squared information ratio.

Note that Equation 5 is not practical for comparisons of investment skill involving negative IR because the sign is lost in squaring.

$$SR^2_P = SR^2_B + IR^2 \quad \dots \text{(Equation 5)}$$

Equation 5 implies that the active portfolio with the highest information ratio will have the highest Sharpe ratio. Therefore, the expected information ratio is the best criterion for choosing between several actively managed funds with the same benchmark. All other things remaining the same, an investor should choose the investment manager with the highest level of skill (as measured by the information ratio), because investing with that manager will produce the highest Sharpe ratio for the investor's own portfolio.

Determining the Optimal Amount of Active Risk

The optimal level of active risk is the level of active risk that yields the highest Sharpe ratio for the investor. For unconstrained portfolios, the optimal level of active risk (also known as the optimal amount of aggressiveness) is computed as:

$$\sigma^*(R_A) = \frac{IR}{SR_B}\sigma(R_B) \qquad \text{... (Equation 6)}$$

where:
$\sigma^*(R_A)$ = Optimal amount of active risk
IR = Information ratio of the actively managed portfolio
SR_B = Sharpe ratio of the benchmark
$\sigma(R_B)$ = Standard deviation of the benchmark return

See Example 1-4 for computing the optimal active risk and the Sharpe ratio.

Example 1-4: Computing the Optimal Level of Active Risk and the Resulting Sharpe Ratio

An actively managed portfolio has an information ratio of 0.40 and an active risk of 12%. The benchmark portfolio has a Sharpe ratio of 0.50 and a total risk of 20%.

1. Compute the optimal amount of aggressiveness in the actively managed portfolio.
2. Compute the Sharpe ratio of a portfolio constructed with this amount of active risk.
3. Verify that the Sharpe ratio computed in Question 2 is in fact the maximum possible Sharpe ratio.

Solutions:

1. The optimal amount of active risk for the portfolio is computed as:

$$\sigma^*(R_A) = \frac{IR}{SR_B}\sigma(R_B)$$

$$\sigma^*(R_A) = \frac{0.40}{0.50}20\% = 16\%$$

2. If the active portfolio is constructed with the optimal amount of active risk (16%), the Sharpe ratio of the portfolio would improve to:

$$SR^2_P = 0.50^2 + 0.40^2$$

$$SR_P = 0.64$$

---

3.   The Sharpe ratio of the combined portfolio is computed by dividing the return on the portfolio in excess of the risk-free rate by the total risk of the portfolio.

We will use the information ratio of the active portfolio to compute the active return, the return on the active portfolio in excess of the benchmark.

We will then use the Sharpe ratio of the benchmark to compute the excess benchmark return, the return on the benchmark in excess of the risk-free rate.

The sum of those two would give us the excess active portfolio return, the return on the active portfolio in excess of the risk-free rate. This is the numerator in the Sharpe ratio calculation.

Then we will compute the standard deviation of the combined portfolio using the active return variance and benchmark return variance.

At that stage, we would have all the components required to compute the Sharpe ratio.

The information ratio of the active portfolio represents the ratio of the return on the active portfolio in excess of the benchmark (or active return) to active risk. Therefore, the active return on the active portfolio (with the optimal level of aggressiveness) can be computed as:

$$IR = \frac{\text{Active return}}{\text{Active risk}} = \frac{R_A}{\sigma(R_A)}$$

$$0.40 = \frac{R_A}{\sigma(R_A)}$$

$$0.40 * 16\% = R_A$$

$$R_A = 6.4\%$$

The Sharpe ratio of the benchmark is computed by dividing the return on the benchmark in excess of the risk-free rate by the standard deviation of the benchmark. Therefore, the excess return on the benchmark can be computed as follows:

$$SR_B = \frac{R_B - R_F}{STD(R_B)}$$

$$0.50 = \frac{R_B - R_F}{20\%}$$

$$R_B - R_F = 0.50(20\%) = 10\%$$

Therefore, the total return on the active portfolio in excess of the risk-free rate can be computed as the active return plus the excess return on the benchmark, which equals $6.4\% + 10\% = 16.4\%$.

By definition, the total risk of the combined portfolio is the sum of (1) benchmark return variance and (2) active return variance. Given the optimal risk of the active portfolio (16%) and the total risk of the benchmark (20%), total portfolio risk can be computed as:

$$STD(R_P)^2 = STD(R_B)^2 + STD(R_A)^2 = 0.20^2 + 0.16^2$$
$$STD(R_P) = 0.2561 \text{ or } 25.61\%$$

The maximum possible Sharpe ratio of the combined portfolio can then be computed as 16.4%/25.61% = 0.64.

Notice that our initial actively managed portfolio had active risk of 12% (provided in the example), but the optimal level of active risk has been computed as 16%. In order to increase active risk while preserving the information ratio, we would need to short the benchmark and increase the size of the actively managed fund. Specifically, we would need to increase the size of the actively managed fund 16/12 = 1.33 times, while shorting the benchmark by 0.33 times to fund the increase.

We now illustrate the same concepts using risk–return charts.

In Figure 1-1, we plot the risk–return characteristics of individual assets (circles), the benchmark portfolio (triangle), and the optimal portfolio (square). Since we have excess return on the *y*-axis and risk on the *x*-axis, the slopes of the two lines drawn in the figure are Sharpe ratios. Notice the following (this material is really a recap from Level I):

- The Sharpe ratio of the benchmark portfolio (slope of solid line) is higher than the Sharpe ratio of most individual assets. This is due to diversification.
- The Sharpe ratio of the optimal portfolio (slope of dotted line) is higher than the Sharpe ratio of the benchmark portfolio and all individual assets.
- Once the investor has zeroed in on the optimal portfolio, she can retain this higher Sharpe ratio while at the same time adjusting her level of expected return and risk by adding cash to her portfolio or borrowing.

Figure 1-1: Portfolio Risk and Return

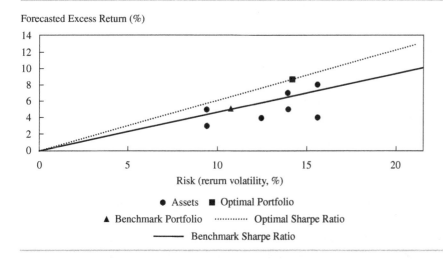

Before moving on, let's add some numbers. Assume that the optimal portfolio has an expected excess return of 8.7% and volatility of 14.2%, which results in a Sharpe ratio of 0.61 (=8.7/14.2). Further, the benchmark has an expected excess return of 5.0% and a return volatility of 10.8% for a Sharpe ratio of 0.46.

In Figure 1-2, we plot the same individual assets (circles), benchmark portfolio (triangle), and optimal portfolio (square), but this time along their expected active return–active risk characteristics. Note the following:

- The benchmark portfolio plots at the origin, as it has zero expected excess return and zero active risk.
- Individual assets can have both positive and negative expected active return compared to the benchmark.
- The optimal portfolio has a positive expected active return, and the slope of the solid line is positive. The slope represents the expected information ratio of the optimal risky asset portfolio (forecasted active return divided by active risk).
  - To add numbers to the explanation, assume that the optimal portfolio has an expected active return of 3.8% and active risk of 9.4%, which gives it an information ratio of 0.40.
- An investor can apply varying levels of aggressiveness to the portfolio while maintaining the (optimal) information ratio of the optimal portfolio by taking appropriate positions on the active portfolio and the benchmark portfolio.

Figure 1-2: Portfolio Active Risk and Return

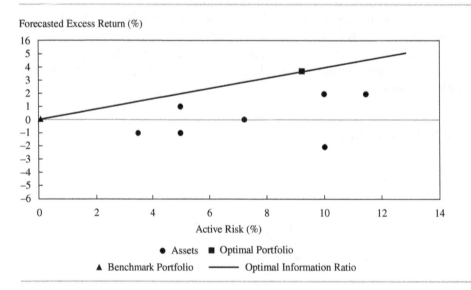

Before moving on, make sure you understand the following:

- The information ratio measures active return per unit of active risk, whereas the Sharpe ratio measures excess return per unit of total risk.
- Information ratios are used to examine the relative value added by active management.
- The information ratio is unaffected by the aggressiveness of active weights (deviations from benchmark weights), as any change in active return is offset by an equal proportional change in active risk.
- The potential improvement in an active portfolio's Sharpe ratio relative to the benchmark's Sharpe ratio is a function of the squared information ratio.
- Therefore, the expected information ratio is the best criterion for constructing an actively managed portfolio, and the *ex post* information ratio is the best criterion for evaluating the past performance of actively managed portfolios.

LESSON 2: THE FUNDAMENTAL LAW

LOS 51c: State and interpret the fundamental law of active portfolio management including its component terms—transfer coefficient, information coefficient, breadth, and active risk (aggressiveness). Vol 6, pp 483–495

LOS 51d: Explain how the information ratio may be useful in investment manager selection and choosing the level of active portfolio risk. Vol 6, pp 483–495

FUNDAMENTAL LAW OF ACTIVE MANAGEMENT

The fundamental law offers us a framework to use in evaluating active portfolio management strategies. It can also be used to determine active asset weights, estimate the expected value added from an active strategy, or measure realized value added *ex post*.

Active Security Returns

Investors aim to maximize the portfolio's active return while limiting the portfolio's active risk. The active return on an individual asset, R_{Ai}, is computed as:

$$R_{Ai} = R_i - R_B$$

where:
R_i = Return on asset i
R_B = Return on the benchmark

Going forward, we will use μ_i as our notation for the forecasted active return on a security or the security's expected active return. Note that this expectation is subjective; it is not an expectation based on any equilibrium pricing model.

Figure 2-1 illustrates how we should think about the parameters in the fundamental law of active management.

- The correlation between active weights and realized active returns (the base of the triangle) reflects realized value added through active portfolio management.
  - Recall that value added is defined as the difference between realized returns on the actively managed portfolio and the benchmark portfolio.
- The correlation between forecasted active returns and realized active returns (right diagonal leg of the triangle) represents signal quality, which is commonly referred to as the information coefficient (IC).
  - All other things remaining the same, investors with higher IC will add more value over time. If forecasts of active return do not correspond with actual realized active returns, there is little hope of adding value through active management.
- The correlation between forecasted active returns and active weights (left diagonal leg of the triangle) represents the extent to which the investor's forecasts are translated into active weights in the portfolio. It is commonly referred to as the transfer coefficient (TC).
  - If a manager does not execute on active return forecasts by taking appropriate positions, there is little hope of adding value.

Figure 2-1: The Correlation Triangle

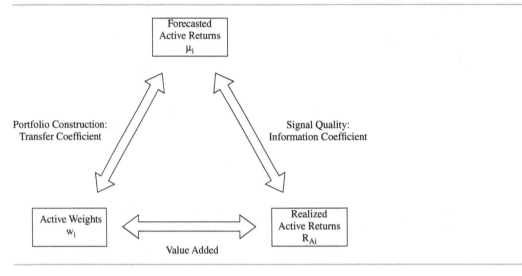

With a conceptual understanding of value added and the factors that influence it, we now move into some math.

Assuming that active returns on individual securities are uncorrelated, the mean-variance-optimal active security weights, subject to a limit on active portfolio risk, are given by:

$$\Delta w_i^* = \frac{\mu_i}{\sigma_i^2} \frac{\sigma_A}{IC\sqrt{BR}}$$ ... (Equation 7)

where:
Δw_i^* = Active security weight
μ_i = Active return forecast
σ_A = Active portfolio risk
σ_i = Forecasted volatility of the active return on security i
IC = Information coefficient
BR = Breadth

- The active return forecast (μ_i) for each security is typically scaled using the Grinold rule:

$$\mu_i = IC\sigma_i S_i$$ ... (Equation 8)

  - S_i represents a set of standardized forecasts of expected returns across securities, sometimes called **scores**.

- Equation 7 ought to make intuitive sense.
  - The larger the forecasted active return for a security (μ_i), the larger its desired active weight (Δw_i^*).
  - The greater the forecasted volatility of active return for a security (σ_i), the lower its desired active weight (Δw_i^*).
  - The greater the desired active portfolio risk (σ_A), the larger the individual active weights (Δw_i^*).

- We mentioned earlier that the information coefficient (IC) is the *ex ante* or anticipated correlation between active return forecasts and realized active returns.
  - As a correlation coefficient, IC can lie anywhere between −1 and +1.
  - However, an investor would pursue active management only if the *ex ante* (expected) IC is positive.
- BR, or breadth, represents the number of independent active decisions made by the investor per year in constructing the portfolio. For example:
  - If a single-factor model is used, and decisions about the active return on a security are independent from one year to the next, breadth simply equals the number of securities, N.
  - If an investor makes quarterly or monthly forecasts about a security that are independent over time, breadth equals the number of securities times the number of rebalancing periods per year.

See Example 2-1.

Example 2-1: Scaling Active Return Forecasts and Sizing Active Weights

Consider four individual securities whose active returns are uncorrelated with each other. The investor believes that Securities A and B will outperform, while Securities C and D will underperform over the next year. She therefore assigns scores of +1 to the first two, and −1 to the other two. Active return volatilities for the securities are provided in this table:

Security	Score	Volatility
A	+1.0	20%
B	+1.0	40%
C	−1.0	20%
D	−1.0	40%

1. Assume that the expected accuracy of the investor's active return forecasts is captured by an IC of 0.25. What are the forecasted active returns on each of these securities using Grinold's scaling rule?
2. Given that the four securities' active returns are uncorrelated, and that forecasts are independent from year to year, what is the breadth of the investor's forecasts?
3. Assume that the investor wants to maximize the expected active return of the portfolio subject to a limit of 10.0% on active risk. Determine the weights that should be assigned to each security.

Solutions:

Security	Score	Active Return Volatility	Scaled Expected Active Return $\mu_i = IC\ \sigma_i\ S_i$
A	+1.0	20%	$(0.25)(20\%)(+1) = 5\%$
B	+1.0	40%	$(0.25)(40\%)(+1) = 10\%$
C	−1.0	20%	$(0.25)(20\%)(−1) = −5\%$
D	−1.0	40%	$(0.25)(40\%)(−1) = −10\%$

1. Grinold's scaling rule for active return forecasts is given as $\mu_i = IC\ \sigma_i\ S_i$. The scaled active return forecasts for the four securities are computed in this table:
2. Since active returns are uncorrelated with each other and forecasts are independent from one year to the next, the investor has made four separate decisions (one for each security). Therefore, BR = 4.
3. Active weights for the four securities are computed in the following table, using Equation 7. Note that $\sigma_A = 10.0\%$.

Security	Expected Active Return	Active Return Volatility	Active Weight $\Delta w_i^* = \dfrac{\mu_i}{\sigma_i^2}\dfrac{\sigma_A}{IC\sqrt{BR}}$
A	5.0%	20%	$[(0.05)(0.10)]\ /\ [(0.20^2)(0.25)(4)^{0.5}] = 25.0\%$
B	10.0%	40%	$[(0.10)(0.10)]\ /\ [(0.40^2)(0.25)(4)^{0.5}] = 12.5\%$
C	−5.0%	20%	$[(−0.05)(0.10)]\ /\ [(0.20^2)(0.25)(4)^{0.5}] = −25.0\%$
D	−10.0%	40%	$[(−0.10)(0.10)]\ /\ [(0.40^2)(0.25)(4)^{0.5}] = −12.5\%$

The Basic Fundamental Law

Based on Equation 3 (from earlier in the reading), we can assert that the expected value added from an actively managed portfolio is the sum product of active security weights and forecasted active security returns:

$$E(R_A) = \sum_{i=1}^{N} \Delta w_i\ \mu_i$$

If we were to use optimal active weights for each security (computed using Equation 7) and the forecasted active security returns (computed using Equation 8), the expected active portfolio return is given by:

$$\boxed{E(R_A)^* = IC\sqrt{BR}\ \sigma_A} \quad \dots \text{(Equation 9)}$$

Note that the * indicates that that actively managed portfolio is constructed using optimal active security weights (Δw_i^*).

Equation 9 presents what is known as the basic fundamental law (see Example 2-2). Optimal expected active return is a function of three parameters:

1. The assumed information coefficient (IC).
2. The square root of the breadth (BR).
3. Portfolio active risk (σ_A).

Dividing both sides of Equation 9 by active risk (σ_A) allows us to express the information ratio of the unconstrained optimal portfolio as a function of just the IC and BR:

$$E(R_A) \ * \ / \sigma_A = IC\sqrt{BR} \, \sigma_A / \sigma_A$$

$$\frac{E(R_A)}{\sigma(R_A)} = \text{Information ratio}(IR^*) = IC\sqrt{BR}$$

Example 2-2: The Basic Fundamental Law

Building on Example 2-1, we continue to work with the four securities whose active returns are uncorrelated and forecasts are independent from year to year. Relevant information is reproduced in the following table:

Security	Expected Active Return	Active Return Volatility	Active Weight
A	5.0%	20%	25.0%
B	10.0%	40%	12.5%
C	−5.0%	20%	−25.0%
D	−10.0%	40%	−12.5%

1. Assume that the benchmark portfolio is equally weighted across these four securities and the forecasted return on the benchmark is 15%. Compute the portfolio weights and total expected returns for each of the four securities.
2. Calculate the forecasted total return and active return of the managed portfolio.
3. Calculate the active risk of the managed portfolio.
4. Verify the basic fundamental law of active management using the expected active return and active risk of the managed portfolio. In computing active return forecasts and active weights, we assumed that IC = 0.25, BR = 4, and active risk = 10.0%.

Solutions:

1. The benchmark weight for each security is 25% (=100%/4). The total weight of each security in the active portfolio is calculated by adding the active weight to the benchmark weight.

Security	Total Weight	Total Return Forecast
A	25% + 25% = 50%	15% + 5% = 20%
B	25% + 12.5% = 37.5%	15% + 10% = 25%
C	25% + (−25%) = 0%	15% + (−5%) = 10%
D	25% + (−12.5%) = 12.5%	15% + (−10%) = 5%
	100%	

The expected total return on each security is computed by adding the active return forecast to the benchmark return.

2. The expected return on the portfolio is computed as the weighted average of the returns expected from each security in the portfolio:

$$E(R) = (0.50)(20) + (0.375)(25) + (0)(10) + (0.125)(5) = 20.0\%$$

The expected active return equals the expected total return minus the benchmark return:

$$E(R_A) = 20\% - 15\% = 5\%$$

Note that the expected active return can also be computed directly as the weighted average of the active returns expected from the securities in the portfolio:

$$E(R_A) = (0.50)(5) + (0.375)(10) + (0)(-5) + (0.125)(-10) = 5\%$$

3. The active risk of the managed portfolio is computed as the square root of the sum of the products of each security's active weights squared and active volatility squared:

$$\sigma_A = [(0.25)^2(20)^2 + (0.125)^2(40)^2 + (-0.25)^2(20)^2 + (-0.125)^2(40)^2]^{0.5} = 10.0\%$$

4. The basic fundamental law of active management states that:

$$E(R_A) = IC\sqrt{BR}\sigma_A$$

Inserting the values of IC, BR, and σ_A, we do indeed obtain a value of 5.0% for active return:

$$E(R_A) = 0.25 * \sqrt{4} * 10.0 = 5.0\%$$

Note that we can compute the information ratio by dividing active return by active risk: 5.0%/10.0% = 0.5; or by multiplying the IC by the square root of BR: $0.25 * \sqrt{4} = 0.5$.

The Full Fundamental Law

In the previous section, we developed a framework for deriving a set of unconstrained optimal active weights. Practically speaking, however, investors face some strategic constraints (e.g., limits on short selling, limits on turnover, etc.) in portfolio construction. Going back to the correlation triangle (Figure NaN), the transfer coefficient (TC) captures the correlation between forecasted active security returns and actual active weights. Specifically, TC is the following risk-weighted correlation:

$$TC = COR(\mu_i / \sigma_i, \Delta w_i \sigma_i)$$

From Equation 7, we know that forecasted active security returns are positively related to optimal active weights. Therefore, the transfer coefficient can also be expressed as the correlation between optimal active weights and actual active weights: $TC = COR(\Delta w_i^* \sigma_i, \Delta w_i \sigma_i)$.

-   The transfer coefficient can take on any value between −1 and +1.
-   The more stringent the constraints placed on the portfolio, the lower the TC.
-   At TC = 0, there is no expectation of value added from active management.

- At TC = 1, there are no constraints placed on the portfolio and there is perfect correspondence between active weights and forecasted active returns.
- The TC can be negative if relative weights are negatively correlated with current expected returns, because the portfolio requires rebalancing.

The full fundamental law, one that accounts for the transfer coefficient, can be expressed as:

$$E(R_A) = TC\,IC\sqrt{BR}\,\sigma_A \qquad \text{... (Equation 10)}$$

Note that there is no * with the expected active return here because the portfolio is constructed with constrained active security weights. The full fundamental law (henceforth referred to as the fundamental law) asserts that active return is the product of four parameters:

1. Information coefficient (IC).
2. Square root of breadth (BR).
3. Active risk (σ_A).
4. Transfer coefficient (TC).

We can now express the portfolio's information ratio (IR) as:

$$E(R_A)/\sigma_A = (TC * IC * \sqrt{BR} * \sigma_A)/\sigma_A$$

$$\frac{E(R_A)}{\sigma(R_A)} = \text{Information ratio (IR)} = TC * IC * \sqrt{BR} \qquad \text{... (Equation 11)}$$

See Example 2-3.

Example 2-3: The Full Fundamental Law

We continue with four securities whose active returns are uncorrelated, and continue to assume that forecasts are independent from year to year. Relevant information (from previous examples) is reproduced in the following table. The last column in the table presents actual weights of each security in a **constrained** (not optimized) portfolio. We are working with IC = 0.25, BR = 4, and σ_A = 10.0%.

Security	Expected Active Return	Active Return Volatility	Optimal Active Weight	Actual Active Weight
A	5.0%	20%	25.0%	8.0%
B	10.0%	40%	12.5%	6.0%
C	−5.0%	20%	−25.0%	9.0%
D	−10.0%	40%	−12.5%	−23.0%

1. Calculate the transfer coefficient (TC). Compare this number with the TC for optimal active weights.
2. Calculate the forecasted active return and active risk of the managed portfolio using actual rather than optimal active weights.
3. Verify the full fundamental law of active management using the active portfolio return, active portfolio risk, and transfer coefficient.

Solutions:

1. The transfer coefficient is the correlation between the risk-weighted expected active returns and actual active weights: $TC = COR(\mu_i/\sigma_i, \Delta w_i \sigma_i)$. The two values for each of the four securities are computed in the following table:

Security	μ_i/σ_i	$\Delta w_i \sigma_i$
A	$5.0/20.0 = 0.25$	$(0.08)(20.0) = 1.6\%$
B	$10.0/40.0 = 0.25$	$(0.06)(40.0) = 2.4\%$
C	$-5.0/20.0 = -0.25$	$(0.09)(20.0) = 1.8\%$
D	$-10.0/40.0 = -0.25$	$(-0.23)(40.0) = -9.2\%$
	$TC = COR(\mu_i/\sigma_i, \Delta w_i \sigma_i) = 0.59$	

*The correlation between the four pairs of numbers was computed using Microsoft Excel.

The TC for the constrained portfolio is 0.59, while the TC for the unconstrained portfolio would be 1.0 (by definition). You can verify this by performing a calculation similar to the one performed previously, but using optimal active weights instead of actual active weights.

2. The forecasted active return for the managed portfolio is calculated as:

$$E(R_A) = (0.08)(5) + (0.06)(10) + (0.09)(-5) + (-0.23)(-10) = 2.85\%$$

The active risk for the managed portfolio is calculated as:

$$\sigma_A = [(0.08)^2(20)^2 + (0.06)^2(40)^2 + (0.09)^2(20)^2 + (-0.23)^2(40)^2]^{0.5} = 9.77\%,$$

which satisfies the active risk constraint of 10.0%.

3. The full fundamental law states that the expected portfolio active return can be computed as:

$$E(R_A) = TC \, IC \sqrt{BR} \, \sigma_A$$

$$E(R_A) = (0.59)(0.25)(4)^{0.5}(9.77) = 2.88, \text{which is close enough to } 2.85\% \text{ computed in}$$

the solution to Question 2.

Note that there is a slight difference between the numbers because the actual active weights and the transfer coefficient were rounded off. Actual active weights are computed using a numerical optimizer using a number of constraints. Those calculations are beyond the scope of this reading.

The transfer coefficient (TC) is also used in the computation of the optimal amount of active risk for a **constrained** portfolio.

$$\sigma(R_A) = TC \frac{IR^*}{SR_B} \sigma(R_B)$$

The formula is similar to Equation 6, but now TC comes into the mix. Note that IR^* is the information ratio of an otherwise unconstrained portfolio. If this optimal level of aggressiveness is built into the portfolio, the resulting maximum value of the constrained portfolio's Sharpe ratio is calculated as:

$$SR_P^2 = SR_B^2 + (TC)^2 (IR^*)^2$$

We mentioned earlier that with no contraints, the active risk of a contrained actively managed portfolio can be adjusted to itss optimal level while preserving the information ratio by combining it with short or long positions in the benchmark portfolio. We work with that concept again, but this time introduce the transfer coefficient into the mix.

Assume that the actively managed portfolio has a transfer coefficient of 0.40 and an unconstrained information ratio of 0.25, while the benchmark has a Sharpe ratio of 0.30 and risk of 15.0%.

The optimal amount of aggressiveness in the actively managed portfolio is calculated as 0.40(0.25/0.30)15.0 = 5.0%.

The Sharpe ratio of an actively managed portfolio constructed with optimal risk is calculated as $(0.30^2 + 0.40^2 \times 0.25^2)^{0.5} = 0.316$.

If the constrained portfolio has an active risk of 8.0%, the active risk can be lowered to the optimal level of 5.0% by investing 5.0/8.0 = 62.5% in the actively managed fund and 1 − 5.0/8.0 = 37.5% in the benchmark.

Finally, note that if TC = 0, the optimal amount of active risk is also 0, which means that the investor should just invest in the benchmark portfolio.

Ex Post Performance Measurement

We now turn our attention to evaluating actual performance, in terms of the realized (not expected) value added.

Whether actual value added is positive or negative, its magnitude is determined by the extent to which the portfolio has positive active weights on securities that outperform and negative active weights on securities that underperform. Basically, actual performance depends on the relationship between relative weights and actual or realized relative returns. The realized information coefficient (IC_R), which reflects how actual active returns correlate with realized active returns, allows us to determine what realized return to expect given the transfer coefficient. Expected value added conditional on the realized information coefficient, IC_R, is calculated as:

$$E(R_A \mid IC_R) = (TC)(IC_R)\sqrt{BR}\, \sigma_A \qquad \dots \text{(Equation 12)}$$

Note that this equation is similar to Equation 10, except that the realized IC has replaced anticipated IC.

Any difference between the actual active return on the portfolio and the conditional expected active return is represented by a noise ter

$$R_A = E(R_A \mid IC_R) + Noise$$ ... (Equation 13)

Equation 13 asserts that the realized value added from an actively managed portfolio can be broken down into two parts:

1. The expected value added given the realized skill of the investor for the period, $E(R_A \mid IC_R)$.
2. Any noise that results from constraints that prevent the portfolio constructed from being optimal.

Similarly, *ex post* or realized active return variance can also be broken down into two parts:

1. Variation due to the realized information coefficient.
   ○ Studies have shown that the proportion of realized variance that can be attributed to this part equals TC^2.
2. Variation due to noise induced by constraints on the portfolio.
   ○ Studies have shown that the proportion of realized variance that can be attributed to this part equals $1 - TC^2$.

This implies that if an investor's TC is low, there is a high probability that when his forecasts are accurate, his actual performance is poor, and when his forecasts are inaccurate, his performance is actually good.

- For example, for an investor with TC = 0.6, 36% ($= 0.6^2$) of realized variation in performance can be attributed to variation in the realized information coefficient, while 64% ($= 1 - 0.36$) comes from constraint-induced noise.

See Example 2-4.

Example 2-4: *Ex Post* Performance

Consider an active management strategy where IC = 0.10, BR = 121, TC = 0.80, and active risk = 5.0%.

1. Compute the expected value added using the fundamental law.
2. It turns out that realized IC = −0.05 (instead of the expected value, 0.10). Compute value added assuming zero constraint-induced noise.
3. Now suppose that the actual return on the active portfolio was −1.8%. Given the −0.05 realized information coefficient, what is the contribution of noise to actual active return?
4. What percentage of active risk variance (or performance variance, tracking risk squared) can be attributed to variation in the realized information coefficient (or forecasting success), and what percentage can be attributed to constraint-induced noise?

Solutions:

1. The expected value added according to the fundamental law is calculated as:

    $$E(R_A) = (TC)(IC)\sqrt{BR}\sigma A = 0.80 \times 0.10 \times \sqrt{121} \times 5.0\% = 4.4\%$$

2. Value added, without including constraint-induced noise, is calculated as:

    $$E(R_A | ICR) = (TC)(ICR)\sqrt{BR}\,\sigma_A = 0.80 \times (-0.05) \times \sqrt{121} \times 5.0\% = -2.2\%$$

    The negative value here indicates that, conditional on the actual information coefficient, the investor should expect a negative active return because the realized information coefficient is negative.

3. The contribution of noise to active return equals the difference between realized active return and the forecasted active return: $-1.8\% - (-2.2\%) = 0.4\%$.

    Given a negative forecasted active return (-2.2%), the positive contribution of noise (0.4%) to active return helped improve the actual active return to -1.8%. Note that the contribution of noise could as easily have been negative, which would worsen the negative value added.

4. Given a TC of 0.8, the contribution of forecasting success to active return variance equals 64%, while the contribution of constraint-induced noise equals 36%.

LESSON 3: APPLICATIONS OF THE FUNDAMENTAL LAW AND PRACTICAL LIMITATIONS

LOS 51e: Compare active management strategies (including market timing and security selection) and evaluate strategy changes in terms of the fundamental law of active management. Vol 6, pp 495–508

APPLICATIONS OF THE FUNDAMENTAL LAW

The exhibits provided in the curriculum in this section are too detailed. Do not lose sight of the forest for the trees here. We list the important concepts/takeaways in the following bullets:

- Given the number of individual assets being considered (N), if the correlations between different assets do not equal zero, the value of breadth will be different from the number of assets.
- The more ambitious the forecasts, the greater the value of the information coefficient (IC) in the fundamental law.
    - For example, consider Assets X and Y, whose active returns are believed to be positively correlated. If an investment manager forecasts that the active returns on these two assets will actually go in different directions (a relatively ambitious forecast), the IC used in fundamental law accounting will increase.

- As another example, consider an active fixed-income strategy. If we determine the allocation across short-term bonds and long-term bonds based solely on the active decision that interest rates will rise across the board, we will attain a particular value for IC. However, if we determine the weights based on an active decision that there will be a change in the shape of the yield curve, the IC will be higher, as we are making a more ambitious active forecast.
- If constraints are placed in portfolio construction, there will be reduction in the transfer of active return forecasts into active weights (i.e., the transfer coefficient [TC] will be lower). This reduction in the TC will lead to a decrease in the expected active return and in the information ratio.
  - As mentioned previously, for an unconstrained portfolio, an increase in allowed active risk leads to a proportionate increase in active risk, leaving the information ratio unchanged.
  - However, when constraints are imposed in portfolio construction, an increase in allowed active risk does not leave the information ratio of the constrained portfolio unchanged. The higher allowed active risk actually leads to more variation in unconstrained active weights, and the constraints actually become more binding, resulting in a further decrease in the transfer coefficient and in the information ratio.
  - Therefore, for a constrained portfolio, the information ratio decreases with the level of aggressiveness of the strategy. Specifically, it decreases at an increasing rate due to an increasingly lower transfer coefficient.

See Examples 3-1 and 3-2.

Example 3-1: Compare and Contrast Active Management Strategies

Consider two active management strategies: (1) individual stock selection with a benchmark composed of 100 securities, and (2) sector selection with a benchmark of nine sectors. Active security returns are uncorrelated, and forecasts are independent from year to year. The expected IC for the individual stock selector is 0.03, while that of the sector selector is 0.12.

1. What is the breadth of each active management strategy?
2. Calculate the expected information ratio for each strategy, assuming that forecasts can be implemented with no constraints.
3. Compute the expected active returns of the two strategies assuming that the active risk constraint on the portfolio is 2.0% per year.
4. Now employ a more realistic assumption that the individual stock selection strategy is constrained to be long only and has turnover limits. If the transfer coefficient equals 0.60, compute the constrained information ratio and expected active return of the strategy.
5. Suppose the aggressiveness of the constrained individual security selection strategy is increased to a portfolio active risk target of 4.0% per year. Conceptually, what is likely to happen to the information ratio, and why?

Solutions:

1. Given that active asset returns are uncorrelated, and that forecasts are independent from year to year, BR for the stock selector equals the number of stocks (100), and for the sector selector equals the number of sectors (9).

2. Expected information ratios are computed as: $IR = IC\sqrt{BR}$

$$StockselectorIR = (0.03)(\sqrt{100}) = 0.3$$
$$SectorselectorIR = (0.12)(\sqrt{9}) = 0.36$$

3. Expected active returns are computed as: $E(R_A) = (IC)\sqrt{BR}\,\sigma_A$

$$StockselectorE(RA) = (0.03)\sqrt{100}(2.0) = 0.6\%$$
$$StockselectorE(RA) = (0.12)\sqrt{9}(2.0) = 0.72\%$$

4. The information ratio of a constrained active management strategy is computed as:

$$IR = (TC)(IC)\sqrt{BR}$$
$$StockselectorIR = (0.60)(0.03)\sqrt{100} = 0.18$$
$$StockselectorE(R_A) = IR\sigma_A = 0.18(2.0) = 0.36\%$$

Note that with these constraints, the stock selector's IR went down from 0.3 to 0.18, while the expected active return went down from 0.6% to 0.36%.

5. If the level of aggressiveness is increased when working with a constrained portfolio, there will be a more substantial difference between constrained weights and optimal unconstrained active weights, resulting in a lower TC. In response to the increase in acceptable active risk, there will be a less than proportionate increase in the expected active return.

   To illustrate, let us assume that an increase in acceptable active risk from 2% to 3% results in a decrease in the transfer coefficient from 0.60 to 0.50 for the stock selection strategy. This will cause the information ratio to fall to $IR = (TC)(IC)\sqrt{BR} = (0.50)(0.03)\sqrt{100} = 0.15$. Expected active return would increase to $E(R_A) = IR\,\sigma_A = (0.15)(3\%) = 0.45\%$.

   Notice that there has been a 50% increase in the level of acceptable active risk, but only a 25% (= 0.45/0.36 − 1) increase in expected return.

   We now move into a brief example illustrating time-series application of the fundamental law. This will illustrate another way of thinking about breadth (i.e., in the context of a market timing strategy, instead of a stock picking strategy).

   Consider an active management strategy of over- and underweighting credit exposure once a quarter across two assets: a corporate investment-grade bond portfolio (IG portfolio), and a corporate high-yield bond portfolio (HY portfolio). The benchmark portfolio also consists of only these two assets. Each quarter, the single dichotomous decision that confronts the manager is either to overweight the IG portfolio (and therefore underweight the HY portfolio) or to overweight the HY portfolio (and therefore underweight the IG portfolio). Next, we just work with some number to illustrate how certain terms are calculated when it comes to active management through market timing. We then highlight the key takeaway as far as the exam is concerned.

In making this dichotomous over-/underweighting decision, if the investment manager is correct 55% of the time, his information coefficient is calculated as IC = 0.55 − 0.45 − 0.10 (= correct calls − incorrect calls).

Since the manager is really making four quarterly rebalancing decisions per year, the breadth of this strategy equals 4 (under the assumption that active returns are uncorrelated over time).

Notice that the breadth here is quite small, and this leads us directly to the key takeaway here. When it comes to market timing decisions, there are so few opportunities to make active decisions that, in order to achieve a high expected active return or a high information ratio, the portfolio manager must have a higher information coefficient.

A simple formula to estimate the breadth in an active management strategy given the correlation between active security returns is BR = $N/[1 + (N − 1)\rho]$. Here, we have assumed that active returns are uncorrelated over time so BR = N = 4.

In a market timing strategy, the expected information ratio can be increased by rebalancing more frequently (e.g., monthly instead of quarterly). However, for this to happen, (1) the manager should be able to maintain her IC at the previous level by still being correct 55% of the time when it comes to monthly rebalancing decisions, and (2) exposure decisions should be independent over time.

Example 3-2: Breadth and Rebalancing in Active Management Strategies

Consider an active portfolio management strategy that involves over-/underweighting decisions regarding four assets. The active returns on Assets A and B have a positive correlation of 0.3, and the active returns on Assets C and D also have a positive correlation of 0.3, while all other pairwise correlations across these assets equal 0. Assume that BR = 3.2 and that portfolio management decisions are dichotomous; that is, each year the manager forecasts two of the assets to outperform and the other two to underperform.

1. Why is the breadth less than the number of assets in this case?
2. If the manager forecasts that Assets A and C will outperform, how will the information coefficient in the fundamental law be affected compared with a prediction that Assets A and B will outperform?
3. If the manager rebalances the portfolio monthly instead of annually, how would the information ratio be affected?

Solutions:

1. The breadth is less than the number of assets in this strategy because the correlations between active returns on Assets A and B, and Assets C and D, do not equal 0.

2. A forecast that Assets A and C will outperform is more ambitious than a forecast that Assets A and B will outperform (as the risk model already asserts that the active returns on these two are positively correlated). The more ambitious the forecast, the higher the information coefficient.

3. Rebalancing the portfolio monthly instead of annually could increase BR by a factor of 12. However, this will be the case only if (1) the information coefficient remains at the same level, (2) there are no constraints in constructing the active portfolio that might cause the TC to decline, and (3) active returns are uncorrelated over time.

LOS 51f: Describe the practical strengths and limitations of the fundamental law of active management. Vol 6, pp 508–511

PRACTICAL LIMITATIONS

Ex Ante Measurement of Skill

Generally speaking, managers tend to overestimate their level of skill (IC). Aside from this bias, there are issues relating to assessing the level of skill accurately and the fact that forecasting accuracy varies across different asset segments and over time. Studies have shown that realized active portfolio risk is a function of (1) benchmark tracking risk predicted by the risk model and (2) the uncertainty of the information coefficient. They suggest that a more accurate representation of the fundamental law is given by:

$$E(R_A) = \frac{IC}{\sigma_{I_C}} \sigma_A \quad \text{... (Equation 14)}$$

The result of accounting for uncertainty in the information ratio (captured by the term σ_{IC}) is that the actual information ratio is lower than predicted by the original fundamental law. The greater the uncertainty regarding forecasting ability, the lower the expected value added.

Independence of Investment Decisions

We have already mentioned that BR does not equal N when (1) the active returns between individual assets are correlated, or (2) forecasts are not independent from period to period. For example, decisions to overweight all stocks in a given industry are not really independent decisions, because the stocks are all affected by similar factors. In this case, BR will be less than the number of securities. Further, when the fundamental law is applied to hedging strategies that make use of derivatives and other forms of arbitrage, BR will be much higher than the number of securities.

We earlier introduced you to the following formula for estimating BR:

$$BR = \frac{N}{1+(N-1)\rho}$$
  ... (Equation 15)

Note that ρ represents the same correlation coefficient in all the other-than-diagonal elements in the risk model. For two securities (N = 2) and a correlation coefficient associated with a near-perfect arbitrage strategy ($\rho = -0.9$), BR will equal 20.0. As a result, the information ratio will be quite high even for relatively modest values of IC.

Another limitation of the fundamental law comes up in the active management of fixed-income portfolios. For stocks, their risk can be decomposed into systematic and non-systematic factors, and since non-systematic risk factors can be diversified away, we can assume that active asset returns (that are driven by systematic factors) are essentially independent. Therefore, BR can be easily determined. However, in the fixed-income arena, almost all bonds are, at least to a certain extent, driven by interest rate risk and credit risk, resulting in some correlation between returns.

Finally, when it comes to market timing active management strategies, more frequent rebalancing can increase the information ratio, but only to the extent that forecasts are independent from one period to the next.

To conclude this section, let's consider an active portfolio management strategy of selecting individual stocks from the FTSE 100 on a monthly basis. Based on IC = 0.10 and BR = 1,200, the information ratio comes to an extremely impressive 3.46. However, before getting too excited, we should consider the following limitations:

- The active returns on the FTSE 100 are probably correlated, as they are, to a certain extent, driven by UK macroeconomic factors. Therefore, the number of independent active decisions made every month is probably less than 100.
- The decisions relating to any stock may be correlated from one month to the next.
- The information coefficient may vary from 0.10 over time. Further, a different IC may actually be accurate for difference sectors.

Other practical limitations of the fundamental law include:

- Transaction costs and taxes are ignored.
- The limitations of mean-variance optimization also apply here.
- There are problems associated with estimation and use of risk models (e.g., identifying the right set of risk factors, nonlinearities, and non-stationary returns).

READING 52: ALGORITHMIC TRADING AND HIGH-FREQUENCY TRADING

LESSON 1: TRADING ALGORITHMS AND HIGH-FREQUENCY TRADING

LOS 52a: Define algorithmic trading. Vol 6, pg 530

LOS 52b: Distinguish between execution algorithms and high-frequency trading algorithms. Vol 6, pg 530

Algorithmic trading uses a computer to find opportunities, place orders, and manage their execution in a series of programmed steps called an *algorithm*. Buy-side firms that purchase participation in markets use *execution algorithms* to find optimal prices for client trades. Trading desks at sell-side firms and independent traders use *high-frequency trading* algorithms to find and execute opportunistic trades, often small in size but designed to be profitable on volume.

LOS 52c: Describe types of execution algorithms and high-frequency trading algorithms. Vol 6, pp 530–534

Execution Algorithms

Execution algorithms attempt to minimize trading impacts of large trades by breaking them down into smaller trades that can be introduced into the market over time. This reduces visibility of the trading strategy to other traders and algorithms as well as better matching supply with demand for the asset.

Approaches to breaking up the large order include:

- *Volume-weighted average price (VWAP)*—Breaks orders into proportions based on historical daily trading patterns.
- *Market participation*—Breaks orders into proportions based on volume experienced over the execution period.
- *Implementation shortfall*—Uses market conditions during the execution period to minimize losses from the decision price to the final execution.

High-Frequency Trading (HFT) Algorithms

Where execution algorithms automate decisions on *how* to place trades into markets, *high-frequency trading* algorithms focus on *when* to trade or *what* to trade. *Event-driven algorithms* systematically analyze whether events confirm or could potentially change asset values. *Statistical arbitrage algorithms* focus on changes in relationships among assets.

HFT Events

Types of HFT-relevant events include:

- *Quote events*—Bid or ask security, price, and volume
- *Trade events*—Bought or sold security, price, and volume
- *News events*—News about securities or economic indicators

In order to accommodate news event algorithms, data providers can tag information useful to HFT participants so that their proprietary programs can snag relevant data (e.g., earnings changes or economic data) from the feed as fast as possible.

Statistical Arbitrage

Statistical arbitrage ("stat arb") seeks to profit from changes in correlation or spread:

- *Pairs trading*— Correlation changes between assets (e.g., options and the underlying). A new algorithm with instruments, parameters, and other instructions is said to be *instantiated* when it is created.
- *Index arbitrage*—Correlation changes between individual instruments and an index.
- *Basket trading*—Correlation changes within a basket of securities included in an index (includes aspects of pairs trading and index arbitrage).
- *Spread trading*—Spread changes between two instruments, particularly popular in commodities markets and usually involving a long position and a short position. Some examples include:
  - *Intra-market spread*—Spread changes for instruments representing the same commodity but different delivery dates (e.g., between July and March wheat).
  - *Inter-market spread*—Spread changes for instruments representing different commodities of the same delivery date (e.g., July gold and silver).
  - *Inter-exchange spread*—Spread between the same commodity in different exchanges (e.g., corn in Kansas City vs. Chicago market).
  - *Crack spread*—Spread between crude oil and petroleum products.
  - *Spark spread*—Spread between input costs (including operating) and output price for units of electricity (i.e., operating margin).
  - *Crush spread*—Spread between commodity and output prices (e.g., soybeans and soybean oil).
- *Mean reversion*—Purchasing oversold or selling overbought instruments to capture profits when the asset returns to its average price.
- *Delta neutral*—Neutralizing option delta to profit from volatility or time decay without regard to price moves of the underlying.

Genetic Tuning

Firms may simultaneously run several algorithms with different instructions for achieving the same result, although only one or two may actually be trading in the market. This Darwinian approach, known as *genetic tuning*, allows survival of the fittest algorithm while dropping less profitable algorithms.

Programming Approaches

Brokers typically offer clients a *black-box approach* that denies users access to knowledge of the programmed steps and may allow limited or no flexibility in setting up or operating the algorithm. Alternatively, traders who want to set an algorithm in motion and forget about it while executing may purchase black-box applications from a third-party provider whose algorithm has earned a good reputation. Black-box algorithms often provide the least costly option, but make earning a profit more difficult because other traders compete for profits from the same strategy.

A *white-box approach* provides additional flexibility over black-box applications by allowing users to integrate with market feeds, control entry and exit points, combine with other algorithms, and view the strategy's progress. White-box strategies cost more, but provide the benefits of some customization and less competition if the user specifies unique parameters.

Larger firms may hire highly talented mathematicians and programmers to design *bespoke algorithms* (i.e., *custom algorithms*). Custom algorithms are very expensive but offer the best profit opportunities because the firm has few competitors in exploiting a strategy.

LESSON 2: GROWTH OF ALGORITHMIC AND HIGH-FREQUENCY TRADING

Algorithmic trading has its roots over 15 years ago when electronic markets allowed capital market firms direct access to their platforms through open application programming interface (API) architecture. Participants realized they had a competitive advantage, and could further stretch that advantage by introducing algorithms that trade faster and often better than human traders.

This shift in technology created many problems and opportunities.

Fragmented Markets

LOS 52d: Describe market fragmentation and its effects on how trades are placed. **Vol 6, pp 536–538**

Market fragmentation (i.e., the same instrument traded in multiple markets) has increased as new markets develop in response to competitive opportunities and new technology.

In response to increased fragmentation, traders developed *liquidity aggregation* that creates a "super book" of quote and depth across many markets. Companies can use methods such as *smart order routing* to introduce orders in markets that offer the best prices and most favorable market impact.

Real-time pricing seeks to price assets using event data aggregated across markets. Pricing may involve spread adjustments to favor customers based on their trading volume and importance to the firm.

New Opportunities

In addition to creating fragmented markets, wider adoption of advancing technology has opened new opportunities:

- *New asset classes*—Although equity and futures markets were initial targets of algorithmic trading, bond markets, foreign exchange, and even energy trading have become algo-friendly markets.
- *Cross-asset trading*—As mentioned previously, arbitrageurs have begun trading across correlated asset classes.
- *Cross-border trading*—Differences in trading platforms and venues have also opened opportunities for cross-border arbitrage in which firms buy low in one country's market and sell higher in another country's market.
- *New geographic areas*—Although available initially only in the United States and United Kingdom, algorithmic trading has spread across the world's larger markets, most recently even Brazil.

Latency and Trading Technologies

Latency describes the delay between receiving information, recognizing significance of events, developing a strategy, and ultimately executing the trade. Low latency (i.e., shortest possible lag) is important in making the trade before competitors (i.e., *first-mover advantage*).

Firms may use an *execution management system (EMS)* that includes one or more of the following features:

- *Tick database*—Records all transactions across all markets for use with the appropriate algorithms. (The tick database may also be used for back testing strategies.)
- *Complex event processing* (CEP)—Uses instantaneous information to adjust existing algorithms or develop new ones with little human involvement.
- *Application programming interface* (API)—Integrates user algorithms with a trading platform using the financial information exchange (FIX) protocol to place and manage orders directly through the trading venue.

Firms may further reduce latency by using supplier-provided virtual private networks (VPNs) or co-locating physical equipment to reduce transmission times.

LESSON 3: RISK MANAGEMENT AND REGULATORY OVERSIGHT

LOS 52e: Describe the use of technology in risk management and regulatory oversight. **Vol 6, pp 538–540**

Using computers allows market participants to trade at an increasingly faster rate, but also exposes firms and the market to extraordinary potential loss. Trading firms can use algorithmic trading tools and techniques to manage risk within the firm, while regulators can use these trading methods for market oversight.

Managing Risk

Firms have often assumed that potential reward outweighs risk, and they have sometimes been proven wrong by various financial meltdowns over time. A desire to protect capital and, in addition, meet increasingly burdensome regulatory restrictions has led to pre-trade analysis that uses algorithms. Brokers can also use these methods to avoid abuse that can damage their reputations.

Pre-Trade Risk Firewall

Real-time pre-trade risk assessment can block trades from going to market if they violate previously established risk guidelines. Firms can also protect against trading errors, especially *fat finger trades* (e.g., buying 1 million shares rather than 10,000 shares).

Brokers offering *sponsored access* (i.e., allowing traders direct access to markets using a broker platform) can block certain trades, often using a CEP platform (i.e., market data connections, modeling tools, and a *complex event processing* program). This is important because the broker retains responsibility for sponsored-access client errors.

Simulation

Traders can model trades using actual historical situations and even potential but highly unlikely events to assess risk before placing a trade, although this typically increases latency. By back testing algorithms before using them for trading, however, traders can assess performance under modeled situations and avoid the latency problems of testing every trade before submitting it.

Regulatory Monitoring and Surveillance

Regulators can use modern technologies (e.g., tick databases, CEP) for enhanced surveillance and detection across markets and exchanges, or even prevent abuses before they occur.

Examples of potential abuses detectable via regulatory algorithms include:

- *Fictitious trades*—Trades entered with the intent to deceive traders or algorithms into responding. Some types of fictitious trades include:
    - *Spoofing*—Placing limit orders not intended for execution but to give the impression of excess demand or supply.
    - *Quote stuffing*—Using an algorithm to place trades and immediately withdraw them with the intent of distracting other algorithms that must process the quotes. Meanwhile, the perpetrator takes advantage of actual situations using a valid algorithm.
    - *Layering*—Baiting other market participants into bidding on a legitimate trade by placing multiple illegitimate orders on the other side.
- *Front running*—Trading ahead of a known large order. For example, a trader with knowledge of a large buy-side purchase enters an order for the same security ahead of the trade with the intent to profit from the increased demand.
- *Wash trading*—Simultaneously buying and selling the same security to attract interest.
- *Painting the tape*—Manipulating orders to give the appearance of movement in a particular direction in order to purchase or sell at a more favorable price.
- *Collusion*—Traders operating together to manipulate security prices or rates (e.g., Libor).

LESSON 4: MARKET IMPACTS OF ALGORITHMIC AND HIGH-FREQUENCY TRADING

LOS 52f: Describe issues and concerns related to the impact of algorithmic and high-frequency trading on securities markets. Vol 6, pp 541–543

Although asset managers often use modern trading technologies to benefit individual clients, and other techniques are available to all market participants, investors and regulatory authorities remain concerned that techniques such as high-frequency trading may disadvantage some participants due to cost and difficulty of gaining access.

Research indicates that smaller investors benefit from lower transaction costs. Lower-cost access to data, off-the-shelf algorithms, widely available low-latency technology, and other factors make algorithmic and high-frequency trading available to even very small teams.

Advantages of Modern Trading

Research indicates that smaller investors benefit from lower bid-ask spreads and other transaction costs as well as increased market efficiency:

- *Execution costs*—Algorithms have replaced more expensive traders as well as creating more competition among trading firms. This brings down trading costs for buy-side firms.
- *Liquidity*—Research indicates many more trades and lower average trade size. This often leads to less market impact from large trades, which can be broken down and introduced to smaller investors.
- *Trading venue efficiency*—Lower spreads lead to increased competition for business, which further decreases trading costs to investors.
- *Market efficiency*—Faster trading technologies allow faster remediation of market inefficiencies and result in lower profits than previous arbitrage opportunities allowed to develop over time.

Disadvantages of Modern Trading

In spite of all the advantages, some traders, legislators, and regulators remain concerned about the negative aspects of algorithmic and high-frequency trading:

- Unfair advantages:
  - *Speed*—Super-fast trading platforms and superior algorithms, along with co-location that results in lower latency, contribute to the idea that big companies have a speed advantage in recognizing and executing profitable trades.
  - *Data access*—Algorithmic traders have access to order books and tick data that may not be available to individual traders with lower volume.
  - *Dark pools*—Special trading venues may be available only to special clients or large transactions at the expense of market opportunities for other investors.
  - *Regulatory inefficiency*—Regulators constrained by budgets and congressional foot-dragging may be unable to keep up with modern technology.
- *Increased market volatility*—Market panic can create rapidly decreasing prices, which trigger stop losses that further accelerate falling prices. Algorithms unemotionally and rapidly implement short-selling strategies that can increase the damage from such flash crashes, although they do not necessarily cause them.
- *Trader risk*—Accelerating market volatility and rapidly executed algorithms can quickly expose traders to undesirable risk levels in the absence of adequate pre-trade firewalls.
- *Gaming*—Higher-frequency trading and regulatory lag allow malicious traders to take advantage of opportunities that may not otherwise be available.
- *Rogue algorithms*—Poorly programmed or tested algorithms may inadvertently trade the wrong direction into market crashes, creating increased losses rather than limiting them. Possibilities for minimizing algorithms running wild are a "kill switch" that pulls algorithms out of overly risky markets or human intervention when position limits exceed parameters.
- *Trading venue overload*—Algorithms respond nearly instantaneously to market conditions, placing or pulling orders with increasing volume over time. Some venues have responded by charging fees for excessive order cancellations. In some cases, the venue responds to overly high levels of order cancellation much in the way an information technology (IT) network responds to a denial-of-service attack by a malicious hacker, rejecting valid orders in an attempt to process invalid orders.